PERCEIVE

CONCEIVE

ACHIEVE

The Sustainable City
A European Tetralogy

PART IV

Aesthetics, Functionality and Desirability of the Sustainable City

Maurice Culot (1939), Architect-town planner, Architecture critic, Professor at the École d'architecture du Prince de Galles, Head of the History and Archives departement of the Institut Français d'Architecture, Paris, Officer of the Arts and Literature.

After completing architecture and planning studies in Brussels, Maurice Culot attended a number of courses in the United States (Frank Lloyd Wright Foundation, Arizona; Paolo Soleri, Scottsdale, Arizona; New York).

In 1969, he set up the *Archives d'Architecture Moderne* in Brussels (keeping of architects' archives, organization of exhibitions, publications).

He taught planning and architecture for 10 years at the École de la Cambre in Brussels.

In 1979, he was asked to head a department at the Institut Français d'Architecture.

He was awarded the *Grand Prix de la Critique Architecturale* [Prize for Architectural Criticism] in 1984.

He is the author of numerous works and studies on 20th-century architecture.

PERCEIVE
CONCEIVE
ACHIEVE

The Sustainable City
A European Tetralogy

PART IV

Aesthetics, Functionality and Desirability of the Sustainable City

Maurice Culot
Institut Français d'Architecture

 European Foundation
for the Improvement of Living and Working Conditions
Wyattville Road, Loughlinstown, Co. Dublin, Ireland
Tel: (+353) 1 204 31 00 Fax: (+353) 1 282 64 56

Cataloguing data can be found at the end of this publication

Luxembourg: Office for Official Publications of the European Communities, 1997

ISBN 92-827-4923-1 Volume IV Aesthetics, Functionality and Desirability of the Sustainable City

ISBN 92-827-4915-0 Volumes I-IV

© European Foundation for the Improvement of Living and Working Conditions, 1997

For rights of translation or reproduction, applications should be made to the Director,
European Foundation for the Improvement of Living and Working Conditions,
Wyattville Road, Loughlinstown, Co. Dublin, Ireland.

Printed in Ireland

AESTHETICS, FUNCTIONALITY AND DESIRABILITY OF THE SUSTAINABLE CITY

FOREWORD

This is the fourth part of the Tetralogy "Perceive – Conceive – Achieve the Sustainable City". The previous parts concern urban eco-auditing and local authorities in Europe, the role of SMEs for the revitalisation of the European cities and the transport and public spaces, connective tissue of the sustainable city. This study concerns the aesthetics, functionality and desirability of the city and their role in the road to sustainability.

A city may be ecologically perfect and economically healthy, but if its inhabitants do not desire to live there and do not take any pleasure in it, its future is questionable. Are urban forms neutral? The study suggests that functionalism is responsible for many of the urban problems and makes a strong case for the return of the traditional city, historic place of sociability, encounters, emotion and culture.

Clive Purkiss
Director

Eric Verborgh
Deputy Director

INTRODUCTION

The first phase of the research programme "Innovations for the improvement of the urban environment" tried to identify projects which had a significant meaning for the sustainable city. I had imagined that city as human and strong, dynamic and complex ecosystem. I believe that such a city is quintessentially cultural and dignified, that it should concentrate the desires of everybody seeking a better environment to live in, work, create and dream.

In its analytical phase, the project looked into the innovative character of four types of actions aiming at sustainability. The first axis was the improvement of the urban metabolism through actions of eco-auditing. The second concerned the enhancement of public spaces, which are also places of mobility and accessibility. The third axis approached the economic foundation of the sustainable city, through the dynamism of SMEs.

This study is concerned with urban aesthetics and functionality which are the basis for the desire and desirability of cities. The quintessential city is made out of places, links and symbols. It is a space of confrontation of desires. To define the desirability of the city and the right to urban happiness, to reconcile the material city with its moral entity, aesthetics and ethics, and finally to present alternatives to the destructive functionalism – these were the challenges which this study tried to meet.

Desiring cities is certainly a precondition for responding to these challenges and Maurice Culot seems to agree with C. Lévi-Strauss (The city is the human invention par excellence) or Louis Mumford (The city is the most advanced work of art of the human civilisation). But cities are ambivalent. There are cities which include, integrate and enrich and also cities which exclude, disintegrate and impoverish. Is there any cause which affects the relationship between urban morphologies and pathologies? Are there any correlations on which one can act, any vicious circles which one can transform into virtuous?

The study condemns functionalism as a cause of further urban fragmentations. Rigid zoning and all the resulting facts (segregation, traffic congestion) have generated more problems than the problems they were supposed to solve. They did not face urban complexity. But each simplification is a fraud. A city cannot be the sum of its districts or its historic facts. Today, mix and diversity, with their synergetic effects, become a major goal for cities. The radiant city of the dawning of the XXIst century has certainly a different face from the city promised by the Charter of Athens. It also has a different smile.

The city is plural by essence, socially heterogeneous, economically diversified, culturally mixed. It should be a theatre and a school for exercising citizenship. It should have citizens who have rights in the city and who can feel responsible for the future of the city. Who remake the city every day. Who make of it a territory of heritage. Who freely elect politicians at the height of the political challenge that is the city. Who cultivate the art of urban governance, moving from procedure and management to responsibility and mission.

But citizens and politicians need proposals, options and alternatives to functionalism. A city cannot be substituted by any other city. Each city has a very unique urbanity.

There are, however, common principles and options and inspiring experiences. The author presents ten cases, each one illustrating a theme of intervention on the collective body of the city. There are cases which reject ordinariness and uniformity, attributes of stagnant cities, asking for freedom of expression in the unity of style and coherence of action.

The author suggests that we should "take the measure of the city", "evaluate its symbolic significance and its suggestive power". He proposes "itineraries for understanding a city's soul", passages which can be dorsal spines of desire, metronomes of the beating heart. From Fornovo di Taro to Poundberry, all the cases have as a common axis the search for beauty, the cardinal value of all human activities. Long regarded as a sign of frivolity and élitism, beauty will always be a source of desires. Urban beauty comes from within, from the soul of cities, from all secret gardens, and it is reflected outside in the public spaces, by definition noble, "islands of freedom in the archipelago of the city". Investing in the beauty of cities is investing in the quality of life and the art of everyday living. It is a prelude to happiness.

This study is first and foremost an essay and it demands improvements, confrontations, perfection.

Voula Mega
Research Manager

CONTENTS

Summary 7

Synopsis 9

Part one

General Considerations

1. The return of desire 17

2. Sizing up the city 21

3. Does meeting all the modern functionality criteria necessarily make a city more desirable? 27

4. Functionalist town planning versus the traditional city 28

5. The traditional city or the good times of life 30

6. The misery of functionalism 31

7. Desire, what desire? 32

8. Functional zoning 34

9. On the subject of public architecture and town-planning competitions 35

10. The power and limits of popular solidarity 42

11. The need for a vision 44

12. The city and the bourgeoisie 45

13. The city is not a tree. The city is a human creation 47

14. Desire and architectural language or the choice of styles 48

15. Functionality, aesthetics and desirability of the city 55

16. Night-time visions 56

PART TWO

CASE STUDIES

1. Brussels, Belgium. Reconstruction of the rue Laeken 63

2. Fornovo di Taro, Italy. Extension of the town 73

3. Chinon, France. Global project and selective measures 83

4. Trouville, France. A testing ground for the urban heritage 93

5. Cergy-Pontoise - La Rochelle - Bordeaux, France. Choice or suffering 103

6. Warsaw, Poland. Greatness and limitations of the symbol 115

7. Poundbury, England. Extension of the city of Dorchester 117

8. USA. New American lessons of value to Europe 131

9. Paris, France. The Goutte d'Or neighbourhood 141

10. Toulouse, France. The delights of imitation 155

PART THREE

Conclusion 167

Recommendations 169

Epilogue 177

Annexes 181

SUMMARY

The starting point of the study is the ideology collapse brought about by the demise of the Soviet regime.

Such a Copernican upheaval rattled the political equilibrium, questioned the nature of progress, disrupted the markets and touched the scientific and artistic world. It also affected architecture and town planning.

Concepts that were formerly banished from discussions on the city, for the sake of moralism and the prevailing functionalist vision, are back on the agenda. These concepts include <u>desire</u> and <u>desirability</u> of the city.

In a series of short essays, the author contrasts functionalist theory, which still dominates town planning in Europe, with the theory based on the European urban tradition. Formulated from the mid-1970s onwards by the Luxembourg theoretician and architect Léon Krier, it now constitutes an operational alternative to functionalism.

The author shows that functionalism is Utopian in essence:
- being moralistic, it ignores the fundamental nature of the men and women it intends to reform;
- being functionalist, it advocates the division of urban activities into monofunctional zones.

These two approaches are the antithesis of the city.

Despite serious challenges throughout the 1960s and 1970s, functionalism has survived. Being prescriptive and quantitative, this new urban order was adopted by the bureaucracies, supported by the practitioners, accepted by the elected representatives, and perceived as inevitable by the people. The new global equilibrium now enables those who are fighting the intolerance of functionalism to achieve significant victories in bringing about architectural and urban pluralism.

The author goes on to sketch ten portraits of recent projects and developments in various European cities, illustrating the theory of urbanism according to the European city-building tradition. Each portrait evokes a theme: the global nature of the city, the character of public space, the concept of imitation, the creation of complex urban neighbourhoods, the integration of the low-rise housing blocks of the 1960s into a living urban fabric, etc.

In conclusion, the author develops a number of recommendations for those elected representatives and officials who wish to see pluralism establish itself and want to implement programmes that enhance functional coexistence and are inspired by the European urban tradition and the constituent concepts of the city, ie the neighbourhood, the street, the square.

SYNOPSIS

To raise the issue of the functionality, aesthetics and desirability of the sustainable city is to suggest that uncertainties, flaws, latent and unfulfilled desires do exist.

It is a fact that the issue could not have been raised officially a few years ago. Neither was it advisable, in architecture and planning circles, to mention the concepts of love, urban art, urban improvements, imitation, charm, colourfulness, etc.

These concepts were banned from discussions on architecture and the city for 50 years, during the supreme rule of functionalism. They were criticized for their frivolity, their élitism, their lack of consistency; they did not take precedence in social issues, they were not scientific and, through lack of arguments, they were identified with the arsenal of the political right.

Now they are back on the agenda – recalled and invoked by books, exhibitions, essays and symposiums.

This study endeavours to show that the question of desire arises because of the existence of objects of desire - not only for the nostalgia-inducing paraphernalia of yesteryear, but also for those modern achievements that are evidence of an alternative to the destruction and loss of the European city.

Without prejudging the results of the emergence of desire, the study presents some theoretical aspects and actual achievements of the alternative to functionalism.
It ends with recommendations aimed at those officials and elected representatives who want a dialogue to be initiated, pluralism to prevail over dogmatism, the European tradition that produced the finest cities to be challenged once again and turned to good account.

How can the harbingers of upheavals, reversals in public opinion, even revolutions, be identified within the flood of information?
One is reminded of Louis XVI writing in his diary «Today, nothing» on the very day when the French Revolution began.

In the wave of enthusiasm that engulfed Europe on 3 October 1990 following the announcement of the reunification of Germany and the fall of the Berlin Wall, who in Italy then sensed that this event was also to trigger the *Mani Pulite* [clean hands] campaign? Actions to which the judiciary turned a blind eye so long as the tacit enemy was Communism and the Soviet regime, would suddenly become punishable and liable to relentless legal proceedings.

However, the world of politics is not alone in facing Copernican upheavals. Economics and art are not immune, nor are architecture and town planning.

Fifty years of town planning and architecture advocating a break with history and tradition have been a patent failure. The Athens Charter – cornerstone of the new urban order – drawn up on Le Corbusier's initiative during World War II, promised a radiant city. The implementation of its precepts has led to urban, ecological and human disaster.
Although functionalism was challenged and its perverse effects denounced as early as the late 1960s, it followed its course, in the absence of an operational alternative, merely altering its appearance as one architectural fashion followed another.

Today, portents of a radical change are proliferating throughout the world.
And everyone is becoming aware that a decisive battle is brewing.
Those opposed to change are striving to maintain the status quo; those in favour of the alternative are joining the resistance and getting organized.
The object of this struggle against the *de facto* tyranny of functionalism is to bring about a genuine pluralism in architecture and town planning.
<u>Suffering or choice</u> is the rallying cry of the resistance. It is also the core theme of Léon Krier's book *Architecture, choix ou fatalité* [Architecture – Choice or Finality] published in 1995 by the *Institut Français d'Architecture*.
The identity of European cities hinges on this cultural conflict.

The functional architects, in favour of perpetuating the break from tradition, are more numerous but not necessarily stronger, since they are on the defensive. They advocate a neutral, abstract architecture and town planning, relying on moralistic apriorisms and excluding those who do not think like them. They accept the finality of zoning and function separation (here the motorways, there the housing estates, the industrial estates, etc) and defend the primacy of the architect as an artist who is above criticism by right. They lay claim to the new forms and to abstraction, whatever the context.

Those in favour of continuity and tradition defend the European identity, relying on ethics and listening to others without apriorism.
They acknowledge the European genius for designing cities – all alike in their conception, yet different in their reality. Cities in which the democratic liberties are earned and defended. They propose to repair, extend and build cities in accordance with this European urban tradition (neighbourhood, street, square), respecting both the context and history.
They are opposed to zoning and want a mix of human activity in the neighbourhoods (excluding whatever is out of place, namely airports, nuclear power stations, polluting or dangerous factories, stadiums, etc).
Their approach is based on imitation and dialogue.

Although the balance of power still favours the opponents of tradition, both camps know that a swing is now possible.

The examples mentioned in the study illustrate some of the operational solutions that can be provided by traditional architecture and town planning for the problems experienced by today's cities.

Functionalist theory dissects the city into separate components before dealing with them in isolation. The theory associated with the urban tradition always perceives the city as a whole, and all the issues raised invariably lie within the global framework of the city.

The crisis facing North American cities has a dual link with capitalism and with the very structure of American society that thinks in terms of communities rather than complex cities.

In Europe, however, where ethnic and social segregation is not a basic element of urban culture, how can the drifting of cities towards chaos, waste and loss of identity be explained?

How has Europe come to lose its ability to build cities that are expressions of its spirit and civilization?

It should be noted, in the first place, that this is a recent phenomenon, associated with the industrial revolutions but chiefly with the massive urbanization following World War II.

The reason for the loss of an expertise going back ten centuries lies essentially in the adoption of functionalism, two inherent elements of which prevent it from producing and devising cities.

The first is the reference to moralism. Functionalism claims to make men and women happy despite themselves. Functionalism wants to moralize society and refuses to consider the conflicting feelings of the human heart that make men and women masterpieces of complexity and contradiction. The functionalists feel that the truth is their property, and they intend to instil it into others.

Functionalism is aimed at a human being who does not exist, at an abstract person, passionless and faultless. The desire to promote the good in such a way inevitably causes frustration and an upsurge in evil. Functionalism predicted the demise of cities and the emergence of a new urban order, but what we see is the disorderly growth and deterioration of cities into suburbs and monofunctional zones. Although the old cities are under continual attack, they are holding out better than expected.

The second factor preventing functionalism from building cities is that its rationale is based on zoning. The separation of functions is the antithesis of the city.

Because it is oversimplified, fragmented and quantitative, functionalism gained an instant foothold in the bureaucracies. Functionalism generates criteria, statistics, specialisms, everything that feeds and sustains a bureaucracy.

All the current laws and regulations governing town planning and the future of cities are derived from functionalism. All are directed against the traditional city for reasons that seem logical when taken separately (hygiene, safety, traffic flows, comfort, etc). Applied simultaneously, however, they destroy and impede the city.

With the emergence of the functionality, aesthetics and desirability of the city, it is now possible to fight the moralistic tyranny of functionalism. The support of a growing audience for the ideas of the urban renaissance encourages more and more developments based on imitation of the traditional cities and their complex organization along the lines of neighbourhoods, streets and squares.

This trend favours the establishment of a pluralistic frame of mind. Pluralism does not mean doing anything anywhere or mixing styles for the sake of it; on the contrary it allows a confrontation of different conceptions, each one having its own logic.

The re-emergence of formerly banished concepts is a good omen for the advent of such pluralism. But it will not just come to the people, they will have to wrest it from the bureaucrats, the politicians, the architects, engineers and planners, as in times past the burghers wrested privileges from the princes, so that the city atmosphere could give men and women more and more freedom.

To assist the elected representatives and the local councillors who wish to contribute to this emergence, the study ends with recommendations that are not exhaustive but partake, once implemented, of an emulation, an urban dynamics, a confrontation of European experiences, of the desire to safeguard and develop the identity of every European city.

This study whose *raison d'être* lies in the recognition of desire – which is nothing but an impulse of the heart, a complex feeling blending nostalgia and projection into the future – concludes with operational recommendations. The city of desire is indeed the precondition of its own durability in the sense that it will be treated, managed, transformed with care and love simply because it is desirable. The city of desire generates a dynamic city which is the natural support of economic vitality.

As suggested by the architect Léon Krier, it will be noted, *inter alia*, that attention should be paid to well-proportioned public spaces. That in the finest and most convenient traditional cities, they make up approximately 35% of the total area, whereas in the new towns, the housing estates and the suburbs, the share of public space reaches 70%, even up to 90%, of the total area. This is a false luxury that generates perverse effects, eg impossible management, lack of places that can be recognized and occupied by the residents, violence and vandalism, etc.

The study recalls that the traditional cities are not random occurrences but the outcome of a

thousand-year-old urban culture. This culture is not extinct or obsolete, it merely needs to be relearnt if we are to understand, *inter alia:*
- that neighbourhoods have a maximum area not to be exceeded, and that this area is based on walking distance;
- that, when building a city, monofunctional zones should be banned, thereby contributing to a significant reduction in traffac flows;
- that architecture and town-planning competitions must be held along pluralistic rather than dogmatic lines if they are to produce meaningful results;
- etc.

In a nutshell, the purpose of this essay is to highlight the forward-looking solutions contained within the traditional cities, the cities of Europe, and to show that these solutions are within reach if there is a political determination to implement them.

PART ONE

GENERAL CONSIDERATIONS

1. THE RETURN OF DESIRE

«... we can perceive an entire world of desires, an emotional world of objects devoid of order and logical structure, and a more elaborate world of representations where cognitive aspects prevail, tending to set into models, to assert themselves in behaviour and in the devising of plans. Where does the urban imaginary have its roots? Is it imposed by the rational organization of space? Does it originate in the desires and images associated with memories? Popular memory is full of evocations relating simultaneously to space and to events, of struggles and dramas that have marked the lives of a city's inhabitants. In what places is this imaginary formulated?»

        Paul-Henry Chombart de Lauwe
        in La fin des villes, Mythe ou réalité [The end of cities - myth or reality]
        Calmann-Lévy, Paris, 1982

With the collapse of ideologies, desire and love made their first appearance on the urban scene. As recent examples in the arena of exhibitions, books and the media, I shall mention L'amour des Villes [The love of cities], an exhibition presented in September 1995 at the Institut Français d'Architecture, now on tour in Europe; a book, Les villes du désir [The cities of desire] by André Antolini and Yves-Henri Bonello (Éditions Galilée, Paris, 1994); a magazine article, «La ville, objet de désir pour tous» [The city, object of desire for all] by Catherine Trautmann, Mayor of Strasbourg and chairperson of the *Communauté Urbaine* (Urbanisme, December 1994, Paris).

Only a few years ago, talking of desire in terms of architecture and town planning was just as improper as mentioning urban art and city improvements before those who prefer collective order repression to the dynamics of individual life.

Those words smacked of heresy and concealed concepts related to the bourgeois ethics whose death had already been proclaimed by the French writer Emmanuel Berl in 1928 (Emmanuel Berl, Mort de la morale bourgeoise, Gallimard, Paris, 1928).

The *Robert* dictionary of the French language defines desire as a realization prompting one to want to obtain a known or imaginary object whereas desirability refers to the desirable character.

Very early in the 20th century, the signs appeared of a desire crisis in the western world. This takes the particular form of a shrinking or acceleration of time. In other words, today's man is tempted to do things quickly and therefore in many cases badly, for fear that he will stop wanting to do them too soon.

That is the point where confusion arises between science and conscience, work and toil, pleasure and happiness, desire and need.

The dismembering of European cities is akin to a tragedy of desire, and the theme of the desirability of cities is really topical: *can the city desire survive in today's political space and if so, how?*

But can the question of desire, of the desirable character of the modern city be answered? Is it not, in essence, beyond the quantitative and qualitative analysis grids? Admittedly, the European press regularly publishes lists of cities rated in order of preference for their quality of life, but then the criteria focus on physical, economic, structural and political aspects. But is desire not first and foremost a heartbeat, an emotional state, an unforeseen impulse answering the call of mysterious laws? A noise, a smell, the coldness of the air, a smile are sufficient to trigger the surge of adrenaline that suddenly makes the world desirable. When the object of desire is the city and the urban imaginary, it is in most cases aroused by clichés and life experiences – unforgettable moments of urban life one wants to relive. It is also a collective desire for justice that expresses itself in public. Desire therefore has a dual link with nostalgia and projected lust. Nostalgia and desire always refer to known places, and the images of the traditional city are, in most cases, the background, the necessary décor for memories and moments of emotion.

Desire and memory arise and develop from shared places and familiar situations: a wedding and a church square, a loving moment and a city square, a ray of sunshine and a fountain, a walk with friends in a picturesque neighbourhood, etc. Public space is, par excellence, the favoured site of city desire, the receptacle of memories and nostalgia. Being rooted in history, it can attain the 4th dimension and introduce the ingredients of desire – imagination, fantasy, mystery, the unforeseen, the inexpressible, falling in love…

The emergence of desire would then be most frequently associated with the feeling of being part of an adventure, all the city desires forming a corpus continuously sustained by successive generations of actors and active spectators. Historical and archaeological authenticity is not required. Desire and dreaming are related and we have all experienced, in our personal lives, that it is often necessary to forge in order to look more real. Plausibility is more important than certified truth. One can experience a city desire while walking along the Tourny lanes in Bordeaux – a magnificent 18th-century development – or while sipping a *fino* with tapas in the Spanish *pueblo* of Barcelona – a stucco reconstruction of picturesque streets and squares of the different provinces of Spain built for the 1929 Iberian-American Exposition. The European quarter of Brussels definitely impresses by its dimensions, the pedestrian causeway of the district of La Défense in Paris is definitely convenient and Otto von Sprekelsen's Great Arch spectacular, but these places speak an abstract language which has little capacity for holding the desire of men and women.

Desire and moralism are antagonistic. In other words, I can copy without being accused of theft, imitate without regressing. This freedom granted by desire is universal and requires no other quality than the ability to surrender to emotion. And to appreciate desire and the conditions of its emergence, it is preferable to refer to the platitudes of sentimentality than to the intellectual fashions generated by the mass non-conformism that followed the avant-garde movements of the 20th century. The practitioners of architecture are not prepared for this Copernican upheaval of values, since the current teaching methods for the profession of architect and planner are based almost entirely on the aphorisms of mass non-conformism. Aphorisms advocating originality of form at any price, the never-seen, the exceptional as standard practice…

That is why architects often live in charming places while they produce, for others, inhuman places whose existence they justify at best by the kingly right of the artist, at worst by a profusion of technical, administrative, financial or moralistic reasons. Although an intellectual, deliberately abstract and emotionless approach does not prevent its originator from acknowledging and appreciating desire, it nevertheless leads him, in most cases, to suppress the conditions of its arousal in others.

The philosopher Porcius Latron (57 to 4 BC) had already formulated the idea that *rational thinking is possibly our most sentimental deed.*

The writings of the avant-garde architects of the 1920s and 1930s in Europe (which were later to answer for the city's loss of meaning) are revealing in that respect. What is more romantic than the rational ideas of Le Corbusier, whose dream was to build an airport in the heart of Paris, to replace the streets with buildings set on piles among greenery (he justified this solution by explaining that they would offer better resistance to the blast of explosions and bombs!)? Rational thinking is indeed frequently a delusion concealing slogans and sentimental and romantic notions. To study the conditions for the emergence of desire, it is essential to listen to all those who show some sensitivity (innate or acquired through education, family and friends) to the environment, a capacity for delight, a freshness of spirit that makes them prefer what is pretty, charming, antiquated, fresh, picturesque, pleasant, full of memories, civilized, orderly, etc, to what is abstract, ugly, distressing, coarse, threatening, disturbing, etc.

Functionalism cannot generate desirable urban solutions and atmospheres because it imposes its viewpoint instead of sharing it. Functionalism is perceived as inevitable. It is not rational but abstract and, as such, cannot appeal to the urban imaginary which incorporates memories of real events and places, the love and nostalgia of the men and women of a democratic Europe for the places they love and respect and would wish to see imitated and used as a source of inspiration for the future.

To claim the acknowledgement of desire as a key element of the urban imaginary may seem arrogant compared to the weight of functionalist statistics and standards.

However, to quote André Antolini and Yves-Henri Bonello, «*We know that ideal cities tell a story as beautiful as it is irrelevant. There is no debt without acknowledgement, and there can be none without common desire. The city is the acknowledgement of one single desire. It can be grasped only by the fullest possible integration*» (Les villes du désir, op. cit.).

There lies the aporia of the city. It can be dismantled piece by piece but can never be reassembled. What exists cannot be invented. As soon as this fact is established, the only solution, after so many setbacks, is a return to wisdom, ie <u>copying</u> and <u>imitating</u> the best features of the cities we have inherited…

The couple formed by desire and rational thought engenders the imaginary. Rational thought is effective and exerts its power of persuasion only insofar as it relies upon the heritage built up by successive generations, ie the traditional city.

The English historian Mark Girouard winds up his book <u>Une ville et des Hommes</u> [A City and Men] (Flammarion, Paris, 1987) with these words, *«I am only a five-minute walk from the open-air market, six churches and chapels, five cinemas, four good restaurants and several bad ones, and a score of pubs. I am twenty minutes away from Piccadilly Circus. This neighbourhood has some drawbacks but it suits me down to the ground»*.
This is an excellent and colourful definition of desirability.

2. SIZING UP THE CITY

«It seems that the human head needs intelligibility, or at least the impression of integrating the scattered elements that assail it from every direction at an unpredictable pace. Perhaps a more painful lucidity makes the heads of our contemporaries spin, when the truths have lost any stability, when the Earth has swapped the status of fixed and massive centre of the universe for that of a spinning, quasi-imperceptible outpost, when the customary, religious, farming, hunting, handicraft and artistic skills have broken down. Rightly so, perhaps, their heads have detached themselves from the circles, the wholes, the units and the knowledge that looked too much like man, like man's fantasy, like human-head satisfaction. But these bore the features of his desire and undoubtedly the form of his own toil. That similarity and connaturality always generated pleasure and an attraction which has vanished.»

> Pascal Quignard
> in <u>Une gêne technique à l'égard des fragments</u> [A technical difficulty with fragments]
> Fata Morgana, Paris, 1986

Living in Paris is a unique experience for the city dweller who loves his city, enjoying its beauty and pace.

Among the factors contributing to this uniqueness, one stands out because of its symbolic significance and power of suggestion. It is that the Parisian can have the feeling, at any time, that the city is his, that he is in control of it despite its excessiveness. In times of doubt, of mourning, of love's uncertainties, of psychological vulnerability, when a major decision has to be taken, when we are overwhelmed by the tragedy of life or when we muse over the meaning of human endeavour – every one of us feels the need to be comforted before making a fresh start (a feeling similar to the experience art lovers may have when visiting a museum).

This capacity to revitalize the human machine is the privilege of many large cities endowed with a strong historical identity.

The Middle Ages coined the maxim «The city air gives freedom», as the city dweller enjoyed more freedoms and privileges than his enslaved rural counterpart.

Adapted to today's contingencies, the formula could read: «The city air restores hope».

Sizing up the city is grasping it in its essence.

All at once it is history, the present, the future; it is crowds of people and grandiose perspectives, the seasons and a spring day containing the right amount of carbon monoxide to give the air a bite.

Ville, j'écoute ton cœur [City, I listen to your heartbeat] is the title of a Savinio novel dedicated to his city, Milan. Ville, je prends ta mesure [City, I size you up] is more accurate for Paris.

The sublime perspectives, the Champs-Élysées, the Place de la Concorde, the famous monuments, the Arc de Triomphe, the Opéra are impressive, conjuring up the grandeur of a capital and a nation, but they do not give the measure of the living city. The great modern projects – Centre Georges Pompidou, Opéra Bastille, Très Grande Bibliothèque – capture the imagination of tourists and foreigners but do not necessarily meet the Parisians' expectations. The Louvre pyramid, once the novelty has worn off, makes entering the museum unnecessarily difficult for all those for whom contact with a work of art is a physiological need.

The measure of a city is taken on foot, along routes where sequences are linked together, arousing images, nostalgia and hopes. In Paris, the most suggestive is the route from the Observatoire to the Palais Royal. It begins at the entrance of the Jardin du Luxembourg, a stone's throw from the Closerie des Lilas where writers and artists have lingered – Hemingway in bygone days, Philippe Soller today. A walk through the gardens recalls the vastness of nature tamed by the genius of gardeners. Skirting the Senate, the stroller walks down the rue de Tournon, one of the capital's finest thoroughfares, with its flared design punctuated by the porches of the grand mansions opening out on courtyards and gardens, just round the corner from the Marché St-Germain with its rows of arcades saved at the last minute from demolition. Beyond the hustle and bustle of the boulevard St-Germain – recalling the myth of St-Germain-des-Prés – you reach the narrow rue de Seine, lined with art galleries, you walk past the famous Roger-Viollet agency, a must for all those who use pictures (publishers, film-makers, advertising agents). A tiny porch that looks like a secret passage leads to the Place de l'Institut de France (formerly Collège des Quatre Nations, founded by Louis XIV to impart French culture to the young gentlemen of conquered provinces). On your way, you will cast a glance at the oval stairway of the Bibliothèque Mazarine erected by Biet in 1824. Slowly cross the Passerelle des Arts with its iron arches and wooden floor slab recently rebuilt after years of shilly-shallying with the boatmen, stop in the middle of it, stand in ecstasy before the Vert Galant peninsula, the Pont Neuf and the Île de la Cité, the towers of Notre-Dame, then turn 180° to the Gare d'Orsay (now a museum of the 19th century), the Grand Palais, the Tuileries. Enter the Louvre through the Cour Carrée, whose architecture was unified under Napoleon I by the architect Fontaine. Hurry across the rue de Rivoli – whose arcades have been imitated time and time again in other capitals – to the courtyard of the Palais Royal, play leapfrog over the Colonnes de Buren until you reach the gardens surrounded by galleries, with their timeless shops including the decorations and medals store that sends out all the Legions of Honour, the Orders of Merit and other education and farming medals.

Now that the point has been made and the city sized up, there is nothing to stop the inspired stroller proceeding via the rue Drouot and the rue des Martyrs to the Sacré-Cœur, and taking in Paris at one glance.

This axis has the obvious advantage of being secant, contrary to the Louvre-Arc de Triomphe axis – which is essentially monumental, rectilinear and homogeneous – punctuated by the chant of prestigious names such as Louvre, Tuileries, Concorde, Champs-Élysées, crossroads of the Étoile.

However, Paris is not the only European city to feature one of these exceptional routes. A stroller in Turin, setting out from the Duomo, passes by the Royal Palace, the Piazza Castello, the via Roma, the Piazza San Carlo, a sublime baroque square, the via Roma again to the Porta Nuova and the Station. The measure of London, a city of fragments, is taken from Regent's Park (Gloucester Gate, for instance) to Portland Place, recently refurbished with superb custom-designed street furniture, to Langham Place and its conical-spire church, the BBC of the early 1930s, and the mansion faithfully rebuilt after the devastation of the war years, leading at a slant to the impressive arcades of Regent Street, Piccadilly Circus, the National Gallery and the Thames.

All these routes are not necessarily touristic, commercial or pedestrian, but they are itineraries along which the soul of a city may be captured.

To maintain these routes (the London one is spoilt at Langham Place by an out-of-place modernist building of the 1960s), to restore and rehabilitate them, as has just been done in Paris, is essential. Some cities (Berlin, Amiens, Brest, Stuttgart, etc) have lost them as a result of the war. Others have downgraded them through neglect. Brussels, for instance, deliberately destroyed, peace year after peace year, its North-South thoroughfare where the soul of Flanders and Till Eulenspiegel fraternized with Burgundy and the valiant, rock-splitting knight Bayard. A route that residents' associations are busy reclaiming through sheer perseverance, thereby displaying an urban public spirit which is unique in Europe.

Those thoroughfares are the backbones of city desire. It is not necessary to signpost them, to urge morning joggers to use them, to direct hordes of tourists through them, to turn them into pedestrian malls or souvenir lanes. The main thing is that they exist and that we know they can be relied upon – as one can rely upon a democratic charter or the presence of a distant relative or friend whose mere existence is enough to provide reassurance. These itineraries are the city dwellers' guardian angels, regulating the heartbeat of the city. They are the living legacy of previous generations.

Those horizontal routes, those noble axes are matched by vertical axes, the dark twins that plunge into the depths where the heart of the city secretes another city.

Horizontal and vertical axes communicate, and this dialogue generates the erotic dimension of the city and the people's desire for it. Everyone in the city is free to explore those axes according to their tastes, their desires, their tendencies, their perversions. Vice and virtue work together to channel the passions so that the city may awake every morning in peace.

The fathers of the functionalist city wanted to restrict what they saw as evil. Today we are harvesting the fruit of their prudishness, namely gratuitous violence.

The point is not to create seedy areas from scratch, but to avoid hindering the urban sedimentation process that generates secret, taboo and hazardous places – places where dissoluteness rules.

If the active citizen is unable, at any time, to size up his city, if he cannot think *«it is mine»* whenever he feels like it, his desire for it will inevitably wane. His disenchantment will loosen the bond, break his pledge of loyalty to his city, and the active citizen will have no more power to influence the masses and prevent the triumph of the consumer ideology.

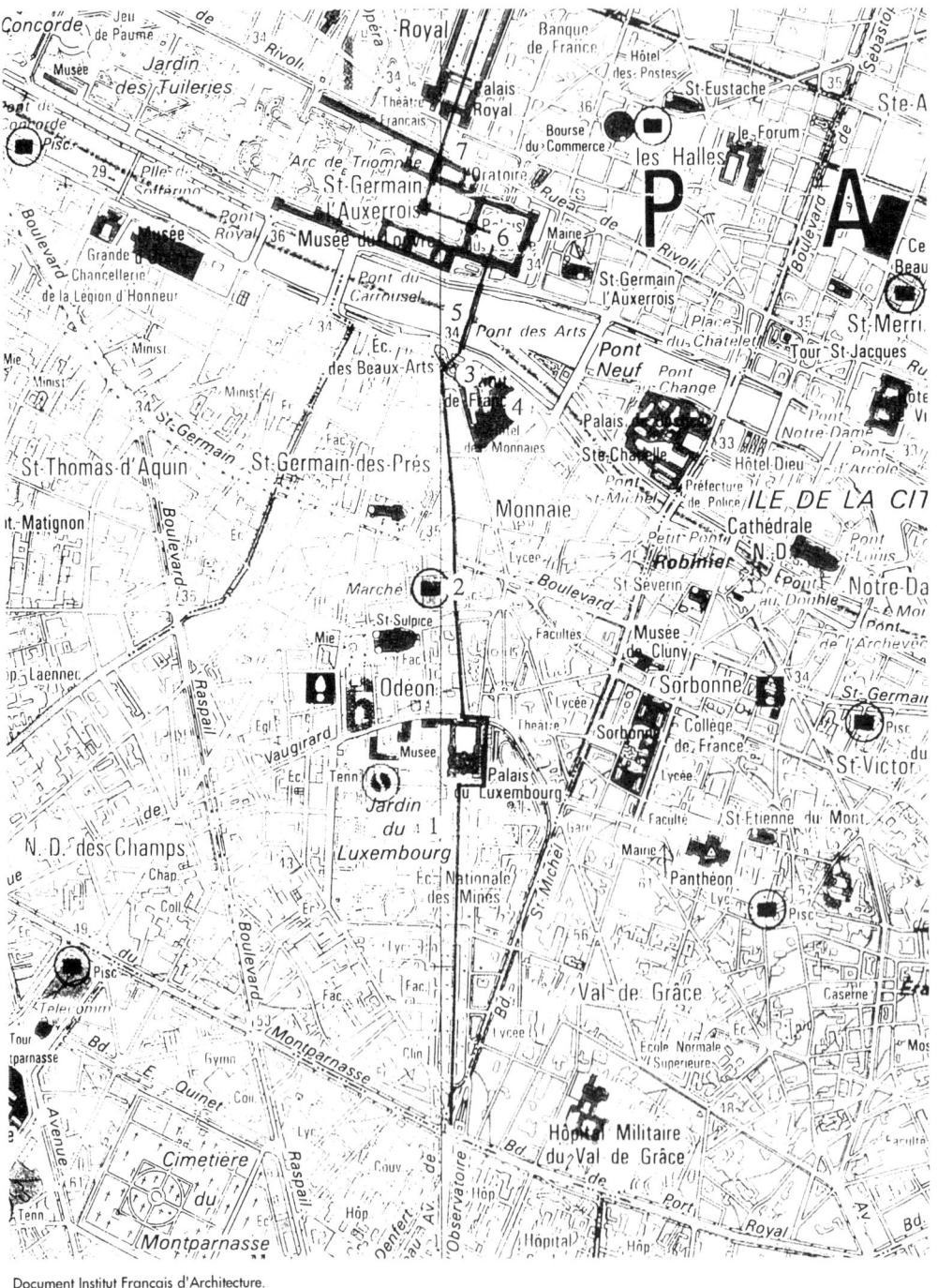

Document Institut Français d'Architecture.

1. Jardins du Luxembourg and Sénat.
(I.F.A. / DR.)

2. Marché St-Germain.
(I.F.A.)

3. Institut and Passerelle des Arts.
(I.F.A. / DR.)

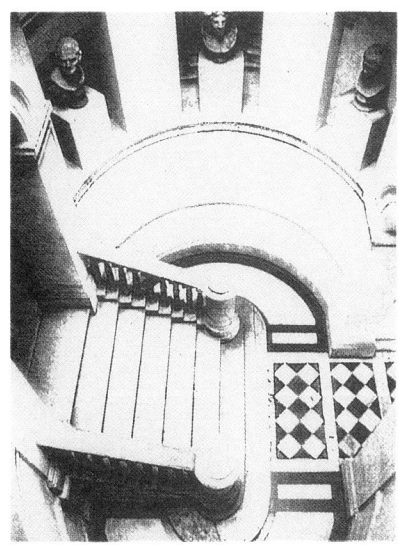
4. Stairway of the Bibliothèque Mazarine.
(D. Delaunay / I.F.A.)

5. Passerelle des Arts and Île de la Cité.
(I.F.A. / DR.)

6. Cour Carrée, the Louvre.
(I.F.A.)

7. Rue de Rivoli.
(I.F.A.)

8. Palais Royal.
(I.F.A.)

25

L'EXRESS – The cheapest – The dearest – LIST OF TOP CITIES – Housing, taxes, everyday life…
L'Express / I.F.A.

3. DOES MEETING ALL THE MODERN FUNCTIONALITY CRITERIA NECESSARILY MAKE A CITY MORE DESIRABLE?

The attraction of one city more than another is frequently discussed in sociological and market surveys. These have revealed that industry executives and high-ranking French officials have a preference for the medium-sized cities of Grenoble and Annecy. These are sought after for the quality of life they provide, for their proximity to unspoilt nature, lakes and mountains, for their charming historical centres, for their driving facilities, and frequently also because it is possible to live in a residential suburb, in a detached house or a flat outside the city! A long way, at any rate, from the realities of large cities that many French people dread, rightly or wrongly so, eg traffic jams, stress, violence, fear of promiscuity, even perhaps of designated aliens whose mere presence is sufficient to depress the property market, who are accused of lowering education standards, of sustaining drugs networks…

The answers to those surveys very seldom conjure up the city in its richness, its complexity and its comprehensiveness, as Mark Girouard encapsulates it in one sentence loaded with life and wisdom. It may also be that the questions relating to city desire are inappropriate and that asking them is enough to crush a feeling that is too diffuse, inexpressible, inextricably moulded by city life itself. A life that has fashioned and been fashioned by successive generations, or even *a contrario,* because today's city dweller feels that the city moulds him more than he is capable of moulding it, because decisions are now taken almost on a world-wide basis. We are aware of the dangers of relocating manufacturing centres from region to region, from country to country, from continent to continent, but the local or national measures taken in support of town planning, zoning and motor-vehicle traffic can also be mentioned. An example of this is the recent introduction of <u>red routes</u> in Paris – right-of-way streets in which parking is prohibited. Their purpose is to facilitate the traffic flow, but the continuous flow of traffic makes the Parisians' lives much less convenient and pleasant. Shops and restaurants are going bankrupt, residents are moving. Steps to control and reduce through-traffic would no doubt be more relevant to those living inside Paris.

4. FUNCTIONALIST TOWN PLANNING VERSUS THE TRADITIONAL CITY

Functionalist town planning, as formulated in the first half of the 20th century and applied massively in the second, is characterized by the separation of functions concept (zoning), the priority given to mechanical flows and the rejection of the enclosed block and the street to promote living in the green spaces of maximum sunlight. The functionalist principles and their derivatives are all directed against the traditional city – hence against the very notion of city – and they found a fertile breeding ground in the psychological and social context of the post-war years.

World War I had driven both the victors and the vanquished to despair. *«There was a century of middle-class love spent here. This was the last love battle»,* says Dick Diver in Scott Fitzgerald's Tender Is The Night, one of the most remarkable voices of the «lost generation». Radical changes in human society, as in nature, occur in the wake of disasters. The Great War brought about sudden changes in lifestyles, upset class relations, but had little impact on the way cities were rebuilt. Between 1915 and 1925 the authorities opted in most cases for a reconstruction style recalling the urban atmosphere of pre-war years. Some streets were widened, some alignments straightened, some fragments combined, and reconstruction architecture fluctuated between a rational art nouveau – geometric and inspired by Viollet-le-Duc – Art Deco and various simplified stylistic formulas.
They built garden cities of Dutch and English inspiration, praised for their hygiene and moral qualities in contrast to the overcrowding and promiscuousness of the existing cities.
On the other hand, however, maintenance and rehabilitation of the old urban areas were no longer on the agenda. Modernist architects began to muse over extensive works, pooled commissions, standards, prefabs; they dismissed cottage industries, local projects, small buildings, maintenance work. What mattered then was making a clean sweep, a fresh start unfettered by history, by a past whose injustice and evil had just been illustrated by the war.
The context of the post-World War II years gave them the opportunity to make their dreams come true. The Marshall Plan, extensive road and motorway projects, mass-housing developments, the newly established administrations – everything contributed to reject the constituent concepts of traditional cities. Houses and flats became living units while the historic concept of neighbourhood was abandoned in favour of vicinity units; street continuity made way for alignment set-backs and free sitings; parks and gardens were turned into anonymous green zones and buffer zones.
In France the concept of regionalism, which had been refined and whose originality had been highlighted at the Paris Exposition in 1937, was deemed obsolete at best. More often than not it was associated with reactionary forces if not with the Vichy regime and collaboration, even with the Nazi ideology. And, above all, one should not underestimate the people's tremendous craving for novelty, for sunlight, after five years of darkness. The cities were too grimy and the Americans were praised – with their Jeeps, paratroopers, chewing gum, Lucky Strike, etc. Everybody felt, as the élite had in the 1920s, that a new life was dawning – less static, with broader horizons, blue skies, nylon

stockings, toasters, bathrooms, fitted-out kitchens with windows looking out on nature… The first low-rise and tower blocks set in greenery were greeted with enthusiasm. Radiant children with tears in their eyes, handkerchiefs, the Solex – no longer a bicycle but not yet a motorbike – conveyed the image of a half-rural, half-urban bliss.

The news headlines of the time were eloquent, if not grandiloquent. The moralistic steamroller was on its way, its intellectual backing a charter drawn up in Athens – democracy *oblige* – and wrested by architects who presented themselves as daring pioneers confronted with a bureaucracy of old fogies. The city ceased to matter, except as a curiosity. Only the certified historical centres were looked upon with favour, but only just. The old dwellings were subjected to health inspections; slums were discovered, never to be rehabilitated, earmarked only for destruction. That is how the working-class neighbourhoods disappeared. In Saint-Denis, the areas adjoining the illustrious cathedral of the kings of France were razed to the ground without a single objection. The urban purification business was in full swing. The web of <u>ever</u> stinking alleys, the <u>ever</u> shaky, dirty houses were culled, eradicated by an urbanism endowed with a clear social conscience.

Progress is relentless, abetted ostentatiously by the alienation of global judgement and the teaching of architecture. The few voices raised against the apophthegms of the god Progress were at once labelled backward-looking, nostalgic, élitist. Why should it be otherwise? The clean-sweep system suits everyone – the fools, who are reminded of their own ignorance by the city and its past; the militant left, seizing an opportunity to erase the traces of man's exploitation of man; the humanist right, using zoning as a solution for dealing with shanty towns before tackling the repatriated settlers [from Algeria]; the administrations and ministries of planning, consolidating their power over a city finally reduced to standards; the over-equipped businesses; the architects who can at last experiment, innovate, give life to their façades without having to consider the tastes of their clients or of the abhorred and reactionary bourgeoisie.

The housing estate, great purveyor of procurement contracts, is by definition beyond any criticism and settles *ipso facto* into the functionalist routine, paving the way for future tragedies with a clear conscience. As for offices and head offices, who can resist their determination to flaunt their power and selfishness once they have been released from the convivial corset of the avenue or boulevard?

5. THE TRADITIONAL CITY OR THE GOOD TIMES OF LIFE

The best and most accurate way of defining a traditional city – convenient (functional) and attractive (desirable) – is still to recall some good times spent in a city one loves. Those good times usually encapsulate the soul of the city. Generally speaking, cities were formed and developed around power struggles that were often violent, cruel and bloody but always arbitrated by the moral (not moralizing) code of the bourgeoisie. We are apt to blame the bourgeoisie for being hypocritical, but what would the world be without the mediation of hypocrisy? And does the truth not have many facets?

Haussmann's Paris erased mediaeval Paris, but the city that rose on the ruins was specifically Paris. Just as Berlin at the end of the 19th century was specifically Berlin, right down to its living «barracks» whose courtyards got bleaker as distance from the street increased.

The functionalist city is supposed to be unfettered by speculation, the basic outcome of a scientific, rationalistic and moralizing intent. It is supposed to be the work of specialists, no longer of bourgeois speculators. To define it, we just need to conjure up the image of some French or English new towns, of German towns rebuilt on the Stuttgart model. Beyond the diversity of architectural exercises that claim to distinguish them, those towns are all the same, frozen in the falsely egalitarian moralism that governed their design. Rather than working on the ever-perfectible traditional typologies, functional urbanism chose to ignore them in favour of the clean-sweep and universal standards. Just like the Caligula staged by the French novelist Albert Camus, the functionalist city wants to force its truth on the people and, like the despot, it also has the means to do so:

CALIGULA:
Men die and they are not happy.
HÉLICON:
Come now, Caius, this is a truth one can easily live with. Look around you. That is not what keeps them from their food.
CALIGULA:
That means that everything around me is a lie, and I want men to live within the truth! And it so happens that I have the means to make them live within the truth. For I know what they lack, Hélicon. They are devoid of knowledge and what they lack is a teacher who knows what he is talking about.

Moralism kills desire, generates sectarianism, dogmatism if not fanaticism, the bureaucratic mind and censorship. Ethics or the moral code, on the contrary, regulates the course of desire and the systolic heartbeat which is unsettled by passion alone. Desire and moralism are contradictory. Desire and ethics are in agreement.

6. THE MISERY OF FUNCTIONALISM

And yet the functionalist city (as opposed to the traditional city that always attempts to be pretty, solid and convenient) is less in control of its destiny than it claims to be. In the same way as the entourage of a despot or dictator teems with schemers, disciplinary autonomy generates rivalries between administrations, the most powerful of which are generally not those concerned with the city. Industry does not hesitate to use job blackmail to seek planning dispensations. Ultimately, everyone wants to proclaim his originality through an architectural form that differs from his neighbour's. It is hoped, in a disillusioned if not cynical manner, that if architects are made to compete, the originality of the sublime and inspired achievements of the «artists» will make us forget the mediocrity of the urbanism. Liberated from the private client, liberated from the bourgeois, architecture finds itself in the shackles of the supreme dictator – profit in cahoots with bureaucracy. It is this drifting of functionalism that causes the wreckage of the brightest talents and, gradually, the point is reached where chaos and discontinuity are praised for their own sake. Chaos and discontinuity as the supreme values of modernity. A trip to the new towns of the Paris region (Marne-la-Vallée, Cergy-Pontoise) will immediately convince the most sceptical of the magnitude of the disaster.

Traditional city and functionalist planning – there lies the difference between the human being and the robot.

Being moralistic, functionalism is also doctrinaire and reactionary as it postulates that man is predestined for the inevitability of technological progress (buildings with windows that no longer open and the urbanism of «raised pedestrian walkways» provide a clear illustration of this).

Between the 1950s and 1980s, the darkest and most dogmatic years ever experienced by European cities, all the players (elected representatives, architects, developers) felt they had done their duty and expected to be crowned, applauded, decorated, published. Did they not all work for the good of mankind? In 1883, Paul Lafargue published <u>Le Droit à la paresse</u> [The right to idleness], a refutation of <u>Le Droit au travail</u> [The right to work] of 1848 – a text of considerable import that was the cornerstone of the 8-hour day, the Sunday break and paid leave introduced by the Front Populaire in 1936. The sociologists of the 1950s and 1960s talked of the <u>Leisure Society</u>. Who then would have dreamed of the recessions and wars that would cause that fine structure to collapse? For the cities, however, the harm was done: in the name of an abstract, already blighted progress, the steamroller was on its way. The Europe of cities made way for the Europe of suburbs, monofunctional zones, and protected historical centres.

The fate of a species is talked about when it is on the way to extinction. Now that the cities are under threat and deliberately being destroyed, their future has never been so thoroughly discussed. If mentioning the desirability of the city in these final years of the 20th century is not tantamount to a paradox, it is none the less a purely academic issue which can be addressed this way or that.

7. DESIRE, WHAT DESIRE?

In that case, is it still important for a city to be desirable? In the context of increasingly anonymous and peripheral urban forms and atmospheres, what could motivate a desire to live in one place rather than another?
Is the question even worth asking?
We do not seek out what we desire; we desire what our eyes see and what our senses perceive, so any desire for a city is born of living there. Most young children naturally prefer the country, but adolescence and adulthood bring them back to the city. Also, we always desire something that has a word for it, a word that conjures up an instantly recognizable and identifiable image. The image conjures up known memories. It does not say that its secret alchemy and concentrated essence are easy to produce or reproduce. It is the law of desire that creates luminous memories.

For most women and men, expressing a desire and opting for a city is a question that does not even arise. Education levels, financial means, family ties, ethnic origin, prejudice, hold them close to where they were born and their families live. On the other hand, many of our contemporaries simply do not appreciate urban life, because they prefer the country or feel that the city has more drawbacks (insecurity, high rentals, noise, traffic, pollution, isolation, etc) than advantages. Many people live there not by choice but because they have no option: too old to drive, too poor to leave. In another respect, however, country life – as childlike imagery still represents it nowadays – is more of a fiction than a reality, and today's country dwellers are often no more than commuters. The country generally boils down to a few square metres of garden around the house, on balconies and around blocks of flats. It would nevertheless by wrong to infer that those who live there are not satisfied. They are quite content with their little houses, with mowing the lawn, with their private garage, with polishing the car, with their handyman's basement, with that universe of small favours, little joys and daily gibes. In many cases, holidays are also an excuse for trips to other suburbs beside the sea. Even the time spent commuting is not experienced negatively, as many people value those intermediate time slots between home and work. The distance between home and office in France increased from 7 to 14 kilometres per day between 1975 and the early 1990s. This is where the expression «killing time» takes on its full meaning. When ideological certainties were strong, class solidarity and factory-floor comradeship, militancy and the assertion of male superiority acted as a bond between the outcasts of the city. The rise of unemployment, outbursts of violence and fundamentalism did no more than dent this widespread pattern of life that was less denigrated by its users than by the criticisms of those gazing at it from the outside, hinting at its existence.

DISTANCES

The French commuter is travelling longer distances

According to a survey the distance between home and office increased from approximately 7 to 14 kilometres per day between 1975 and the early 1990s

The increase in urban population, together with suburban sprawl, has caused the French to make longer commuting journeys. These have doubled in length in less than 20 years. In a recent survey the *Observatoire économique et statistique des transports (OEST)* calculated that, in the early 1990s, the French travelled on average 14 kilometres to get to work, as opposed to about 7 kilometres in 1975. Besides the demographic factor, the change in employment pattern - with the loss of small industrial plants and a number of vicinity jobs in particular - has also contributed to longer commuting journeys, forcing the French to travel further. Today, only 45% of them work in the municipality they live in, as opposed to 60% almost 20 years ago.

This lengthening of the journey has altered the means of transport. The French have rather given up walking and cycling in favour of driving. In the provinces, the ratio of motor car to public transport journeys is five to one, dropping to two to one in the Ile de France. In this region, one person in three walks and 2% cycle. In the provinces, fewer people walk (29%) while 4% use a bicycle, a moped or a motorcycle to commute. Walking is mostly preferred for the home-to-school journey, even though the car and especially public transport are becoming increasingly popular with the school community.

However, the *OEST* points out that *«mobility in terms of the number of journeys per person and per day has shown remarkable overall stability since 1976»*. Women and pensioners having greater access to cars has contributed to an increase in journeys, while the rise of unemployment and the introduction of the continuous working day has somewhat hampered mobility.

The generalization of home leisure also reduces the number of journeys. In the early 1980s, one third of the French went to the cinema regularly and 50% watched television. In 1988, 73% stayed at home to watch television, while only 15% still preferred the cinema.

AFP

Libération / I.F.A. / Culot.

8. FUNCTIONAL ZONING

Drawing by Léon Krier.
THE LETHAL WEAPON IS THE DORMITORY TOWN, NOT THE CAR. HENCE THE DAILY BOMBING OF URBAN CENTRES.

«*The most remarkable outcome of functional zoning is to guarantee the maximum consumption of time, energy and land units in performing the daily functions of society as a whole.*

The circulation of persons, goods and information is the main activity of the industrial man-nature metabolism. The roads, motorways, canals, air-traffic lanes, oil pipelines are the arteries of this fragmented society – paradoxically everyone's commonplaces.

The train, the car, the aircraft, the computer, the telephone, the fax machine and television are its principal instruments, the necessary extensions of the human body and mind. They are also the prime causes of environmental problems.

All industrial States, irrespective of their political ideology, encourage and impose the functional zoning of cities and the countryside, disregarding opposition and arguments of any kind. Yet functional zoning is not a neutral tool. It turns a society of active individuals into a mobilized mass society. Functional zoning replaces the organic order of the city and polycentricity with the mechanical disorder of suburbia and the lack of centrality.»

> Léon Krier in
> Architecture, Choix ou Fatalité
> IFA, NORMA, Paris, 1995

9. ON THE SUBJECT OF PUBLIC ARCHITECTURE AND TOWN-PLANNING COMPETITIONS

While ignorance almost invariably leads to intolerance, an awareness of ignorance enables people to excel and stimulates their desire to learn, though it can also generate authoritarian attitudes and a rejection of dialogue, or simply a taste for artful devices, smoke screens and «display».

Today's architecture magazines indicate that a large number of architects have fallen into that habit, expressing themselves in an obscure, incomprehensible, pseudo-poetic language to present their creations.

This language, like that used by some suburban youths, is a rallying symbol, a convention. It expresses support for artistic conformism and points to a scapegoat, the middle-class lover of pastiche whose myth is fostered by exercises in exorcism. Every architecture magazine of our times features a tirade against pastiche, as if this were the greatest foe preventing architects from creating with complete freedom. If I express amusement at the language of architecture magazines, I am accused of regression. Similarly, I can live in a traditional house without incurring criticism, but if I praise it in public, people point the finger at me. There is a total lack of comprehension between the architects who erect barricades of words, and the public that seeks an aesthetic quality most practitioners are refusing to provide.

It is here, on this plurality of choices issue, that the advocates of discontinuity join battle with those of continuity, who propose to take into account the desire for roots and taste for tradition in architecture and town planning.

Now fearing a radical rejection of modern architecture and planning by the people, the practitioners – backed by the administrations – are attempting to overtake the protest movement. A French law stipulates that the architects of public buildings must be selected through architecture competitions. A praiseworthy notion, initially, since it enables young architects without connections to have access to commissions.

An Interministerial Mission for the Quality of Public Constructions (MIQCP) was set up in 1977. Another laudable initiative, but in actual fact the officials of this Mission, sitting on the juries, use all their influence to steer the selection process mostly towards modernist solutions, as though quality could never be vernacular, regionalist, classical, traditional. Looking at the results, it is immediately apparent that public competitions are the Trojan horse of modernism. Juries always comprise staunch supporters of discontinuity architecture. And to this day, no competition in France has led to the erection of a traditional building and development plan. The styles and vernacular architecture are banished, as well as traditional streets and squares – always on the charge that such proposals are the product of a petit-bourgeois and regressive mentality.

However, the competition system is not criticized by the advocates of continuity alone. The modernists themselves are now firmly opposed to it.

In France, the only European country where competitions are almost compulsory for all buildings and structures put up by administrations (State, region, city, housing estates, hospitals, etc), prominent personalities have just taken a public stand against the competition system.

Paul Chemetow, the architect of the Ministry of Finance in Paris, writes in the *Moniteur* magazine of 23 September 1995 that:

«*The competition system, devised as a means of architectural promotion to redistribute public commissions and break the closed circuits of the large building administrations, has evolved over the years as a result of its own expansion. Once an exception to be envied, it has now become the rule to be endured*» [...].

«*The growing number of competitions simply makes it impossible to select juries in a qualified, serene and enlightened manner. For an average of a thousand 'recognized' competitions, 4000 to 5000 architect-days must be set aside every year. Sitting on a jury has therefore become an activity among others, which has found an equilibrium and a compensation in the friendship, clientele and corporate networks.*» [...].

«*The expansion of competitions*», Chemetow goes on, «*losing sight of the main object of reviving architecture, has generalized a mercenary notion, a commercial if not an <u>intellectual</u> marketing. Instead of being an obligation – in many cases oblique – a competition should be the freely chosen hallmark of the contractor's architectural requirements. To restore the impact of competitions and, above all, to turn them into models by restricting their numbers, it is essential to...*».

Paul Chemetow concludes that the competition policy should soon be discontinued, and he suggests, *inter alia*:

«*Promoting direct commissions decided on the basis of a portfolio or simple audition. A contractor in charge of a project should only consider those architects with whom he would be prepared to work,*» [...]

«*Allowing the public authorities at every level to grant direct commissions in proportion to the number of public competitions organized.*» [...]

«*Authorizing the direct allocation of housing schemes up to 100 homes.*»

Joseph Belmont – a top-ranking French civil servant, former Director of Architecture at the Ministry of Planning and one of the most fervent supporters of public competitions – has also made a complete about-turn and is now even harsher:

«*Architecture competitions have no future as they are by nature dedicated to architectures of exception (...). The ensuing policy of architectural exception, as typified by the Great Projects, has resulted in a kind of hypertrophy of exception leading to an impasse*». (*Le Moniteur*, 18 August 1995).

In France today, modernist architecture has become the official style of the Fifth Republic. The great projects sponsored by President Mitterrand partake of the same ideology: imposing on the people an aesthetic view that is rejected by most of them. The media publicity surrounding these projects is so intense that whoever opposes them is bound to be seen as a reactionary.

To silence the critics, over the past ten years some elected representatives have resorted to a more subtle approach. Playing the snobbery card, they have awarded any potentially contentious projects to the top names of world architecture, either directly or through competitions. Artists with broad media coverage, whose mere names are meant to silence any critics. Initially tested in large cities, this strategy was then extended to provincial towns.

In 1975, ITT made its siting in Brussels conditional upon the construction of a tower block overlooking the charming abbey of La Cambre in a residential area.
This project, instantly censured by the residents, was at the root of the protest movement that led to the creation of 100 citizens' associations in Brussels. To justify the ITT tower project, the Mayor responsible for town planning first resorted to employment blackmail, then argued that the tower had been designed by Gropius (who had died two years earlier!), and that any criticism of the final work of a grand master of modern architecture was inconceivable.
A few years later ITT moved its main office to Paris.

In Paris the Louvre pyramid – which is an aberration in terms of distribution – attracts endless queues of visitors, whatever the weather. It is not open to criticism since it is the work of a famous American architect chosen by the President of the Republic.

European cities are now engaged in relentless struggles to set up business districts round the TGV stations, eg Lille, Brussels, Lyons, Bologna… Here again, to prevent public opinion outcries, the projects are entrusted to top architects.

In Lille, the TGV station and the development of the surrounding area gave rise to a town-planning experiment which turned into a resounding economic flop.

However, such appeals to stardom and snobbery are not always successful. In cities where there is an awareness of the environment and associations are active, the projects of the stars of architecture are subject to criticism like any others.

In Bologna, the State Railways persuaded the Mayor to accept a demolition project for the old station – a historical monument and a monument to democratic resistance – to be replaced by a huge business district with 4 towers more than 100 metres high, in the vicinity of the historical centre. To have this irresponsible project accepted, the Italian State Railways selected a top architect, the Spaniard Boffil, who justifies glass and stainless-steel towers by presenting them as a reflection of the famous brick towers of the city centre! In Bologna, however, after the initial amazement had subsided, an international protest campaign was launched, with the architect of the Historical Monuments Division, various associations, the University of Bologna and even railway engineers mobilizing to fight the Boffil project.

In Belgium, in 1995, the Walloon Government organized a competition for the construction of the Walloon Parliament in the heart of the city of Namur. Judged by a jury consisting mostly of modernists, the competition crowned Mario Botta's project.
The model exhibited in the city attracted thousands of visitors who, almost unanimously, came down against the project that would have disfigured an exceptional site at the foot of the citadel. In the face of the public's determined response, the Walloon Government wisely abandoned the project.

More and more mayors who believed themselves to be above any criticism from their electorate are beaten at the polls because of their planning policy and architectural choices.

In 1992 the Mayor of Biarritz was defeated, within his own majority, for proposing the destruction of the municipal casino erected in 1930. A member of the majority opposed it, early elections were held and the mayor was thoroughly beaten. Not only did the new mayor have the casino restored, he also had the entire beachfront redeveloped and a project investigated for a protection perimeter extended to a large part of the city.

In Dax, south-west France, the mayor had entrusted the construction of the new thalassotherapy centre to the French architect Jean Nouvel. This talented architect erected an interesting though incongruous building beside the Hotel Splendid, an Art Deco masterpiece. The mayor was defeated in 1995, precisely for having encouraged the construction of this building.

The Mayor of Nîmes suffered the same fate after having commissioned Norman Foster to build a glass-and-metal reference library on the site of a neo-classical theatre that had been damaged by fire but could have been rebuilt as it was.

The fact that discontinuity architecture and planning have become the only official expression has further widened the gap between the public and architecture. Architects are increasingly seen as predators, despite the media campaigns promoting their unforgettable creations.

Very recently, the French Architects' Associations wrote an open letter to the Minister for Culture (L'architecture n'est pas soluble dans le patrimoine [Architecture cannot be dissolved in the national heritage], 13 September 1995) in which they conclude that «architects are still fully determined to assert the creative values of their art and to place these at the disposal of the French nation». This claim is all the more amiss since everyone knows that only a small proportion of the 33 000 French architects can pride themselves on being artists. This is not a criticism but an observation that anyone can make with their own eyes – mediocrity and racketeering being common occurrences. It would obviously be healthier and more beneficial for the future of architecture if professional institutions focused on the architect's trade rather than his art. Otherwise, the image of architecture is bound to deteriorate further. One masterpiece can never erase the thousands of errors oppressing the daily lives of residents, while the existence of an increasingly impregnable wall dividing the architects from the public can hardly be seen as a positive factor.

All over Europe, citizens' initiatives are gaining ground. Their purpose is no longer to force the architects' viewpoint on the residents, but to ensure that the legitimate wishes of the main party concerned, ie the public, are taken into consideration.

There is an increasing number of significant cultural campaigns, such as the events initiated by the Vision d'Europe association, in Bologna, with a three-yearly exhibition on Urban Renaissance. On the initiative of The Classical Architecture League, The Art of Building Cities movement was set up in the United States in 1992 as the successor of Beautiful America. These non-conformist initiatives take active steps to salvage the prestigious heritage of tradition, for after the collapse of ideologies there is no reason why architects should continue depriving themselves of the tools that fashioned the most successful architectures and urban projects. In other words, the concepts of copying and imitation must be reinstated in colleges, debates, magazines and symposiums. This is the only way to restore pluralism, genuine freedom of choice and a firm balance between the advocates of discontinuity and those of continuity.

It is therefore essential that the practitioners and their institutions, associations, colleges and schools stop defending their members in the name of their individual right to express their art with complete freedom. Such a stance is dogmatic and all the less democratic since it is now becoming impossible to criticize. Everyone, including those responsible for the worst aberrations, is claiming the artist's right to free expression, even at the detriment of the people's legitimate wishes.

Some architects are indeed artists; most of them do their job (or should be able to do it), some are interested chiefly in the commercial aspects, others in the social, technical or legal aspects. The main thing is not to turn all those architects with such diverging concerns into as many geniuses. The temptation to do so is understandable, as it is one way of forcing architects upon a public that has increasing doubts as to their problem-solving ability. But a move in this direction can only intensify mutual incomprehension.

It is suicidal for a profession to consider that the mere virtue of enrolment in a school of architecture automatically makes one an artist. One of the first steps that can be taken in favour of architects is to stop idealizing their image and presenting them as artists whose work is *ipso facto* regarded as sacred. Continuing to favour the VIP system in teaching and within the profession instead of promoting the learning of a trade can only generate more frustration and destructive antagonisms. To defend architects properly within their diverse profession, we should start with the defence of architecture, of cities, of the living environment. As for the true artists, history shows that, even in the worst circumstances, nothing but death has prevented them from expressing themselves. If we want to defend architects, we must begin with defending architecture, cities and the living environment.

THE ART OF BUILDING CITIES

CLASSICAL ARCHITECTURE
A conference at the Art Institute
July 9-11, 1995

Programme of the conference The Art of Building Cities, Chicago, 9-11 June 1995.
Cover drawing by J. Montgomery.

THE ART OF BUILDING CITIES

The Art of Building Cities is a conference and exhibition being held to explore how architectural and urbanistic principles of traditional city planning can create new sustainable cities and towns that are environmentally and socially balanced.

We feel that today architecture is at a crossroads. It is time for architects to contribute again towards a genuinely civic social structure; a meaningful built environment in which to conduct our lives. The surviving traditional city and its architecture present an alternative model that is rooted in and embodies civic and democratic life. Its language is legible to all. Traditional buildings and towns remain useful long after their original function has disappeared. We can see this in cities around the world where the urban fabric is hundreds of years old yet has adapted well to new uses and has accommodated new technologies.

The Art of Building Cities will examine how to generate new livable communities with a sense of place and civic identity by facilitating accessibility and cultural interaction. Good cities embody respect for their citizens and sensible stewardship of the earth.

THE CLASSICAL ARCHITECTURE LEAGUE
Stephen Chrisman, Michael Lykoudis, Thomas Noble

FROM ABOVE: Barrett and Buch with Duany and Plater-Zyberk, The Green at Blount Springs, AL; John Simpson & Partners, Coldharbour Farm, England

41

10. THE POWER AND LIMITS OF POPULAR SOLIDARITY

At fêtes and fairs in the Belgian city of Charleroi, the townspeople – proletarians and bourgeois together – readily identified with the lyrics of a song:

«Charleroi country, the finest place on earth in my eyes,

yes, that's you...»

These lyrics express the conviction of this 19th-century songwriter who, having admired monuments and cities all over the world, concludes that the Black Country – with its collieries, its mines, its slag heaps, its iron and steel plants, its mining cottages – is the ultimate in Beauty. Similar popular songs are to be found in other European mining towns, eg Roubaix, Lille, Manchester or in the Ruhr. What a visitor finds most hideous and cannot wait to leave behind is seen by the townsfolk as most desirable. Nonetheless, the song was not written to give them heart and those of Charleroi are not sadists. From what we know, the songwriter was no cynic but a much loved child of Wallonia.

So the beauty of the Charleroi country, 250 kilometres from Paris, exists even though it can be seen only through the eyes of the locals – the chosen few who detect it within a large nondescript industrial town, now in full decline, filled with smoke and dust, devoid of any significant monuments or recognizable urban framework and, what is more, afflicted with a poor climate. A beauty that lies both in the tremendous solidarity of the industrial world and its capacity for working and having fun together (fairs and Rabelaisian drunken binges) and in the grandeur of the industrial plant, of the smelting furnaces casting a reddish glow on the night, of the black slag-heap pyramids. The beauty of hell, as it were, and Hieronymus Bosch is not far. The recession has thoroughly defeated industrial activity. Today, many are the poor – unemployed, aliens (Africans, North Africans, Turks) and those who simply cannot afford to live in Brussels – who come to live in Charleroi. They are taking over from the Spaniards and the Italians, the early immigrants who were attracted by jobs in the coal mines (now closed). The town of Charleroi continues, in their eyes, to be a «fine place», if not the finest, and solidarity seems to have endured despite the factory closures.

Such solidarity, such capacity for sharing is encountered in the working-class areas of large cities, in the ethnic Asian and Italian neighbourhoods. It is both an obstacle to integration and a bond promoting it – a function that was often fulfilled in the 19th century by the station areas. Solidarity is a cohesive force for the men and women facing the difficulties of manual labour, emigration and poverty.

But these areas are also breeding grounds for drugs, fanaticism, illiteracy and violence. Though it is not a matter of turning the old industrial towns into cities of art, it is nonetheless urgent to turn the slum areas into neighbourhoods and integrate these into a town before human kindness runs dry.

Hieronymus BOSCH, The Garden of Earthly Delights, detail of Hell, Prado Museum, Madrid.

HIERONYMUS BOSCH'S HELL.

The disturbing beauty of Hell is attractive. Who among us, in our thoughts, have not transposed Bosch's images into the real world? Cities originate from our resistance to the force of those images which artists produce both to tempt us and to divert.

11. THE NEED FOR A VISION

Solidarity therefore expresses itself regardless of urban form, and the suburban way of life – exclusive or popular – has become the norm. On the other hand, historical centres have been preserved with varying degrees of success. Consequently, the criticism of modern urbanism can no longer rest, as it used to, on people's misfortunes and hopes, but only on the affirmation of the traditional city as a global reference, as an image of the world, and as a means of protecting people from egoism and amnesia. In this sense, the traditional city is a topical issue. The loftiest human endeavours collapse if they are not sustained by a vision. A vision, in the American sense, of a project fortified by enthusiasm, propelled into the future, which is implemented as it is developed.

The Athens Charter proposed universal, undifferentiated solutions applicable anywhere in the world. What urban Europe needs today is the opposite, ie specific solutions, with local roots, but driven by a process that can be initiated and adopted anywhere in Europe. The purpose of this is to safeguard identity while avoiding a regression of regional and national identities. This echoes Winston Churchill's words, «you are alone and I acknowledge you alone», to those who rallied England from every corner of oppressed Europe.

Functionalism may arouse curiosity. For instance, the Grande Arche at La Défense in Paris, with its monumental stairs, links up with the tradition of powerful architecture. It rarely arouses desire and, in most cases, it imposes itself rather than gains acceptance.

It is therefore to the dustbins of functionalism that we should turn to salvage – as ecology demands – all that has been dumped, sullied, discredited. They contain everything that was used to create, develop, repair, complement and extend the traditional cities – an incredible clutter where lie, pell-mell and abandoned, the concepts of copying, imitation, mimicry and pastiche, false antique, the styles and the neos, the art of patina. Let us explore the cellars and the lofts.

12. THE CITY AND THE BOURGEOISIE

«But social hardship and urban segregation, the confrontation between conspicuous wealth and poverty within the cities have never destroyed the city as a concept, since these are contradictions it has always managed to absorb, at least up to the industrial period.»

>André Antolini and Yves-Henri Bonello
>in <u>Les villes du désir</u>
>Éditions Galilée, Paris, 1994

In <u>Mort de la Morale bourgeoise</u>, published in 1928 (Éditions Gallimard, Paris), Emmanuel Berl settles the score with the French bourgeoisie: *«the bourgeois is basically a spiritualist. The revolutionary is basically a materialist. This old battle is nowhere near being settled. I do not like those who cry, 'down with money'. They always end up crying, 'long live money,' to defend castes and privileges in the name of the spirit. This is indeed the line of attack used by revolutionaries such as Lenin and Marx.»*

Berl, a bourgeois himself, despises bourgeois spiritualism. He counters it with materialism, which is *«courage in thought and irreverence at heart»*.
The Great Depression of 1929 put an end to the intellectual controversy. There followed an ideological confrontation that stirred up conflicts, aggravating the two extreme camps: Fascism and Communism.

Emmanuel Berl's work is now enjoying an *a contrario* topicality. The ideologies have bowed out to the market economy. The concentration of capital and internationalization of markets are the new rulers. Have they ousted the bourgeois civilization for good? To answer «Yes» would be embarrassing, as all bourgeois-less city experiments have failed. Would Florence and Bruges have prospered without their ingenious merchant bourgeoisie? Would Art Nouveau have flourished in Europe without the wishes and will of an industrial bourgeoisie both dynamic and bold? If the answer is «No», if the bourgeoisie still has a place in the city, how can we create the conditions for its rebirth?
Asking the bourgeoisie, along with a skilled artisan class, to come back and play a significant part can only be effective, of course, if provisions are made so that it can fulfil its responsibilities.
The first of these, if it cannot abandon zoning and large-scale urbanism, is at least to exercise strict control over them. For if the bourgeoisie is to take part in the restoration and reconstitution of the city's urban fabric, the magnitude of the undertakings should obviously be within its reach.
To this end, an urbanism based on plots and streets must be restored – an urbanism that would define different-sized plots of land that the bourgeois could purchase and on which they would plan various

projects, eg housing, small-scale industries, businesses, shops, craft industries, etc.

«The wolves have entered the city», sang the late Serge Reggiani; the bourgeois are possibly – definitely – hypocrites but they are not wolves. If the European city is exhausted, it is through too much bureaucracy generating too many anti-city standards and circulars; too many facilities given to big predators, to anonymous speculators, to the wolves who can take the risk of ruining a city without suffering the same fate.

For Berl, the bourgeois only uses bourgeois culture to gain access to the aristocracy and stand apart from the poor. *«Culture and bourgeoisie are one and the same thing»* he writes, *«culture is a values system raised against the proletariat.»*

«The bourgeois can only oppose cultural values to industrial values», Berl goes on. Precisely: the city is built as much around cultural and symbolic values as around rational arguments.

Ecological disasters in the former Eastern Bloc, the insane waste of land and resources are a perfect illustration of what happens to industrial values unchecked by cultural values.

The bourgeois is an individualist. He is also an idealist, *«...the bourgeois is such a lover of idealism that, in his mouth, this word is always a compliment. To have an ideal, to deny the reality of things (...A woman is a projected thought; a city, the petrifaction of a dream,...), in his eyes those two attitudes are fused»* (Berl).

Perhaps *«because it does not think»*, in the words of the singer Jacques Brel, the bourgeoisie has a global viewpoint. The bourgeoisie does not feel the need to define what bourgeois thinking is. It is bourgeois thinking. Taken individually, almost all its components are intolerable and irritating, as the bourgeois' dramatic contradiction is always to aspire to the individual and always ends up denying it. All this is known. Even so, the most generous social concepts do not combine to make a city; and the bourgeoisie – with its burden of turpitudes and ridicule – has erected and managed cities that are robust or elegant, classical or picturesque, fine or ugly but always interesting, always cities.

The virtue of bourgeois thinking, inexpressible as it is, lies in being pragmatic and effective when the time has come to start building. And if it is not directly involved, it acts through its sons and daughters – so much so that reaction to the bourgeoisie still comes within the bourgeois ethics.

Obviously, it is not a matter of resurrecting the old bourgeoisie but of promoting the emergence of a young, modern, pluralistic, active bourgeoisie – comprising active citizens engaged in community life – bearing with it the blueprint for rebuilding the European city.

13. THE CITY IS NOT A TREE. THE CITY IS A HUMAN CREATION

«*Now then, let's face it: we have become incapable of founding cities. As Baudrillard points out, 'Old cities have a history, American cities have a savage extension [...], the new towns have neither – they dream of an impossible past and an unlikely break-up!' We are at the same stage as Athens when it was conquered by Philip in 338 – devoid of its founders' aspirations.*»

      André Antolini and Yves-Henri Bonello
      in <u>Les villes du désir</u>
      Éditions Galilée, Paris, 1994

In an essay published in 1966 under the title <u>La ville n'est pas un arbre</u> [The city is not a tree], Christofer Alexander showed that the functionalist city was a doomed Utopia, and that its tree structure was incompatible with that of a traditional city which is always represented in network form. But that was merely an observation, not yet a project. The Luxembourg architect Léon Krier was the first, in the 1970s, to draw attention to the fact that the European city is man's only genuine creation. Léon Krier has attempted to highlight the constituent elements of the city, the organization and size of the neighbourhood, the mix. He developed a consistent city project, backed by a critique of zoning and a comparative analysis of the constituent concepts of European cities.

Krier shows that the European city is based on the invariant concepts of neighbourhood, street and square; that these comply with criteria of size (walking distance) and management (beyond 35% of public space, a city is no longer manageable. In the suburbs, the proportion of public space often reaches 70 to 90%).

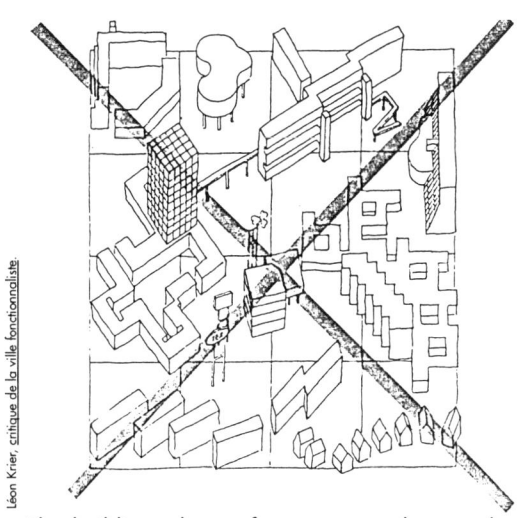

The buildings do not form a space that can be circumscribed. The public space is fortuitous.

14. DESIRE AND ARCHITECTURAL LANGUAGE OR THE CHOICE OF STYLES

Modern European architecture is a victim of the metaphor. In other words, things are no longer called by their name, and so they lose their meaning and their reality.

A street is no longer a street but «a sequential dialogue of autotomized faces» or «a random glimpse of the daily illusion»; a block of flats is «a receptacle of life», «a space liner»; a neighbourhood is «a fractal dynamic-chaotic fragment».

The metaphor – glory of the speculative Roman rhetoric, conveying the object-bearing image to another object and making it lighter – is reduced by some architects, teachers and critics of architecture to a pun, to infantile poetry, to a hotchpotch of fragments borrowed, indiscriminately, from the language of philosophy, science, economics,...

There is one effective remedy for this metaphor epidemic: a return to the styles.

Any desire consists of one part nostalgia and one part project (one part projection into the past, one part projection into the future).

But we can only desire a human being, an object, a feeling, a city that we already know, that we have seen before, whose features and beauty have been called to mind,...

No one longs for an abstraction.

In a civilization such as the European civilization, in which arts and crafts are a significant and valued heritage, many women and men have an interest in fine monuments, urban perspectives, baroque, classical or picturesque squares, patterns of criss-crossing or right-angle streets,...

If an architect, an engineer or a planner designing an architecture and town-planning project asked themselves this question: «will this project appeal to most people, will they adopt and cherish it?», some of the problems would already be solved. The practitioners should therefore inquire into the tastes of a given city, region or country in order to assimilate them.

Well-formulated images (where the context is always taken into account) speak for themselves, for the principles and the social values they underlie.

For the public at large, architecture is primarily a question of style and context, while the architects have long been concerned with the styles.

From the 1920s onwards, the international style, modernist moralism and the teaching of architecture have generally prohibited the use of the styles. Their teaching and learning have waned, and private architecture alone (bourgeois housing) has proceeded according to stylistic criteria with the support of a minority of creators and contractors.

According to Professor Vincent Scully:

[passage in English]

«*The Modern architects of International Style had largely taken abstract painting as their model,*

and they came to want to be as free from all constraints as those painters were, free from everything which had always shaped and limited architecture before, in part from statics itself (forms must float) and from roofs, windows, trim and so on, but most of all from the restraints of the urban situation as a whole: from the city, from the community. Their buildings were to be free of zoning laws, and from the need to define the street, and from all respect for whatever already existed on and around the site. They were to be free – like Lever House or Pan Am building or the Whitney Museum or even the Guggenheim Museum – to rip the old urbanism apart or to outrage it, or, perhaps most truly, to use its order, while it lasted, as a background before which they could cavort. Most of all they had to be abstract; they could not under any circumstances be inflected toward their surroundings by Classical or vernacular details or stylistic references of any kind. Such would have constituted an immoral act. Here was another madness to complement the others. It is still prevalent today among many architects who, baffled by the complexity of reality, still insist that architecture is a purely self-referential game, having to do with the city or with human living on any sane terms. Such architects claim to reflect the chaos of modern life and to celebrate it. Some of them pretend to worship the automobile and the 'space-time continuum', like Marinetti before them idolizing violence, speed, war and Fascism in the end.»
[Sic – end of passage in English]

(op. cit. <u>The New Urbanism</u>, postscript, 1994)

At this juncture, returning to a stylistic approach may be the most effective means of initiating a new dialogue between architects and clients (as demonstrated by the success of the new American communities built around stylistic themes).
Obviously, it is not a question of returning to the stylistic conventions of the past but of reflecting on a new concept linking the choice of styles to the context, to identity and local culture, to history, limited means, human resources, etc.
What style should be used to add to a neighbourhood, build a street, put up a public building?
What style is compatible with the existing environment which may be homogeneous but is frequently made heterogeneous by the contributions of successive periods?
Naturally, each of us have our own tastes and our own ability to fashion the styles. Many architects cannot afford to use the classical orders, the pediments and colonnades for which their architectural training and skill are very inadequate.
There are numerous stylistic sources, however, and everyone can find something suitable in them.
Some examples follow, in no particular order:

<u>The Mediterranean Spanish style</u>
Valued for its colourfulness, (it can easily be given an artificial patina) and its capacity for

solving complex programmes, eg for a house. Composition errors, which are unforgivable in classical architecture, are less noticeable here.

The Basque regional style of south-west France
This style features extensive red-tile roofs on two gradients, thick walls painted white, timber framing and shutters painted red (originally with ox blood) or green. In the 1920s, some architects created an updated version full of freshness and grandeur.

The art deco style
Of particular interest for its dual nature, both cosmopolitan and mindful of local cultures, and its capacity for combining such decorative arts as stained-glass windows, wrought iron, wood panelling, etc. It is the most optimistic of the modern styles.

All the vernacular styles popular in the 1920s
Pueblo style, Art Deco Pueblo, Maya style, American Colonial, Moroccan, neo-Norman, South African, etc.

The neo-classical style
This is the bourgeois variant of high style – practical, quiet and simple. Everything lies in the proportions and the texture. This style is particularly suited to our times which are characterized by excessive gesticulating and gossip.

The international style of the 1920s
It produces emotions similar to those aroused by the modern paintings of that period. It demands absolute precision and considerable maintenance. It is better earmarked for wealthy communities bordering the sea, where the combination of white façades and ocean blue guarantee great poetic effects.

The *beaux-arts* style
It is rarely used in Europe where reconstituting the urban fabric is more of a priority than building operas and banks. The United States, however, still has the necessary financial means and architectural skills, as evidenced by Thomas Beeby's new Chicago library.

The exotic styles
Chinese, Turkish, Mozarabic, Churrigueresque, Aztec, etc.
These, however, can only be used on rare occasions. When an exotic flavour needs to be introduced into a neighbourhood that is either featureless or very homogeneous, with repetitive architecture.

In the late 1920s, the Carreras factory was built on the site of a park lined by a crescent of houses. The factory blotted out the park and caused a housing blight. Nevertheless, its neo-Egyptian Art Deco aesthetics introduced a note of exoticism into this working-class neighbourhood of London.

In the 1970s/1980s the building was stripped and turned into an ordinary office block. The exoticism has vanished, plain unattractiveness has prevailed, the houses continue to deteriorate.

Document Culot / I.F.A.

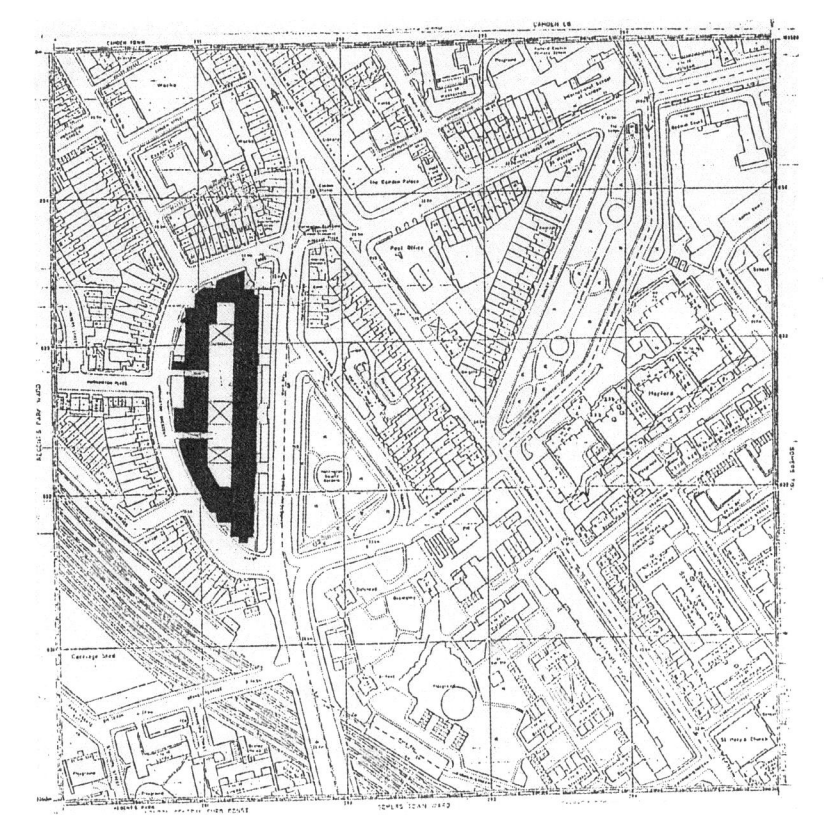

As an example, I will mention the Carreras building erected in the <u>neo-Egyptian art deco style</u> of the early 1930s in Camden Town, London. That is where the famous <u>Craven A cork-tipped</u> cigarettes were made.

The packets bore the symbol of a black cat that appeared in two giant models, two sculptures of slender black cats which flanked the entrance to the building.

The building had been erected on the site of a park lined by a <u>crescent</u> of houses. This was a terrible planning error. But in those depression years, CAMDEN the Red could not afford to turn down a factory project. The injudicious siting (responsible for the area's long-term degradation) was offset by the style of the building. Every morning, the factory workers were cheered by the sight of the temple-factory that conjured up dreams of Egypt and its mysteries.

Unfortunately, Carreras had to close in the 1980s and the new owners took great pains to strip all the neo-Egyptian art deco motifs. Even the two cats fled before the slaughter. The magic has gone; what remains is a poorly sited mediocre office block. This wanton act of vandalism alone warrants the establishment of an international society for the protection of neo-Egyptian art deco buildings, the setting up of an introductory course in this style at an American university (Europe is not ready yet), and the formation of a competitive association to promote an appreciation of this style and reward exemplary achievements.

The styles debate – which is bound to gain considerable momentum in the years to come – carries along with it and rejuvenates the potentially creative concepts of copying, forging to look real, identical reproduction, pastiche, mimicry, imitation – which concepts are banished from European schools of architecture. Yet there is an entire universe to be explored and, into the bargain, centuries of lessons to be drawn, of projects to be completed in the excitement of knowledge. Here again America – prejudice-free and open to research – leads the way.

A victim of the metaphor, European architecture also suffers from the demise of the client. In other words, the client accepts anything that is sold to him under the label of creativity or functional rationality. The three symptoms of this demise are:

- The anonymous nature of today's clients (multinationals, insurance companies, speculators, etc) for whom architecture is a commodity among others.

- Idealization – through the press, exhibitions, teaching – of the architects' image, while it is common knowledge that most of them are unable to live up to the public's expectations.

- The absence of a plain alternative to the inevitability of «*progress*». With few exceptions, architecture colleges and magazines, professional associations and cultural institutions are totally impervious to architecture and urbanism, both of which assert a link with tradition.

The freedom architects believe they have gained by eliminating the client's role is of course an illusion. Without educated and demanding clients, architecture becomes totally subservient to the law of maximum profit at any price. And if the architect's imagination is not channelled, structured by the debate with the client, with the civil society, it will invariably end up generating aberrations.

The development of the city of Brussels from the 1950s onwards is a clear illustration of that scenario. A martyr not of wars (it was spared) but of modern architecture and urbanism, Brussels in the 1960s/1970s gave rise to the term *«brusselise»*, to denote the destruction of a city in peace time!

It is true that the Belgian capital was subjected to unprecedented speculation pressure:

- a universal exposition in 1958 (responsible for devastating road works);

- the siting of NATO;

- the siting of the Common Market institutions, whose urbanistic impact on the neighbouring areas had been miscalculated by the Belgian authorities.

Those huge programmes, requiring prompt completion, overtook the local officials who left a clear field for the road engineers, the private and public developers, the architects.

In the space of a few years, a fine provincial capital was wrecked. It witnessed the demise of its shady boulevards, its fountains, its monumental buildings such as post offices, theatres, food markets, etc.

Entire neighbourhoods were razed to make way for a business centre pompously named Manhattan. The project turned into a disaster. The residents of the city centre were driven out by speculation and municipal negligence.

Today, those dark years seem remote and the planning policy has changed radically. Many developments already bear witness to this urban renaissance.

There are many reasons for such a Copernican upheaval, eg the appointment of new political and administrative staff, the citizens' vigilance and, primarily, the action taken by two cultural associations, the Archives d'Architecture Moderne (AAM) and the Atelier de Recherche et d'Actions Urbaines (ARAU). Both associations, set up in 1968, have been instrumental in arousing and formulating a civic urban awareness.

AAM published books and a magazine, organized exhibitions illustrating – through original architecture documents – the architectural quality that characterized the periods prior to the fateful 1950s. AAM also regularly submitted counter-projects showing that there was indeed an alternative to the destruction of the city – an alternative that lay in the very spirit of architectural and urbanistic tradition.

ARAU, for its part, offered the residents a political reading of the city and proposed an educational line of action. The object was not to topple the politicians but to force them to set up the conditions for a public debate on town-planning matters. ARAU patiently prepared the residents' associations in particular and the civil society in general to decipher the true intentions lurking behind the laws, the architects' projects and the statements of the developers and politicians, and then to criticize them constructively. The reconstruction of the rue de Laeken – which involved the demolition of a tower block and the building of homes in the long-derelict centre – is one of the most successful and eloquent results of such an education.

15. FUNCTIONALITY, AESTHETICS AND DESIRABILITY OF THE CITY. DESIRE AND MORALISM ARE A BAD MATCH

Desire is not a consideration in the formulation of 20th-century urbanism, which is supposed to be primarily scientific. Desire and all its derivatives – love, liking, lust, attraction, passion – is nonetheless a feeling many city dwellers experience for their city. Functionalism consists in favouring the separate functions rather than the city as a whole. Functionalism takes the city to pieces and separates them on the ground into industrial estates, small business areas, housing estates, historical areas, hospital zones, commercial zones and links them together with mechanical flows.

The power struggles governing the fate of the traditional European cities are of a conflicting nature in the society of men and women. In the functionalist city, scientific intent claims to ignore the power struggles. Such a censorship results in a strengthening of disciplinary autonomy. This autonomy generates perverse effects such as the mighty power of functionalist standards, irrespective of the specific features of the city they apply to, and the quasi-absolute rule of the most powerful administrations, eg transport, public works, town planning, etc.

It follows that the cities which conform to the functionalist criteria are rarely genuine cities and even more rarely desirable ones.
Paying attention to the wishes of men and women, analysing what underlies these wishes and how they can have a positive influence on the development of cities can indeed be an objective.
In that case, however, we should agree to reject the moralistic judgements that are used as an excuse for the errors of functionalist urbanism. That also means that the historical concepts of the European city should be taken into account. Those of a constituent nature, eg the neighbourhood, the street, the balance between public and private space; and those of a symbolic, theoretical and aesthetic nature, eg the city as a backdrop for men's and women's lives, copying, imitation, the issue of the styles and their function, mock antique, patina, etc.

16. NIGHT-TIME VISIONS

Bruges: the contrast between street and monument lighting, throughout the entire historical centre of Bruges, creates a permanent relationship between walking and urban landmarks, close-up views and vertical perspectives.

Doc. M. Culot / A.A.M. Bruxelles.

The perception and the memory we have of a city can be influenced both by daytime and night-time atmospheres. Bruges, in Belgium, turns into a different city at night, as beautiful as it is by day. The relationship between the network of streets and the emerging lit-up monuments is well and truly magic. The Concha de San Sebastien becomes an unforgettable sight at nightfall. In Italy, the centres of Modena and Bologna are beautifully illuminated by selective lighting.

Since the 1960s, however, the lighting of streets and public spaces has deteriorated more often than not, except in specific and isolated instances of historical centres. Many areas and streets of Paris that were so poetic at night are now robbed of any originality by streams and sheets of lighting that makes everything uniform and destroys any mystery. Night has turned into poor daylight. Even more dramatic, however, is the use of coloured lighting (orange, yellow, green) that distorts the buildings and the vegetation and makes the scene look uniform and flat. That kind of lighting should be banned.

The light of a city is a major component of its aesthetics, an ethereal element capable of transforming the urban space, of improving or debasing it, of making it legible or chaotic. It is chiefly in this context that qualitative criteria must prove to be operational. The lighting of cities cannot be left to the sole discretion of appliance retailers, installation firms, power companies, engineering departments and administrations. «Lighting plans» must be devised by architects and scenographers who have the necessary skills.

PART TWO

CASE STUDIES

TEN PORTRAITS ON THE CITY DESIRE THEME

The examples presented in the following pages highlight some aspects of the desirability of the city. The city perceived, experienced, managed as a whole - not as a functionalist city made up of a series of juxtaposed functions. These examples recall, to quote Professor Pierre Grimal in <u>Les Villes romaines</u> [The Roman cities], that *«a human built-up area is not necessarily a city. The mere juxtaposition of individual or family settlements does not make a city. It takes on its true identity only insofar as its dwellers have succeeded in creating the instruments of a collective life»*.

Desire and style

1. BRUSSELS

Reconstruction of the Rue Laeken
1991-1995

Because it was the first European capital to be devastated by speculative and functionalist urbanism as far back as the late 1950s, Brussels is now the first city spectacularly to reconquer neighbourhoods and public spaces, drawing inspiration from its own municipal tradition.

Several building sites and recent developments bear witness to this revival, eg the Carrefour de l'Europe (a new square built at one end of the famous Grand-Place, on the site of a car park); the Place de la Vieille Halle aux Blés (rebuilt in its former triangular shape and according to the land subdivisions); the reconstruction of the picturesque rue de la Chaufferette near the Grand-Place, etc. However, the most remarkable achievement is undoubtedly the reconstruction of a section of the rue de Laeken, carried out on the initiative of AG-Fortis, a large insurance group, and completed in

The Place de la Vieille Halle aux Blés, 1994.
Documents S.D.R.B., Brussels.

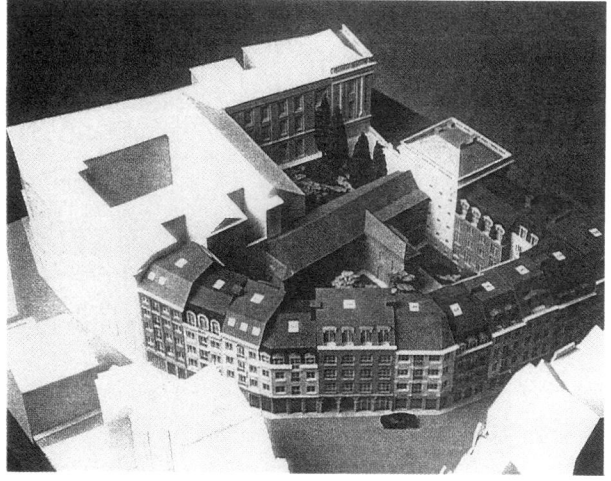

What it will look like in Brussels, 1995.

Partly levelled during the 1960s, the Place de la Vieille Halle aux Blés will be restored to its original triangular shape within a few months. It had been rebuilt on the initiative of Maximilian Emmanuel of Bavaria after the bombing of Brussels by the French in 1695. The neighbourhood was declared unhealthy and extensively razed in 1960, to be replaced by a series of low-rise and tower blocks. Only one was built, and the neighbourhood remained in a state of neglect until 1995.
The reconstruction project was initiated by the Société de Développement Régional de Bruxelles, set up in 1974, which comes under the Government of the Brussels-Capital Region.

This development is indicative of the change that has occurred in people's minds. Only a few years ago, the Atelier de Recherche et d'Action Urbaine (ARAU), a citizens' association, was alone in requesting that Brussels be rebuilt in this manner. Today the Government itself is leading the way.

1995. The ambitious project was to rebuild a vast block in the centre of Brussels, comprising a waste ground produced by excessive demolitions during the 1960s, residential houses, and an office tower known as *Tour bleue*.

On the initiative of the Fondation pour l'Architecture à Bruxelles [Brussels Architecture Foundation] (a cultural association for the promotion of architectural culture), the insurance group held a competition reserved for young European architects under the age of 40.

The office tower was pulled down and the land fronting the rue de Laeken earmarked for housing and divided into seven plots – each large enough for two houses or a small block of flats.

The jury selected seven European architects or teams of architects (Belgium, France, Spain, England).

The projects were picked for the quality and originality of the plans, the building solutions, and their integrability into a neighbourhood in which the neo-classical style predominates (in the vicinity of a structured development erected in 1840).

The reconstructed street forms a coherent complex and the houses fit together naturally.

Beyond the unanimously acclaimed aesthetic success of this reconstruction and its very reasonable building and rental costs, this project provides lessons that apply to all European cities confronted with the restoration of a destroyed or damaged urban fabric. To visualize Brussels today, we must imagine a group of islands in an ocean of planning errors and monstrosities. Forced to live in a mutilated city, the people of Brussels have an increasingly pronounced desire for preservation and the construction of coherent urban sites and complexes. Sites that are coherent in their complexity, neighbourhoods to be lived in, with shops and tradesmen, facilities, but also stylistically coherent sites.

The modernist architecture of discontinuity is held in very low esteem by public opinion. It is defended only by a majority of architects and architecture teachers and critics.

It was therefore a matter of creating an up-to-date architecture that would revive the styles debate, integrate the desire for urban continuity (respecting the streets and their dimensions), and provide evidence of the European architects' ability to testify their skill.

1st lesson - style

Discredited and rejected by modernist thinking in architecture, the architectural styles are one of the main elements of an architectural reflection on the urban renaissance of cities.

The styles question arises today in new form. It is no longer a matter of using columns, pediments and capitals to build palaces or to hold forth on the origins of the orders, but of choosing architectural styles to suit the time and place (by incorporating data such as the architects' existing local culture, the financial means available, the ability to maintain and manage the blocks, etc).

That is how the neo-classical style was adopted most naturally in the rue de Laeken (if it had been the reconstruction of the Place de la Vieille Halle aux Blés, the programme would have leaned more towards a combination of gabled brick architecture and plastered houses, in keeping with the character of the 17th century).

As the styles are here at the service of the city and its set of streets and squares, once again they

RECONSTRUCTION OF THE RUE DE LAEKEN.

Photos Olivier Hennebert, Brussels.

DEMOLITION OF THE TOUR BLEUE.

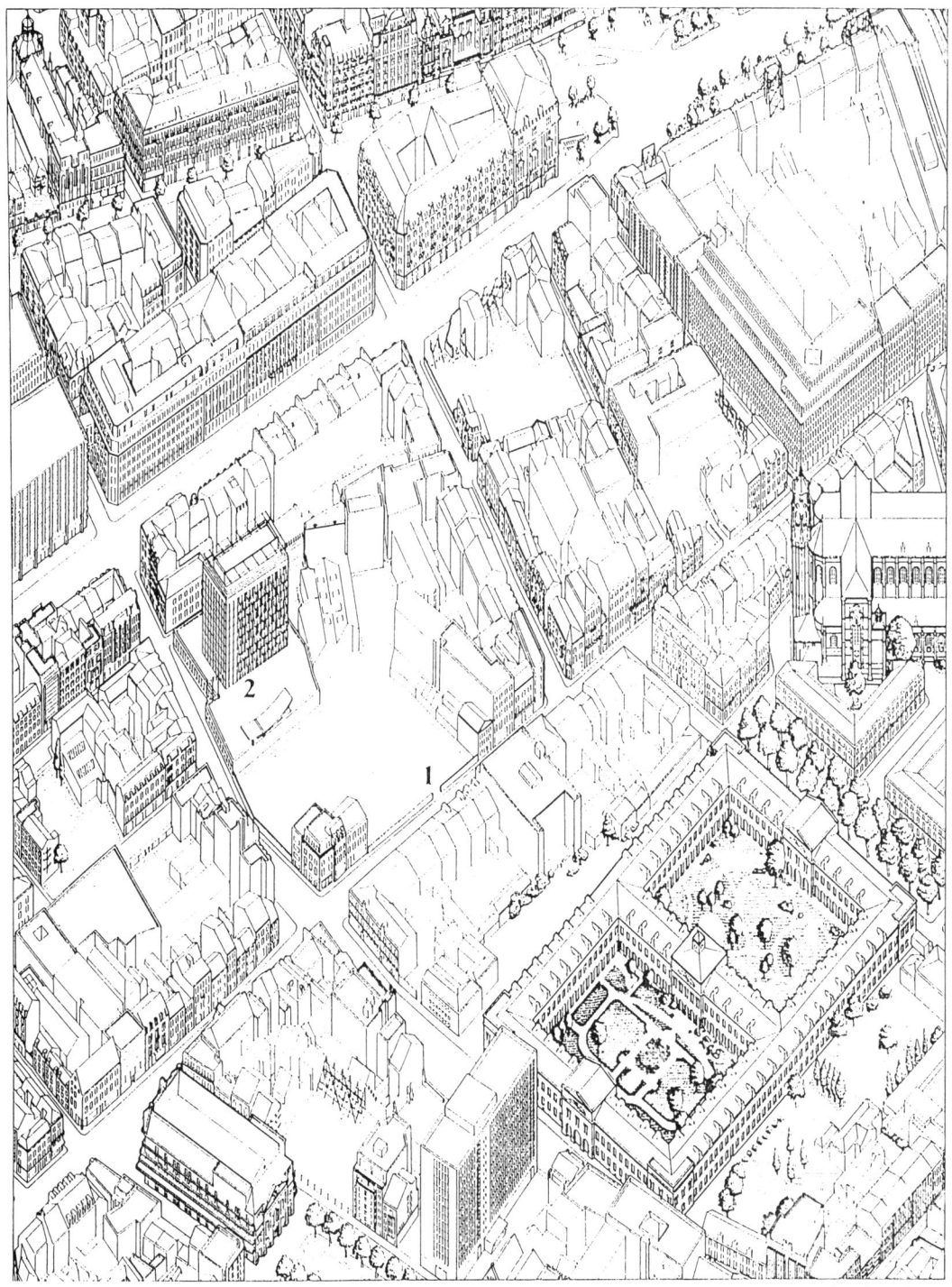

THE NEIGHBOURHOOD AS IT STOOD IN 1989.
1. WASTE GROUND.
2. TOUR BLEUE.

Axonométrie from the Atelier de Recherche et d'Action Urbaine, Brussels.

65

become an educational concern. Rejected and dismissed by the functionalist aesthetics, they are an essential testing ground for the urban renaissance.

2nd lesson - Europe

The advocates of abstract architectures (international, functionalist, brutalist, postmodernist, etc) and their numerous followers have produced all-purpose, interchangeable works with no reference to context.

The rue de Laeken project shows that, if we deliberately choose a common style of reference (in this case, domestic neo-classicism), it is possible to give the complex a homogeneous character while each building retains its own specificity.

Unity of style is not synonymous with triteness and boredom. On the contrary, any observer with an eye for architecture will have no difficulty in noticing the differences between the houses built by the various European architects.

Whoever takes the trouble to look at the new houses in the rue de Laeken will indeed hear accents of Bilbao, Bologna, London or Toulouse. The Basques emphasized the ground floor with the powerful arcature encountered in the palace-houses of their beautiful provinces. The English made care for detail a point of honour, showing a mannerism that is particularly appreciated at a time when polyvinyl chloride woodwork is appearing indiscriminately all over Europe. The Toulouse architects brought to Brussels the memory of the monumental proportions of Toulouse's large brick façades. The Italians coupled the street corner to a baroque crest that houses a most curious flat. The Brussels architects built a tower-house whose internal layout is inspired by the spaces imagined by Victor Horta at the turn of the century.

The rue de Laeken demonstrates most clearly that a reference to Europe is not synonymous with vulgarization and standardization. On the contrary, such a reference makes it possible to integrate the local and specific aspects to produce works that are both beautiful and original and give the impression of being timeless and part of the European culture.

The architects responsible for the reconstruction of the rue de Laeken are Joseph Altuna, Sylvie Assassin, Javier Cenicacelaya, Barthélémy Dumons, Jean-Philippe Garric, Philippe Gisclard, Marc Heene, Michel Leloup, Valérie Negre, Liam O'Connor, Marie-Laure Petit, Nathalie Prat, John Robins, Inigo Salona, Gabriele Tagliaventi. The Brussels-based Bureau d'Architecture Atlante coordinated the projects and monitored the building operations.

Sylvain Desauw / Fondation pour l'Architecture, Brussels.

THE RECONSTRUCTED HOUSES (LEFT) AND THE NEW OFFICE BLOCK VIEWED FROM THE LARGE CENTRAL GARDEN.

Sylvain Desauw / Fondation pour l'Architecture, Brussels.

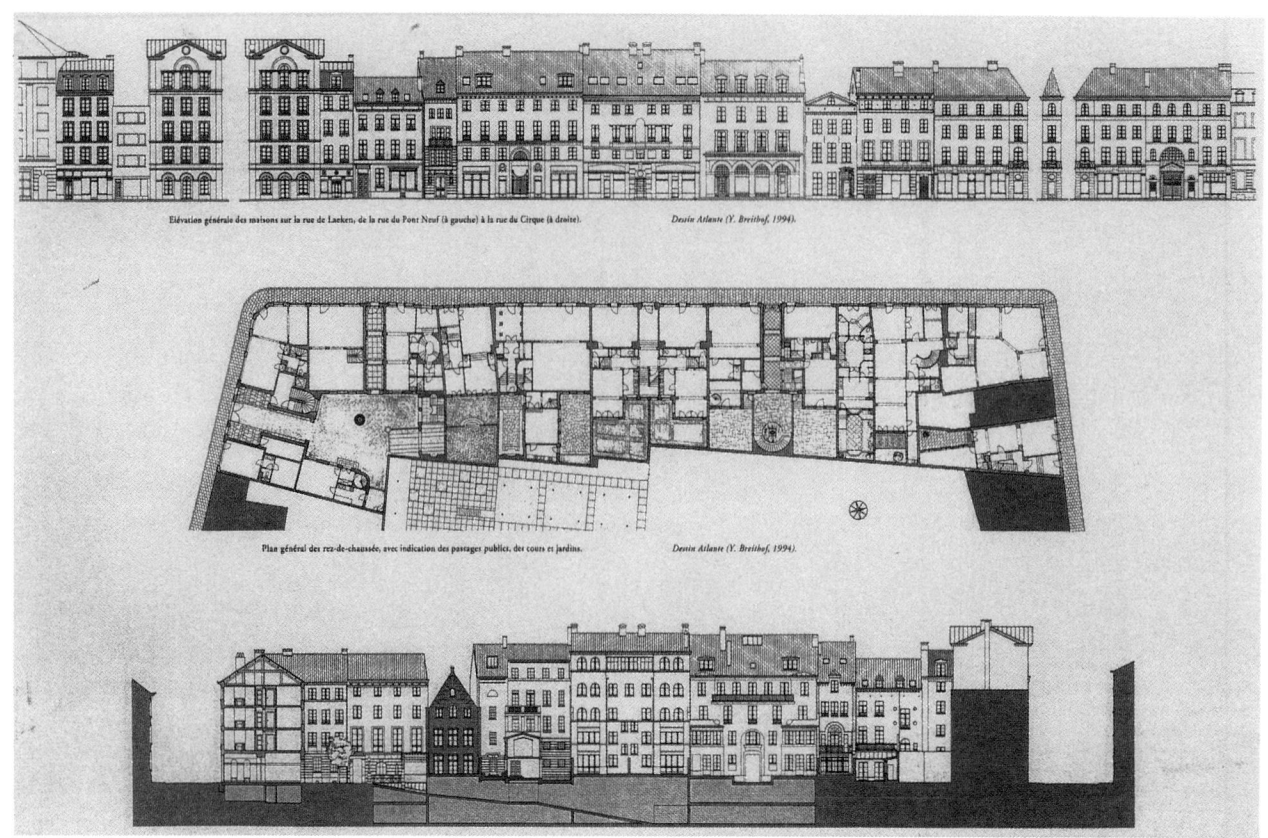

FRONT ELEVATION, GROUND-FLOOR PLAN AND BACK ELEVATION OF THE STREET AS RECONSTRUCTED.

Fondation pour l'Architecture, Brussels.
CATALOGUE PUBLISHED IN 1995 TO MARK THE COMPLETION OF THE RUE DE LAEKEN RECONSTRUCTION WORKS.
(1989-1995, The reconstruction of a historical street in Brussels – Call to young european architects – AG 1924, member of the Fortis Group, Fondation pour l'Architecture)

Sylvain Desauw / Fondation pour l'Architecture, Brussels.

TOWER-HOUSE RECONSTRUCTED ON THE CORNER OF THE RUE DE LAEKEN (G. TAGLIAVENTI & ASSOCIATES, ARCHITECTS).

Against the proliferation of developments in the suburbs: the neighbourhood

2. A DESIRE FOR ECOLOGY
THE EXTENSION OF FORNOVO DI TARO

Italy
1992

2. A DESIRE FOR ECOLOGY
THE EXTENSION OF FORNOVO DI TARO

ITALY
1992

The industrial revolutions, the urban expansion they have caused, the unprecedented growth that followed World War II have erased the distinction between town and country. The 19th century had perceived the threat that loomed over the «sprawling towns». Engineers, architects, landscape gardeners had devised networks of parks and gardens whose object was to recreate an artificial nature inside the big cities. The 20th century has been unable to plan the growth of cities, and the countryside has made way for suburbs and monofunctional zones.

One of the great tasks awaiting the 21st century will be to curb the power of the cities and limit the waste produced by the service sector, and to reclaim rural space in the suburbs which will need to be rebuilt in accordance with traditional planning models, following the patent failure of functionalist experiments based on zoning.

Italy still featured perfect rural areas and landscapes in 1950. It spoilt them irretrievably, in less than 50 years of carelessness, with disorderly suburban developments. Though Italy has succeeded in preserving its historical centres, it should now possibly be viewed as the European country that has paid least attention to preserving its countryside and planning its city outskirts.

This is why the experiment of the small town of Fornovo di Taro can be given as an example. Situated 10 kilometres from Parma in one of Italy's most prosperous regions (no unemployment), the town needs new housing and sites to develop its small-scale mechanical and crafts industries. The hillside land is unsuitable for building due to its instability. To prevent a scattering of buildings, the municipality decided to pre-empt land on the plateau overlooking the town in order to set up a new neighbourhood designed to accommodate 1500 residents.

This neighbourhood will be built in the image of a small traditional town, with a mix of activities and housing laid out in blocks bounded by lanes and streets. There will be a clear-cut boundary between this new neighbourhood and the countryside, which will begin at the boundary itself.

This new neighbourhood will of course be built in stages, but the blocks and streets will be delineated and laid out from the outset. The blocks will be surrounded by stone walls 2 metres high, in the local tradition, and the buildings will be added as the development proceeds. The new neighbourhood's public spaces will account for between 25 and 35% of the total area, which is in line with the ratio prevailing in Italy's finest cities.

To provide this neighbourhood with the typical atmosphere of the small towns of this Italian region, the road system will include many narrow streets and 4-metre-wide lanes.

The completion of such a project requires a departure from the current construction and town-planning laws in Italy, where the building of narrow streets is prohibited. As in other European countries, planning legislation was enacted in accordance with the prescriptive models derived straight from the Athens Charter (land divided into zones), and with functionalist criteria – particularly in traffic terms – that are incompatible with the urban reality of traditional European cities.

A departure from those standards will be made possible by an agreement with the Region and, for Italy, the extension of Fornovo di Taro is a testing ground for the reconstruction of cities according to traditional concepts.

CULTURA E SOCIETÀ'

Parte da Orta uno stimolante progetto urbanistico

Le colline di Fornovo 2

Un «satellite» per millecinquecento abitanti

di FRANCESCA DALLATANA

Orta e il suo lago: una sintesi di turismo e di ospitalità, una lunga tradizione che viene da lontano. Risale alla metà del 1800, circa, l'inizio di una consuetudine che per questa cittadina lacustre si è tradotta in indotto economico, che l'ha resa ricca.

Sicuramente meta, oppure tappa, del Grand Tour, «fossile» per antonomasia del turismo moderno, l'esperienza giovanile di viaggio, molto in voga nell'aristocrazia europea, nei secoli XVII e XVIII, Orta è anche un felice connubio tra natura e architettura. La varietà degli stili, l'uno diverso dall'altro, quasi fosse un campionario di edifici, costruiti tra il '500 e il '700, sottolineano ulteriormente l'originalità, la bellezza e l'indipendenza di questa cittadina a nord del Piemonte; quasi un piccolo stato nello Stato dove si è persino battuto moneta.

E' qui che hanno avuto inizio due interessanti esperienze didattiche: la scuola di senologia, del professor Veronesi del Centro per la diagnosi dei tumori dell'Università di Milano, e un laboratorio di architettura, una scuola post-universitaria avviata dallo scorso 1992. Due iniziative didattiche eterogenee ma del tutto nuove nel loro genere. La seconda è un'esperienza di lavoro alla quale hanno preso parte neo-laureati in architettura e famosi professionisti europei. Tra i promotori un architetto parmense, per la precisione fornovese, che ha contribuito con la sua cospicua esperienza e con le sue proposte a trasformare il lavoro dell'équipe in progetti praticabili, del tutto operativi, una volta sostenuti dal consenso dei rispettivi consigli comunali.

Pier Carlo Bontempi, che si è occupato recentemente, tra le altre cose, della redazione del piano particolareggiato della piazza del Mercato di Fornovo Taro, ha portato all'attenzione del gruppo di lavoro alcune idee-guida che hanno costituito una buona parte del lavoro di Orta. Uno dei progetti elaborati riguarda l'urbanizzazione delle Caselle, una zona a monte del Comune di Fornovo. Un'area che presenta una doppia problematica: di urbanizzazione, necessaria, imperativa se si considera la carenza di alloggi di un Comune che rischia di diventare un mero polo di servizi per l'insufficiente capacità di recezione residenziale; al tempo stesso, di rispetto del paesaggio. Due concetti che sembrano fare a pugni poiché da sempre l'urbanizzazione è considerata la nemica per eccellenza dell'ambiente naturale.

Il progetto finale porta le firme di Pier Carlo Bontempi e del belga Maurice

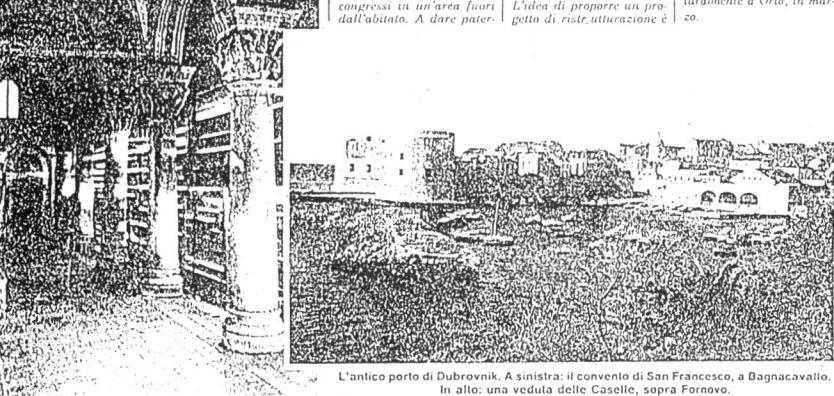

«la Beverly Hills di Fornovo», è già disegnata sulla carta e al più presto arricchirà, di un curato tassello urbano ed ambientale insieme, un comune che da sempre ha convissuto armonicamente con due «presenze naturali», il fiume Taro e il monte della Croce, che ne hanno influenzato lo sviluppo.

Altro tema affrontato dagli architetti di Orta riguarda il recupero del complesso monumentale storico del convento di San Francesco di Bagnacavallo, in provincia di Ravenna. Un corpo monumentale massiccio fuori scala rispetto al corpo minuto dell'abitato. In questo caso si è dovuto procedere al recupero dell'intero complesso architettonico, e alla copertura di un'ala dell'edificio che era stata distrutta, nonché all'integrazione al nucleo urbano. Un lavoro che porta le firme di Peter Wilson e di Bruno Minardi. Anche Orta è stata oggetto di studio oltre che sede di lavoro. Uno dei progetti riguarda un nuovo insediamento turistico-recettivo con strutture per congressi in un'area fuori dall'abitato. A dare paternità a questo progetto sono stati Pier Luigi Nicolin e Renzo Salmoiraghi.

Infine un progetto per l'estero. Per quella meravigliosa città che dalle mine dell'ex Jugoslavia 'affaccia sul mar Adriatico e che reclama a gran voce i fasti di una magnificenza architettonica che non è possibile dimenticare. Dubrovnik (Ragusa) non ha capitolato del tutto sotto i fuochi di una guerra che non risparmia nemmeno ciò che gli uomini hanno costruito per valorizzarla. L'idea di proporre un progetto di ristrutturazione è stata di Pier Carlo Bontempi che alla televisione aveva visto immagini del porto distrutto. Dopo un sopralluogo e dopo contatti con l'amministrazione locale, si è realizzato che a cadere in rovina non era stato il porto vecchio bensì quello nuovo, però militarizzato. Per l'impossibilità di fare rilievi sono stati scelti tre punti della città: tra questi due zone archeologiche dove l'amministrazione comunale locale intendeva intervenire per ricostruire. Il progetto, che porta in calce le firme di Pier Carlo Bontempi, di Franco Povini e di Bruno Minardi, si occupa di tutte e tre queste aree. Il laboratorio di Orta ha solo dato inizio ad uno studio complessivo di recupero della città. Dieci laureandi in architettura dell'ateneo di Venezia, infatti, per le loro tesi stanno lavorando a progetti che prendono spunto dall'idea-guida di Pier Carlo Bontempi. Tra la magia del suo lago e quella dell'isola di San Giulio che le sta di fronte, Orta è stata dunque il luogo privilegiato di studio ma soprattutto di un lavoro di squadra che come primo obiettivo si è posto l'operatività del progetto. Al bando l'astrattezza delle regole di quest'équipe che adesso passa la mano ai consigli comunali per l'approvazione dei progetti. E che concluderà suoi lavori rendendoli pubblici con una mostra che si terrà naturalmente a Orta, in marzo.

L'antico porto di Dubrovnik. A sinistra: il convento di San Francesco, a Bagnacavallo. In alto: una veduta delle Caselle, sopra Fornovo.

In un libro fotografico le più prestigiose sedi dell'Arma

Benemerita Arte
Quando la caserma è un museo

Doc Bontempi - Culot.

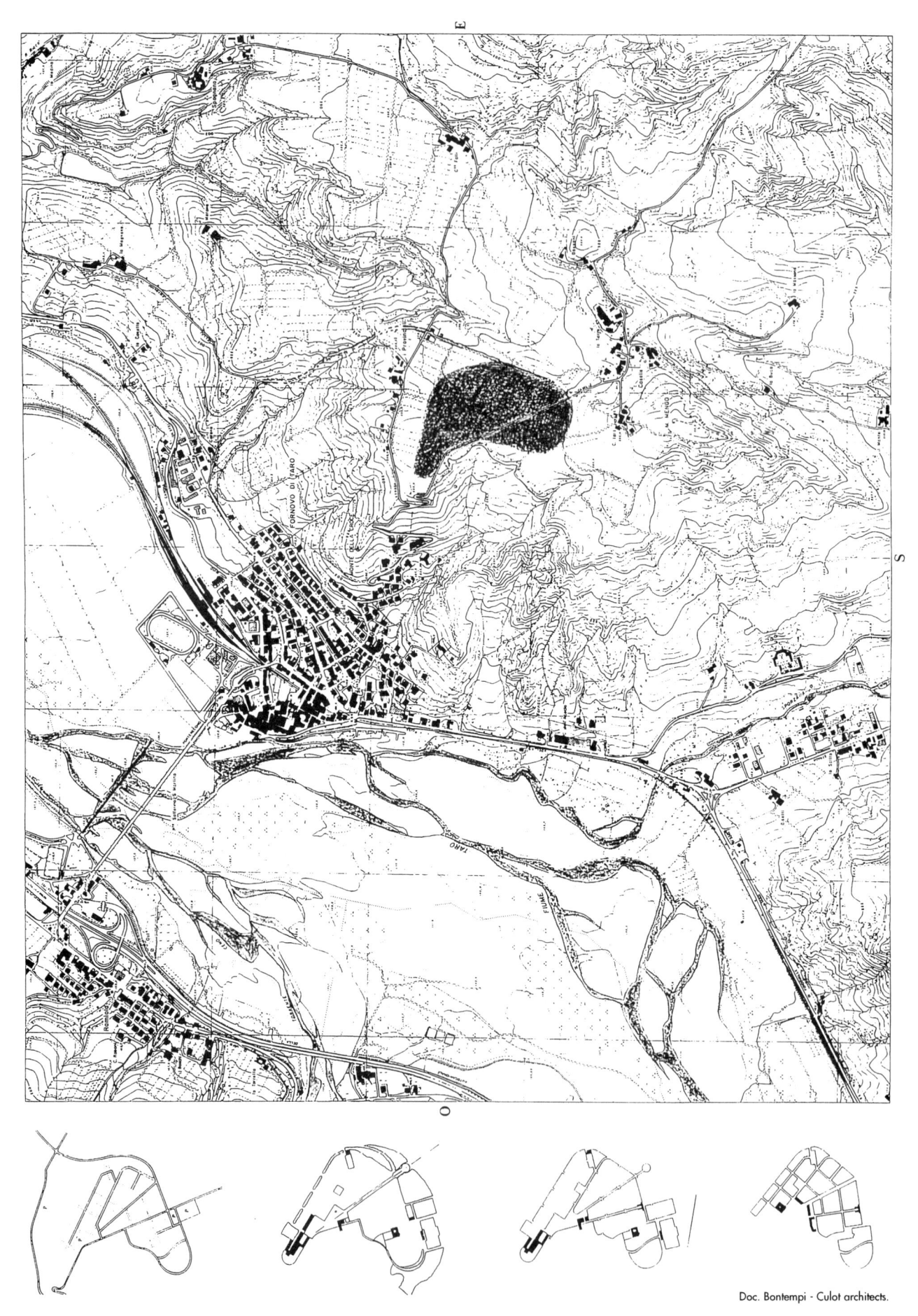

Extension of Fornovo di Taro – General Site Plan

Doc. Bontempi - Culot architects.

Doc. Bontempi - Culot architects.

GENERAL PLAN OF THE NEW VILLAGE OF FORNOVO DI SOPRA, ITALY.
1992-93

Project for a new centre designed to accommodate 1000 to 1500 residents on 12 hectares of land situated on the plateau overlooking the town of Fornovo di Taro, in the Apennines, near the city of Parma.

The project provides for the final extension of the village to avoid the suburbia effect. The plan has been designed as a system of streets and squares, with blocks 50 x 60 metres on average, within which the town will be allowed to grow horizontally (up to 3/4 of building plots) and vertically (3 storeys maximum). All buildings will be erected in alignment with the streets, and the blocks will be surrounded by high walls (2 metres) in the regional tradition.

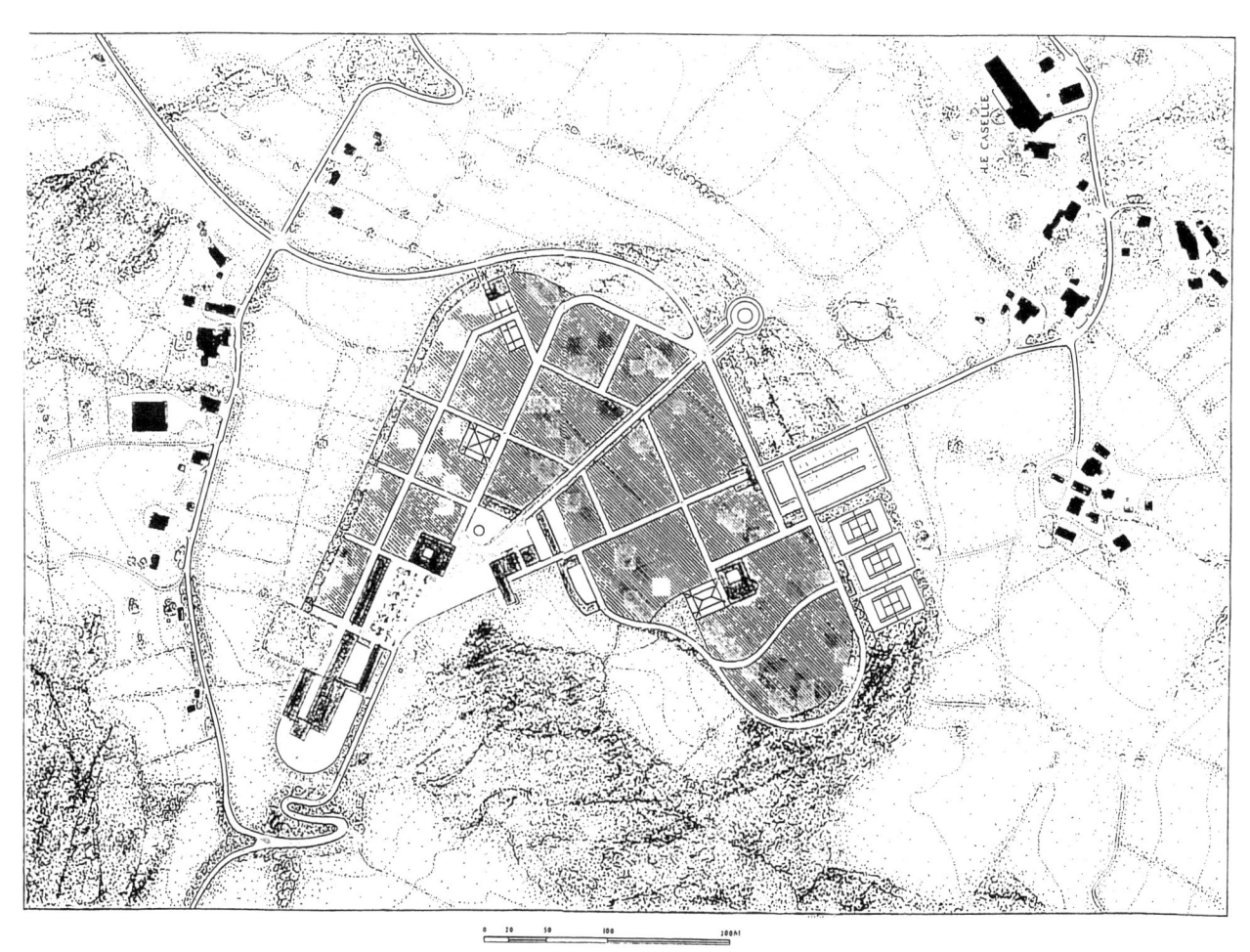

Doc Bontempi - Culot.

Doc Bontempi - Culot.

THE EXTENSION SITE OF FORNOVO DI TARO.
A piece of land on the plateau overlooking the town, where a traditional neighbourhood inspired by the region's villages will be built.

Doc Bontempi - Culot.

THE LAND ON WHICH THE TOWN'S EXTENSION IS TO BE BUILT (HATCHED).

Doc Bontempi - Culot.

FORNOVO DI TARO'S HISTORICAL CENTRE.
Blocks, streets and squares, public space in correct proportion to private space.

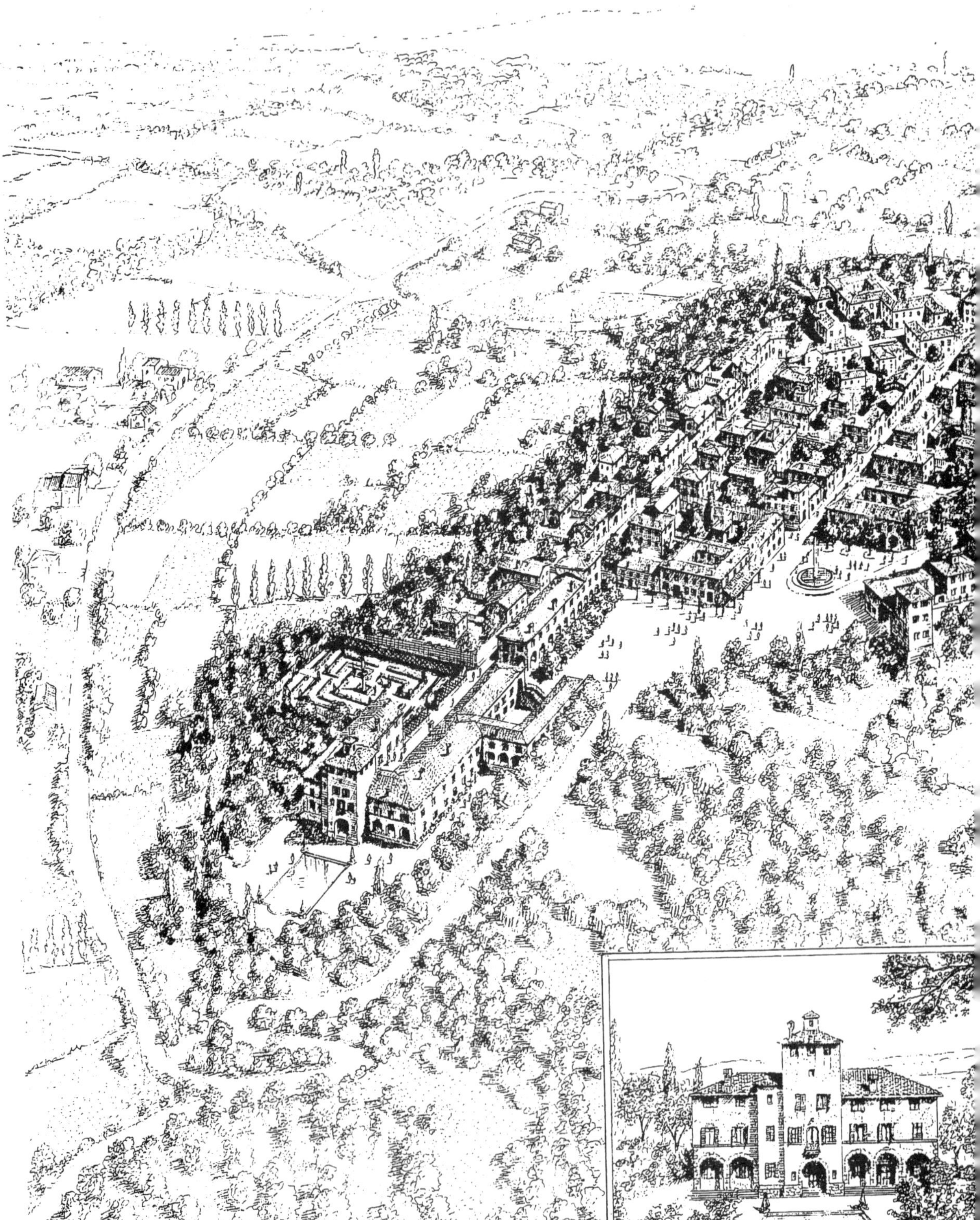

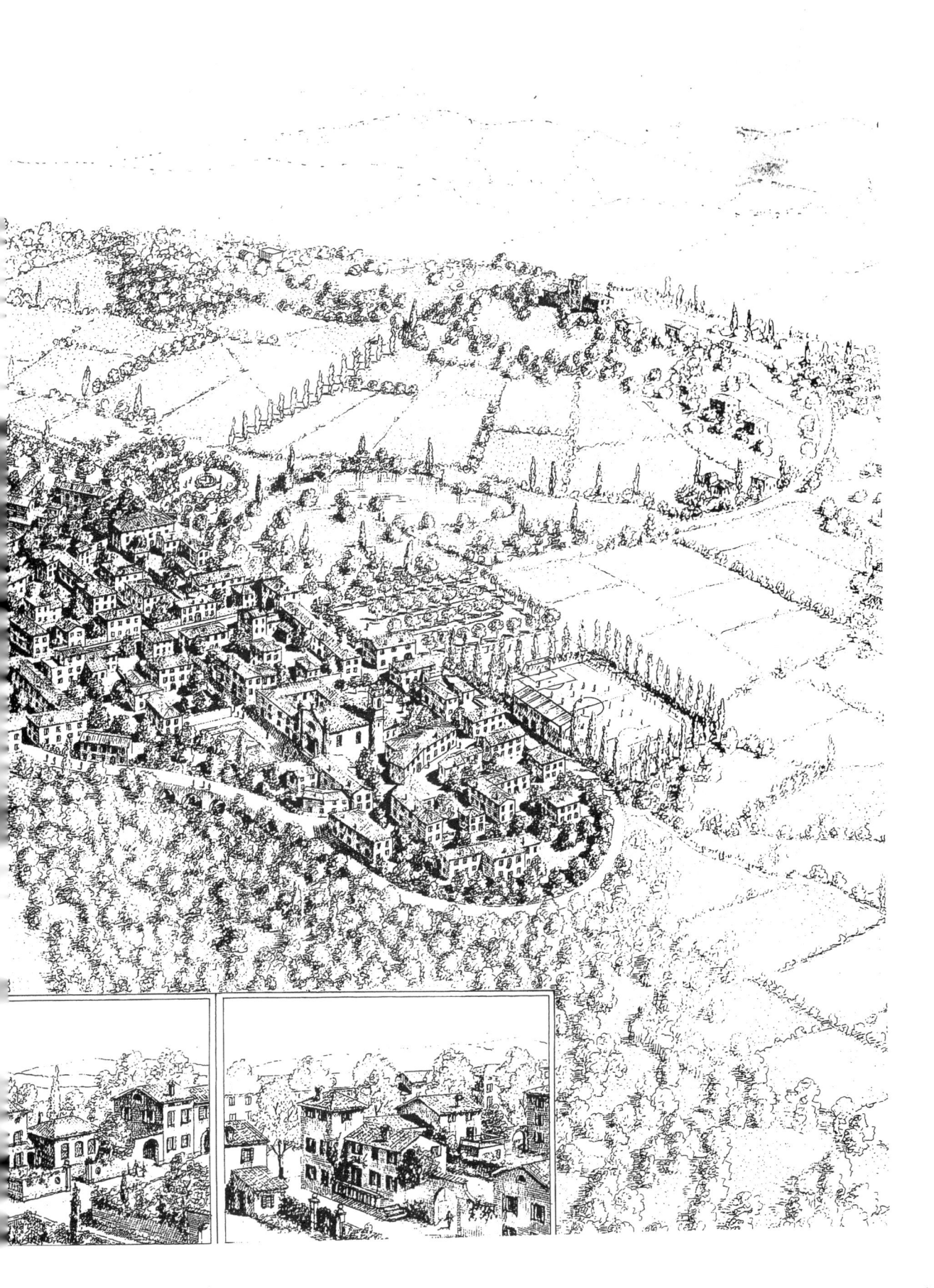

Doc Bontempi - Culot.

Doc Bontempi - Culot.

EXAMPLES OF ARCHITECTURE AND CONSTRUCTION TYPOLOGY FOR THE EXTENSION OF FORNOVO DI TARO.

A LONGING TO EMBRACE THE CITY

3. CHINON, FRANCE

GLOBAL PROJECT AND SELECTIVE MEASURES
1992-1993

CHINON IN THE 19TH CENTURY.
PAINTING KEPT AT THE CHINON TOWN HALL.

The town of Chinon (population: 8000), famous for its castle and its wine, is one of Touraine's fine mediaeval cities. It is now experiencing all the problems of a small French provincial town.
Because it is too close to Tours (50 kilometres), the young will not settle. The town survives chiefly on tourism (shops, restaurants, summer homes) and the vineyards. It is losing its people who prefer to settle in Tours or its suburbs.

Yves Dauge, the Mayor of Chinon, a former town councillor under François Mitterrand's presidency, devised an original policy combining a global view of the future of his city with attention to everyday life. This policy has led to the reopening of the Chinon-Tours rail link and the launching of a European university course on water issues. It has also brought the town's extension under control while protecting the villages and the countryside.

Alongside this general strategy, the Mayor has taken selective measures:

- erection of a Journeymen's House (Chinon is an artistic city suitable for stone restoration work, as the local stone is very friable and requires constant restoration);

- repurchase of the town's only cinema that was in a state of collapse. Its management has been entrusted to a team of young cinema enthusiasts. The impact on attendance has been remarkable;

- purchase of properties for the provision of small squares and pedestrian walkways to open up the urban fabric. Improvement of public spaces, route signposting;

- construction of council housing in the old centre;

- provision of car parks within the town to curb traffic and enable the residents to park;

- etc.

In 1992 and 1993 the Summer Seminar of the École Européenne du Prince de Galles, in association with the Institut Français d'Architecture, was held in Chinon. In close collaboration with the Mayor, the young architects surveyed about 20 sites for which the Mayor wished to gather ideas and images.

All those operations were part of a programme (housing, hotel, public spaces, rehabilitation, access to historical monuments).
The aim of one of the studies was to show that all the council flats built in the 1950s, according to the principles of the Athens Charter, could be reinserted into Chinon's social and urban fabric. After the euphoria of the 1950s this neighbourhood of low-rise blocks has now become a problem area, as it provides no opportunity for employment, no mix.
Like many neighbourhoods built in the 1950s, this complex suffers from an excess of amorphous public space too large to manage. On the other hand, it has no traditional public space (streets and squares).

The study set out to prove that it was possible to integrate the low-rise blocks into an urban fabric and to recreate a busy, lively neighbourhood even though it would lack the aesthetic quality of the old Chinon.

The aim of the project is to build on vacant plots in order to recreate streets, avenues and squares, accommodate craft industries in this neighbourhood and encourage the people to take the initiative in setting up small businesses. It is therefore life that has been favoured here, with its jumble of annexes and billboards, while the issue of building aesthetics can be addressed by planting trees and providing public squares. It is evident that the completion of such a project requires a change in attitude on the part of the Council Housing officials who often prefer cosmetic solutions (the painting of defaced council flats was entrusted to a plastics technician who completely disfigured the architecture of the 1950s, which at least had the merit of being simple and rigorous!). In this respect the concept of council housing is still much too rigid, and the buildings are still seen as a string of isolated items belonging to a bureaucratic accounting system.

The series of measures implemented in 1992-93 has enabled the city to build up a portfolio of ideas and set local forces in motion – a two-way link between global concepts (at town and municipality level) and selective measures at a personal and neighbourhood level.

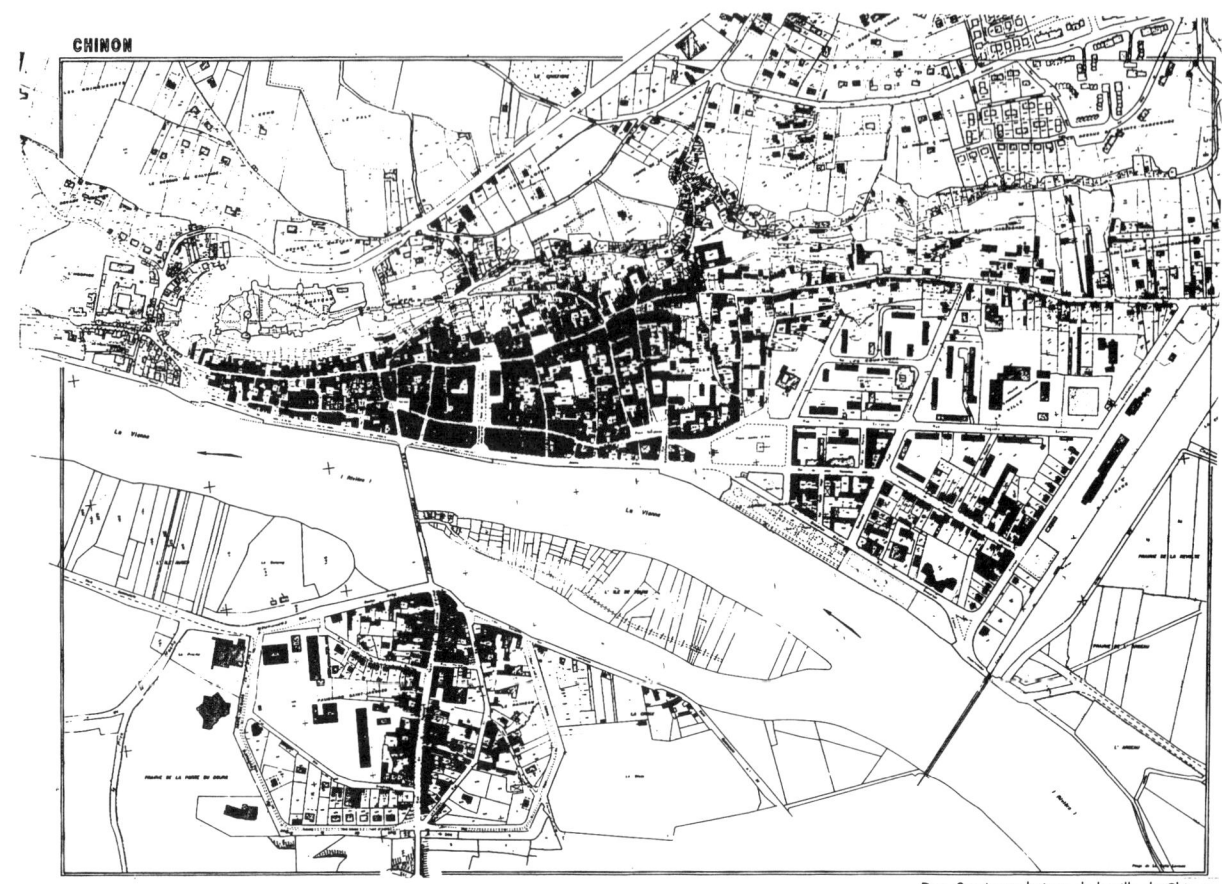

Doc. Service technique de la ville de Chinon.

CHINON TOWN.

Top left: the castle and its rocky outcrop beyond which the vineyards begin.
At the foot of the castle: the mediaeval city, stretching from the hill to the river (Vienne).
The 1950s council-housing area is situated between the old town and the station.

Bottom, beyond the Vienne, the New Town.
The layout of the 1950s low-rise blocks clearly illustrates the urbanistic abstraction arising from the implementation of the Athens Charter and the zoning ideology.
19th-century town extensions, based on a draughtboard pattern, provided a much better solution than the moralistic approach to architecture that longed to impose a way of life derived from demagogic notions of living in greenery, in sunshine, in peacefulness, under roof terraces...

CHINON, CELOT ST-MAURICE.

PRESENT STATE.

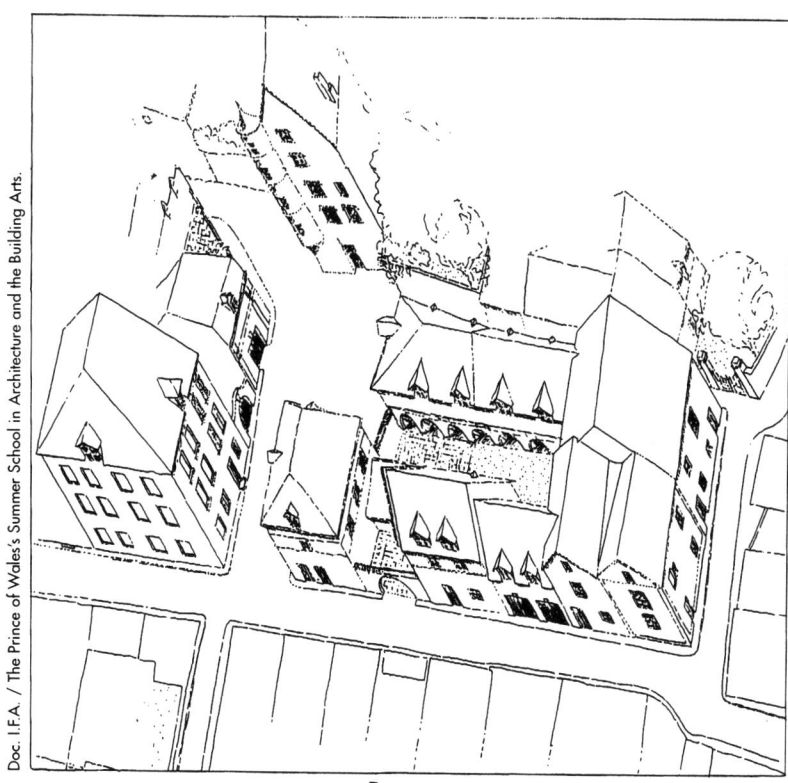

PROJECT.

Chinon's shopkeepers are putting pressure on the Mayor to knock down the Celot St-Maurice, in the heart of the city, and build an open-air car park. The study has shown that some of the houses are architecturally interesting and that these must be preserved. On the other hand, others can be pulled down and replaced by an extension to the adjoining hotel which is looking to expand. Parking space can be provided in the basement.

The project enhances Chinon's features, proposes the building of a small square and provides a solution to the parking problem.

CHINON - ENHANCEMENT AND REHABILITATION OF A SQUARE.

PRESENT STATE.

PROJECT.

The elegant 19th-century theatre in the rue St-Jean was unnecessarily demolished in the 1970s. A square was built on the site but it is adjoined by a school building of insignificant architecture.

The aim of the project is to turn the school into a public market and provide a façade of monumental character in harmony with the square.

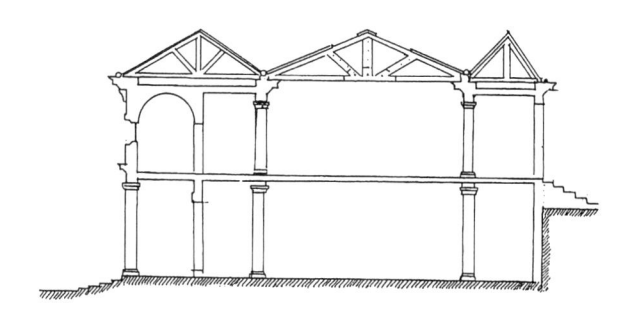

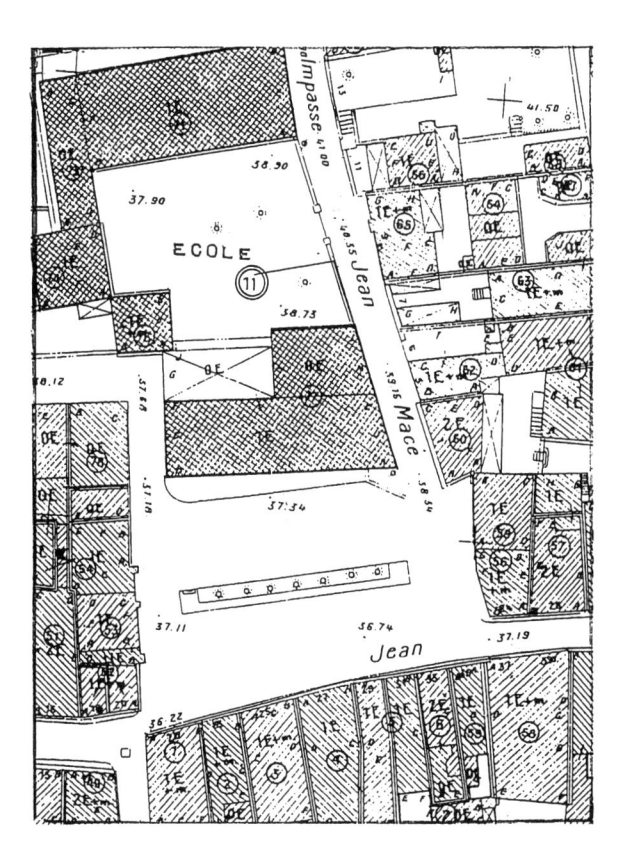

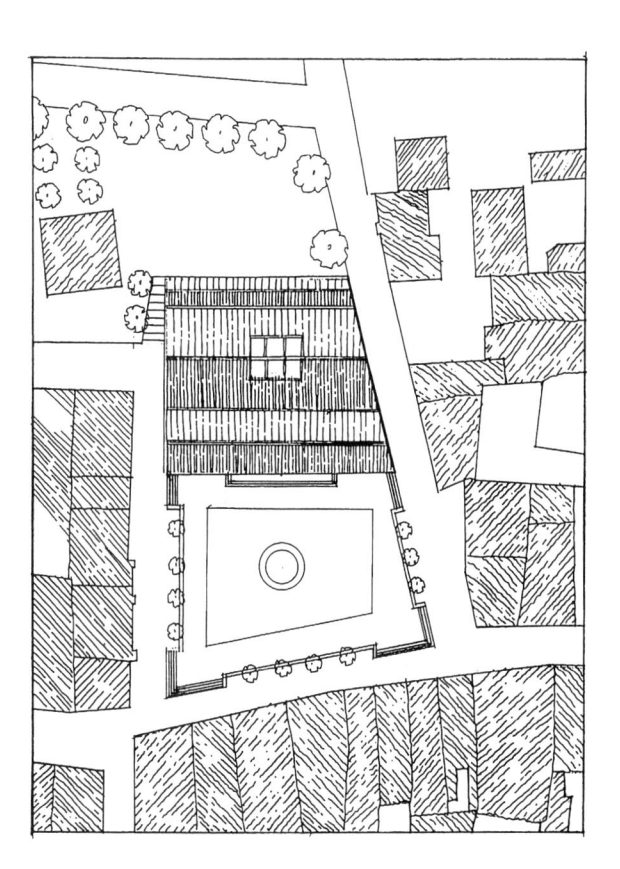

CHINON - ENHANCEMENT AND REHABILITATION OF A SQUARE.

Present state.

Proposal.

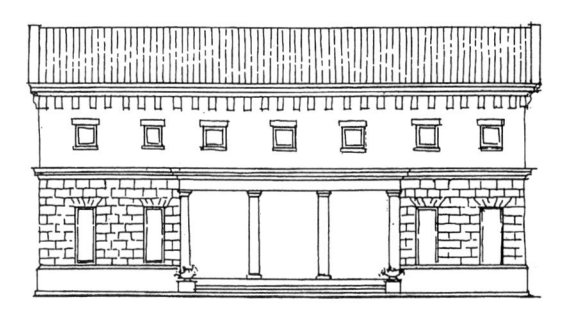

Doc. Carmen Alicia Jerez Gonzalez / I.F.A.
The Prince of Wales's Summer School in Architecture and the Building Arts.

CHINON - CORNER OF THE RUE J.J. ROUSSEAU.

PRESENT STATE.

Maria Saconi / I.F.A.
The Prince of Wales's Summer School in Architecture and the Building Arts.

PROJECT.

The mediaeval corner house was knocked down in the 1960s to make way for traffic. A small featureless garden was laid out on the site. What used to be one of Chinon's picturesque street corners, reproduced on all the old artist-designed postcards, now looks like an ordinary suburban spot.

The aim of the project was to show that a small commercial block can be built on this site, angled back on the ground floor to let the traffic through.

Doc. City of Chinon.

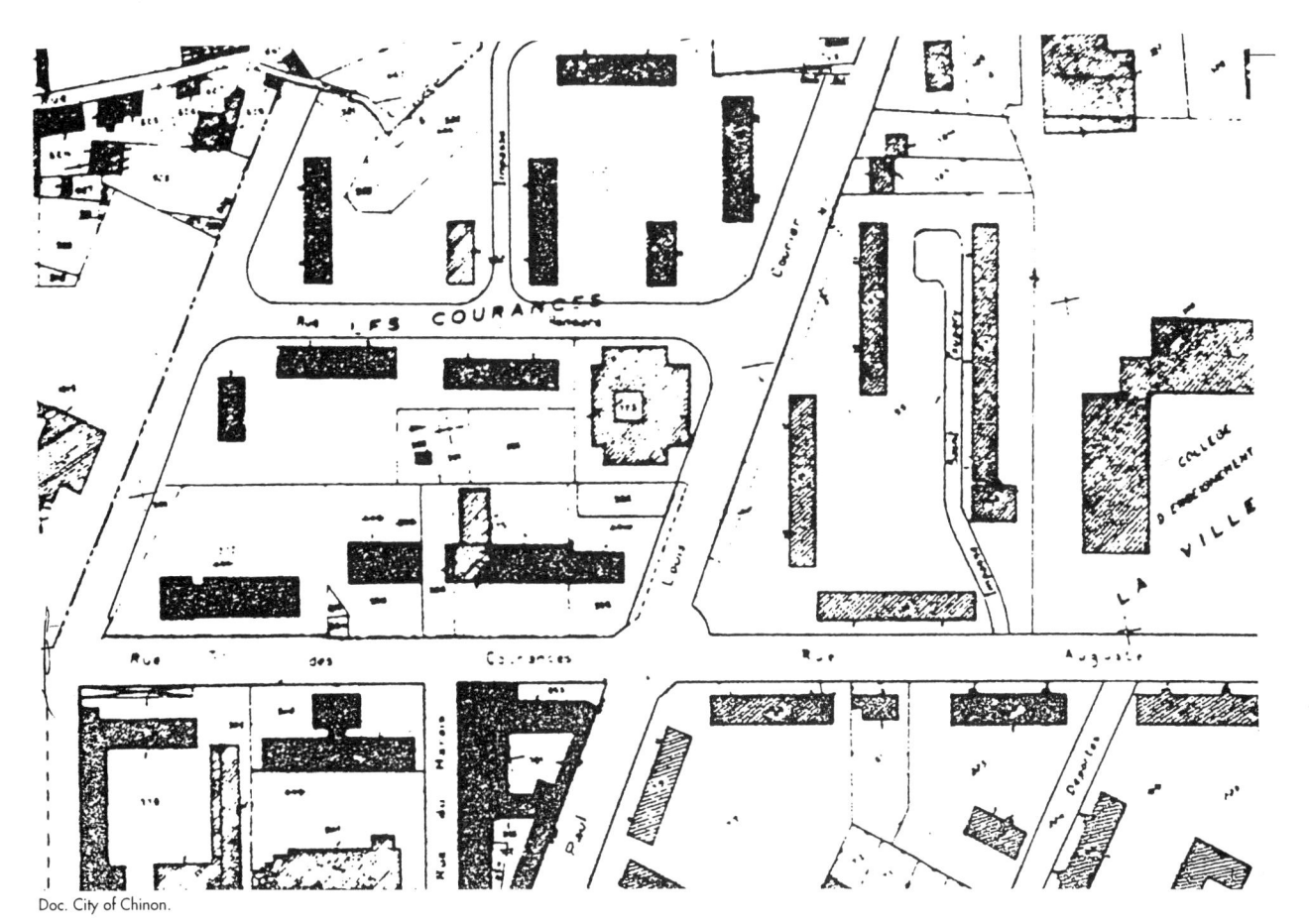

CHINON COUNCIL FLATS – PLAN OF PRESENT LAYOUT.

I.F.A. / The Prince of Wales's Summer School in Architecture and the Building Arts.

PROPOSAL FOR INTEGRATING THE COUNCIL FLATS INTO A LIVING URBAN FABRIC.

4. TROUVILLE

A TESTING GROUND FOR THE URBAN HERITAGE IN FRANCE
1995-1998

On the initiative of the Institut Français d'Architecture and with the support of DATAR, of the Plan Construction Architecture de l'Office Public de Construction du Calvados [Building & Architecture Scheme of the Calvados Public Construction Agency] and of the municipality of Trouville, an experimental project has recently been launched, focusing on the Trouville council housing built in the inter-war period.

Three small council-housing complexes built between 1922 and 1936 have undergone a thorough scrutiny combining the history of Trouville, local architecture and the settlement of the urban area. These dwellings are well situated. In sensitive areas of the old centre that have occasionally been unsettled by too drastic or hasty initiatives, they form streets and squares along which routes have gradually been etched. Any alteration to the buildings therefore modifies – or provides an incentive to modify – the surrounding area. The urban quality of this heritage is one of its greatest assets.

It should be stressed that the residents do not have a negative image of the dwellings. These are not large anonymous or isolated complexes but traditional houses, well integrated into their neighbourhoods, whose architecture is inventive either because of the building system used or the search for the local identity and spirit they bear witness to.

The interior of the fifty dwellings nevertheless requires a new layout to provide more comfort and improved compatibility with modern lifestyles. This must be done at moderate cost, resulting in affordable rentals for the residents.

This implies getting to know the tenants, working with them while providing for the flexibility of the complex, its capacity for accommodating new families, new citizens. A study of the people and the premises.

The principle of the pilot project is as follows:

1. Council housing built in France when the Council Housing Agencies were set up in 1919 and 1940 is recognized as architectural heritage in its own right. It deserves attention and must be rehabilitated in accordance with the original exterior features.

2. The rehabilitation process will be part and parcel of a genuine development strategy for the surroundings of these dwellings. In this way, rehabilitation will be the opportunity for further work.

3. The tenants are associated to the process. Through exhibitions, publications and information meetings, they will be made aware of the architectural quality of their homes. In other words, by giving this small heritage an architectural and social legitimacy rooted in history, we build up the residents' pride, thereby initiating a complex enhancement process.

Reflecting on the rehabilitation of three council-housing units has enabled the municipality of Trouville to identify urban problems and areas requiring urgent attention.

The studies have emphasized the weakness of the urban street framework, the outcome of years of subdivisions into plots, without reference to a global town-planning policy.

Trouville's development has proceeded more often than not at random. The popularity of the seaside gave rise to large properties that were then dismantled and subdivided. Then, in the 20th century, the town continued to expand, relying heavily on successive subdivisions. This lack of planning and the almost systematic recourse to subdivision have now reached the end of the line. The streets of Trouville are suffering from a lack of fluidity. The links with the adjoining municipality of Touques, for instance, are inadequate if not incoherent.

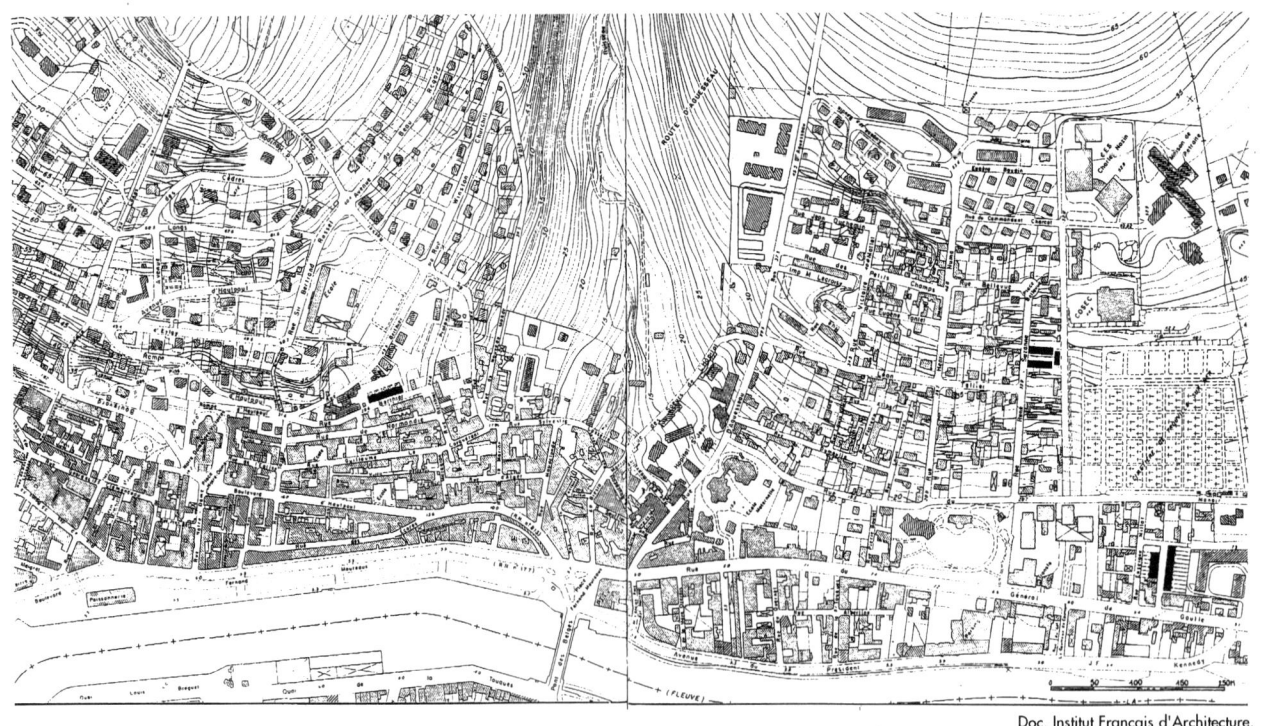

Doc. Institut Français d'Architecture.

Location plan of the three council-housing complexes built in Trouville between the two wars (in black).

At the time, they were all poorly located: by the abattoir, at the foot of a cliff, opposite the cemetery.

Today they are integrated into the urban fabric and, in a familiar reversal of urban history, their rehabilitation will serve as a catalyst for the redevelopment of the adjacent neighbourhoods.

REHABILITATION OF THE RUE FRÉDÉRIC POSTEL AND DEVELOPMENT OF THE ADJACENT AREAS.

Present situation of the streets on the boundary of the municipalities of Trouville and Touques.

This plan highlights the inadequacy of the road links between the two municipalities as a result of:

1. a lack of coordination between the two municipalities,

2. the issuing of subdivision permits lacking any global vision (the subdivision's roads are not interconnected),

3. the lack of a neighbourhood-enhancement strategy, resulting in featureless, lifeless suburbs.

Above: networking proposal.

REHABILITATION OF THE WORKERS' HOUSES IN THE RUE BERTHIER AND DEVELOPMENT OF THE ADJACENT AREAS.

Paul Du Mesnil du Buisson, architect / I.F.A.

The reflection on the rehabilitation of 10 small workers' houses (bottom of the drawing) is turning to the development of the adjacent area, eg construction of new dwellings, development of a waste ground. Council housing acts here as the driving force of the urban process.

The regional rehabilitation agency and the municipality of Trouville are working together and creating a synergy that is beneficial to an entire neighbourhood.

REHABILITATION OF THE WORKERS' HOUSES IN THE RUE BERTHIER AND DEVELOPMENT OF THE ADJACENT AREAS.

Photo I.F.A. / Dominique Delaunay.

PRESENT STATE (1995).

The waste ground by the workers' small houses in the rue Berthier, Trouville.

Paul du Mesnil du Buisson, architect. Drawing by J. Altuna / I.F.A.

PROJECT.

Artist's view of the extended rue Berthier as it could look after development.
The new road, cobbled and picturesque, climbs the hill in stages.
The twin houses earmarked for Trouville families have comfortable terraces looking due south. Underneath are the garages.

97

REHABILITATION OF THE RUE FRÉDÉRIC POSTEL, TROUVILLE.

Photo I.F.A. / Dominique Delaunay.

THE RUE FRÉDÉRIC POSTEL AS IT IS TODAY.

REHABILITATION OF THE HOUSES IN THE RUE FRÉDÉRIC POSTEL AND DEVELOPMENT OF THE ADJACENT AREAS.

The rehabilitation of this street of cheap housing built in 1925 has led to a proposal to build a small square, with some trees and benches – a future meeting place and the symbolic (if not geometric) hub of the complex.

Jean-Philippe Garric, architect / I.F.A.

GENERAL PLANS OF THE RUE FRÉDÉRIC POSTEL.

Left:

In dark hatching, the nineteen houses built in 1926.

Right:

In black, the proposed alterations.
Bathroom units are added, on the garden side, to the houses on the left facing upward.
Towards the top, it is planned to build a new house that will help to delineate a small square.
On the right facing upward, on the garden side, the kitchens are extended outward whereas bathrooms are fitted within the house walls.

REHABILITATION OF THE COUNCIL HOUSING IN THE RUE SUZANNE AND DEVELOPMENT OF THE ADJACENT AREAS.

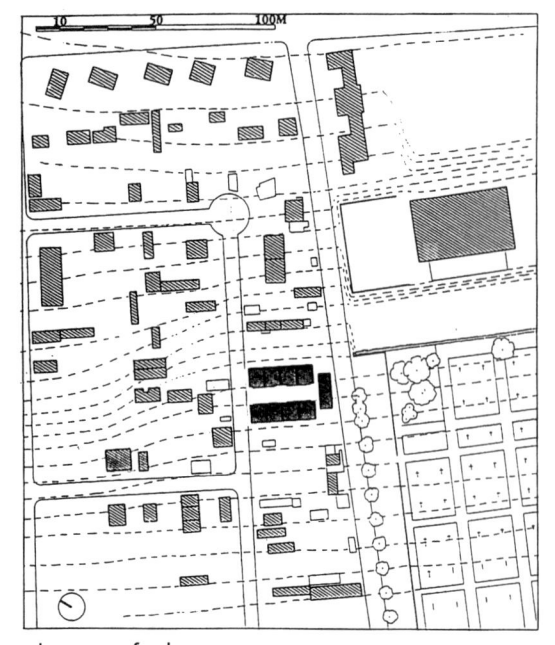

Planning of urban space.
The present oversized road system...

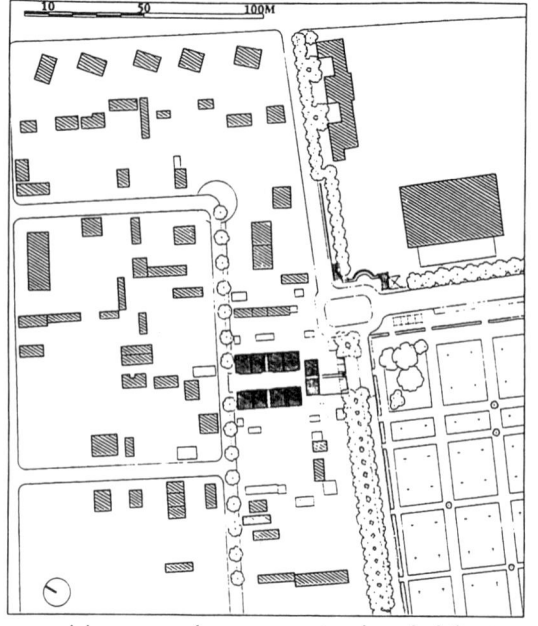

...and the proposal accompanying the rehabilitation of the 1936 workers' garden complex.

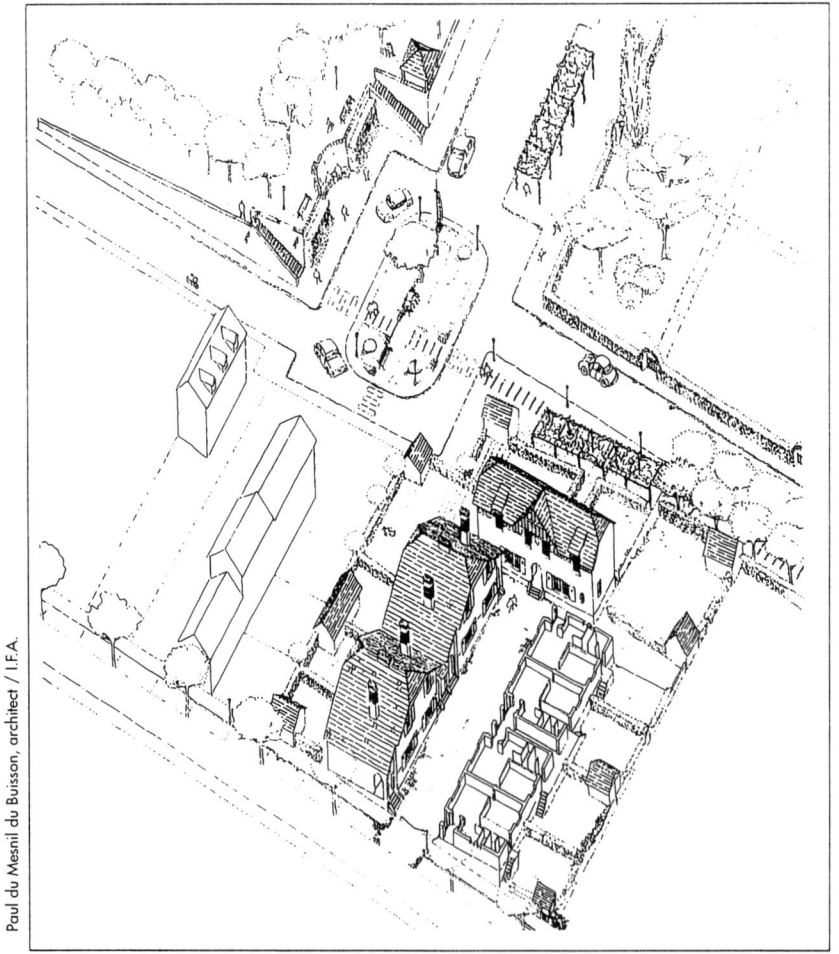

Paul du Mesnil du Buisson, architect / I.F.A.

The layout of the roads and their accessories is still frequently seen as a purely technical process that meets only the traffic and safety criteria. The trunk road bordering the Trouville cemetery is an eloquent caricature of the excessively functionalist attitude epitomized here by a straight featureless road with maximum use of asphalt.

The proposed development aims to transform this appalling environment into an avenue made pleasant by its proportions, its varied perspectives, its shady walks and its traditional urban furniture of street lamps and benches. The new layout revolves around a square marking the intersection of three streets.

The rehabilitation of the houses in the garden complex is used as an opportunity to redevelop the roads of this part of the redesigned neighbourhood.

THE COUNCIL HOUSES IN THE RUE SUZANNE: THE INTERNAL STREET.

CHOICE OR SUFFERING

5. CERGY-PONTOISE - LA ROCHELLE - BORDEAUX

CITY AND NON-CITY
1981-1982

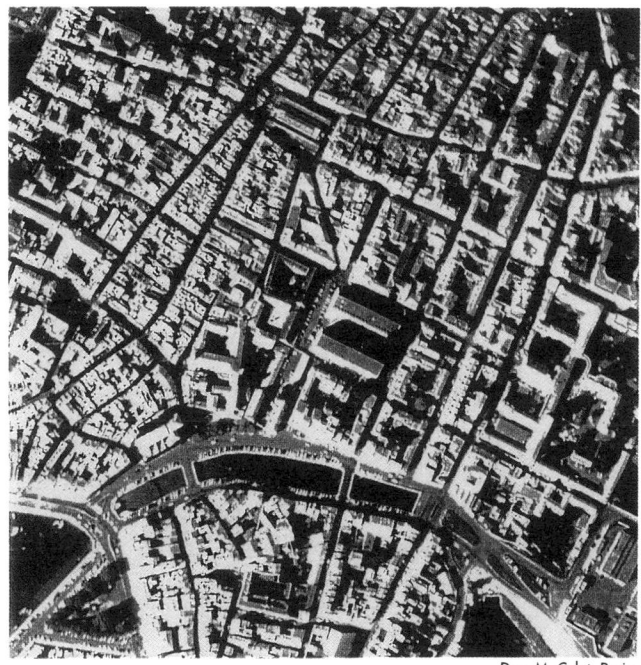

Doc. M. Culot, Paris.

THE CENTRE OF LA ROCHELLE.

The city is compact, long accustomed to defending itself within its walls. There are few squares, due to lack of space. The layout of the city is regular, as a result of both ethics and limited means. A typically Protestant austerity.
The city has only one diagonal, justified by the need to connect an old gate to the Place Royale built during the 17th-century extension. The narrow streets leading to the port were widened as early as the 12th century by fitting arched galleries under the existing houses.

In 1981, the officials of the new town of Cergy-Pontoise commissioned a team (comprising Léon Krier, Lucien Steil and Maurice Culot) to carry out a comparative study between the urban structure of a typical neighbourhood of the new town and that of Bordeaux and La Rochelle, the two French traditional cities.

The results of this study were introduced by a preliminary observation:

The area of the new town (approximately 10 000 hectares) is equal to the area of Paris *intra muros* (within the inner ring road). However, 2 million people live in Paris whereas Cergy-Pontoise, according to its founders, is designed for a population of 200 000.

The mere statement of these figures indicates that these French new towns will experience serious management difficulties when they are no longer supported by the State, and the residents become liable for their repair and maintenance.

It is impossible for 200 000 people to fund, through taxes, the maintenance of such an extensive area and infrastructure. The planning of the new towns is in conflict with any notion of economy. Density is low, the buildings are spread over the entire land area, requiring a huge road network, long linear perspectives, sewerage, lighting.

The only way to save the new French towns from financial bankruptcy is to reduce their expanse, increase the building density and reinforce the mix of activities.

Jean Millier, who took part with Paul Delouvrier in the launching of five new towns in the Paris region in the early 1960s, wrote the following in 1995 [1].

«The standard process for most towns whose extension is not restricted by natural obstacles is slow but steady development. However, while the concentric configuration is acceptable for a town of modest proportions, it has many drawbacks – distance from the countryside among others – for those who live in the centre. This type of development has produced under-equipped suburbs and highly congested centres.
These observations led to the creation, after 1965, of new urban centres around Paris. In 1994 some 715 000 people were living in the five new towns. [...] Generally speaking, the French new towns are capable of incorporating into their programmes various facets of human activity, and they now provide the conditions for the individual and collective fulfilment of their residents. However, the large housing complexes erected at the same time pose acute problems in terms of integrating individuals into society, while these are being physically excluded from the urban process.»
«However», Jean Millier adds, «the future of the new towns is also conditioned by their ability to regenerate, to draw the lessons of their own construction process, to rebuild on their own sites, to increase their density, to provide recognisable public spaces for their residents...»

And that is precisely where the problem lies. Whereas the traditional cities are continuously rebuilding on their own sites, the original design of the French new towns makes them impossible to densify without destroying them almost completely.

The new towns have far too much public space for them to be viable. It should be cut back to a standard ratio of 30 to 35% of the total area.

A traditional city grows denser by raising some buildings, by rebuilding plots or blocks. This cannot be done in the new towns with their isolated, irregular-shaped buildings whose layout does not delineate any specific public spaces nor leads to subsequent densification solutions.

In addition to the waste of time, energy and land illustrated by the comparison between the new and

1. Opening speech at the International Conference on European Towns at the Threshold of the 21st century, Santo Kiriko Conference Centre, Plovdiv, Bulgaria, 18-20 September 1995.

traditional towns, it appears too that the morphology and typologies of the new towns have no sociological reality.

In a traditional city, the urban morphology and the types of blocks and buildings are always the outcome of rational motivations, whereas in the new towns they are merely the product of the architects' and planners' whim and of the implementation of abstract standards detached from the reality and complexity of city life.

An active hub of Calvinism, the largest safe haven granted to the Huguenots by the Edict of Nantes before it was besieged and taken by Richelieu in 1628, La Rochelle's urbanism is typical of a Protestant city, sparing of resources, preferring simplicity to showy urban displays.

Though it lost its city walls in 1628, La Rochelle still bears today the mark of its austere Protestant past.
Because it was a fortress, the town gained density from within, which explains why it has few public squares and why the monuments are often built into the framework. The famous arches themselves were cut under the existing houses, as early as the 12th century, to facilitate the conveyance of goods along the narrow streets.

Bordeaux, on the other hand, is the exact opposite in character: under the stewardship of the Intendants of the King of France, the city improved continuously throughout the 18th century. A city façade was built on the site of the old walls facing the river – a magnificent curtain of coordinated houses drawn across the old mediaeval buildings.

The blocks in La Rochelle are regular and the city has only one diagonal street designed to connect an old city gate to the Place Royale – in the 18th-century patchwork – whose corner buildings are treated as terraced houses. The same solution has been adopted in Philadelphia and many founded American towns where the saving generated by the duplication of a single plan is stronger than the desire for variety. Two hundred years later, on the contrary, the architects of the Art Nouveau strongholds – Brussels, Nancy, Barcelona – will seek out the corner plots that lend themselves to spectacular scenographies.

In Bordeaux, the Chartrons neighbourhood – where the wine is stored before being shipped to England – developed around the port and wine-making activities.
Here the plots are in the form of long narrow strips. The merchants' houses facing the wharves have huge vaulted cellars for the storage of wine. The Chartrons features a block, 300 by 200 metres, with communicating cellars.
This balance between block typology and morphology is lacking in the French new towns which are designed according to the zoning principle.
Neighbourhood diversity is based solely on the (frequently gratuitous) fantasy of the architecture.

This is of course an artificial variety that is not steeped in reality. These typological forms are not only gratuitous, but such an unnecessary exercise makes any future transformation of the new towns even more difficult.

The builders of new towns are very fond of terms such as «streets, squares, forum, agora, neighbourhoods...», yet none of these are apparent when one visits them.

Today's new towns claim to be so different and yet finally they are all alike despite their great architectural diversity, their technical innovations and their different topography and geography.

Traditional cities, on the other hand, are built and rebuilt on simple timeless principles based on the human scale, transcending wars and bloodshed and the hours of misery and joy that have ever been their fate. These towns are the antithesis of today's new towns – all different and displaying a complexity that will always confound the most sophisticated computer.

This comparison of new towns and traditional cities is not only an academic exercise. It points to a genuine educational strategy for cities, including the old ones that should not be split into an untouchable historical centre on the one hand and a testing ground for any architectural and urban fantasies on the other.

With historical knowledge of the formation of city neighbourhoods, of the reasons for typological diversity (always usage-related), with an understanding of the constituent concepts of the European city and of their implementation according to local circumstances, it is possible to formulate solutions that will suit every city.

In other words, the city as a physical and social reality is in a better position to suggest the most appropriate solutions for its own development and evolution.

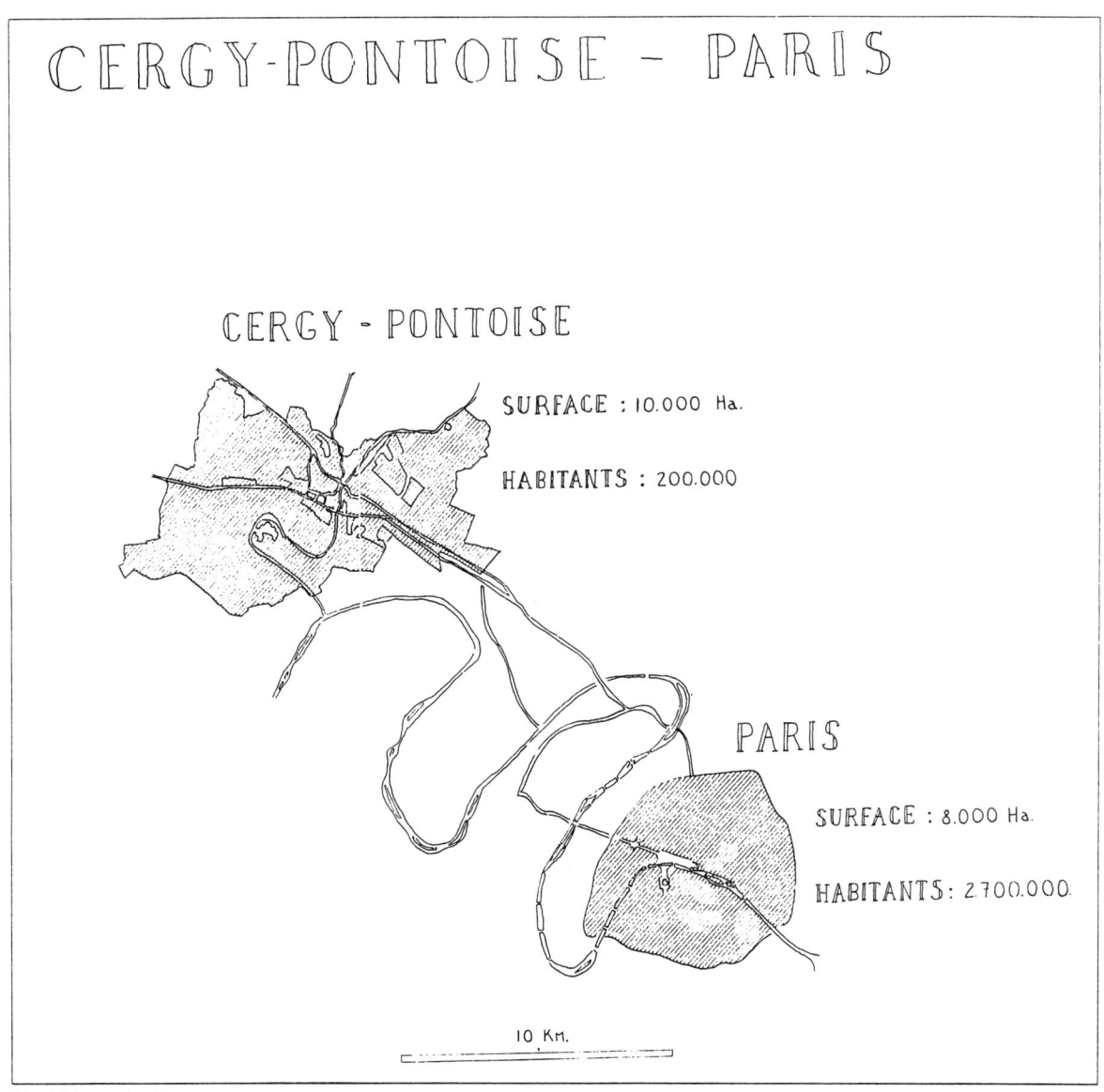

Culot / Krier / Steil architects.

A mere comparison between the population and area figures of the new town of Cergy-Pontoise and Paris *intra muros* suffices to illustrate the costs (social, economic, energy, environmental) incurred by the inadequate urban density of the new towns built around Paris from the 1960s onwards.

PARALLELS: A METHOD OF ANALYSIS.

To highlight the differences between a traditional city and the new towns built around Paris from the 1960s, parallels have been drawn on the same scale between the city of La Rochelle, famous for its beauty and quality of life, and Jouy-le-Moutier, a neighbourhood of Cergy-Pontoise.

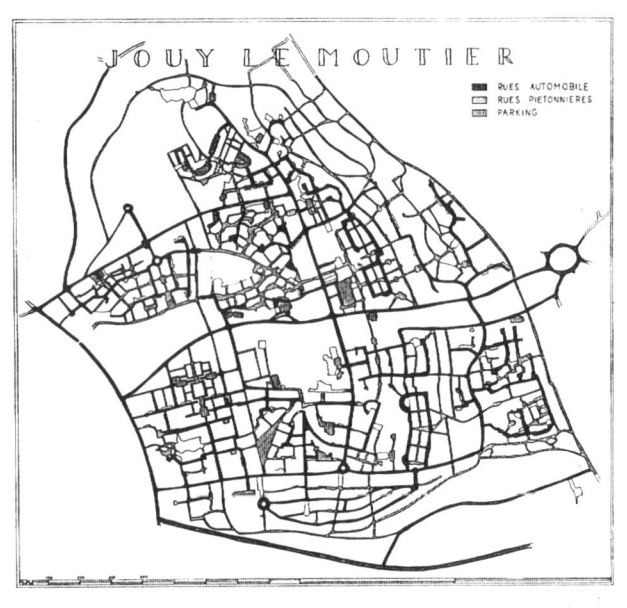

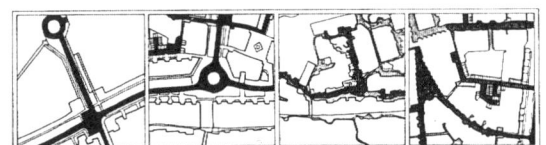

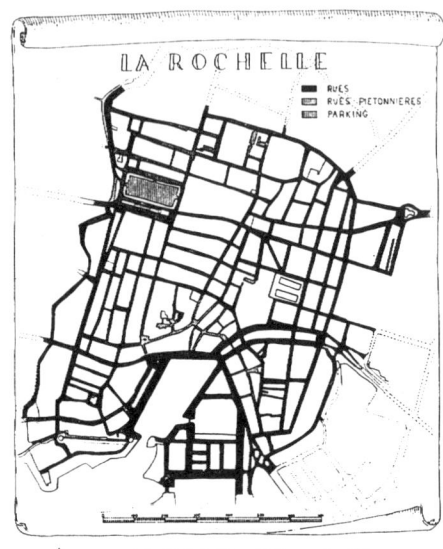

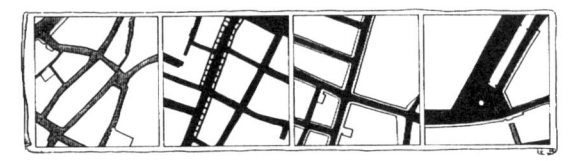

Culot / Krier / Steil architects.

INFRASTRUCTURE PARALLELS.

In the new town:

There are no streets, no avenues, no boulevards but only a rhizome-patterned network. A motorway divides the site, branching off to serve dead ends and culs-de-sac. Public space is always poorly defined and poorly recognizable.

In La Rochelle:

The streets are graded according to priority and neighbourhood character. The wharves are wide because of the goods they handle; the busiest streets leading to the port were widened back in the 12th Century by cutting arcades under the existing houses.
Each public space is recognizable and has its own density.

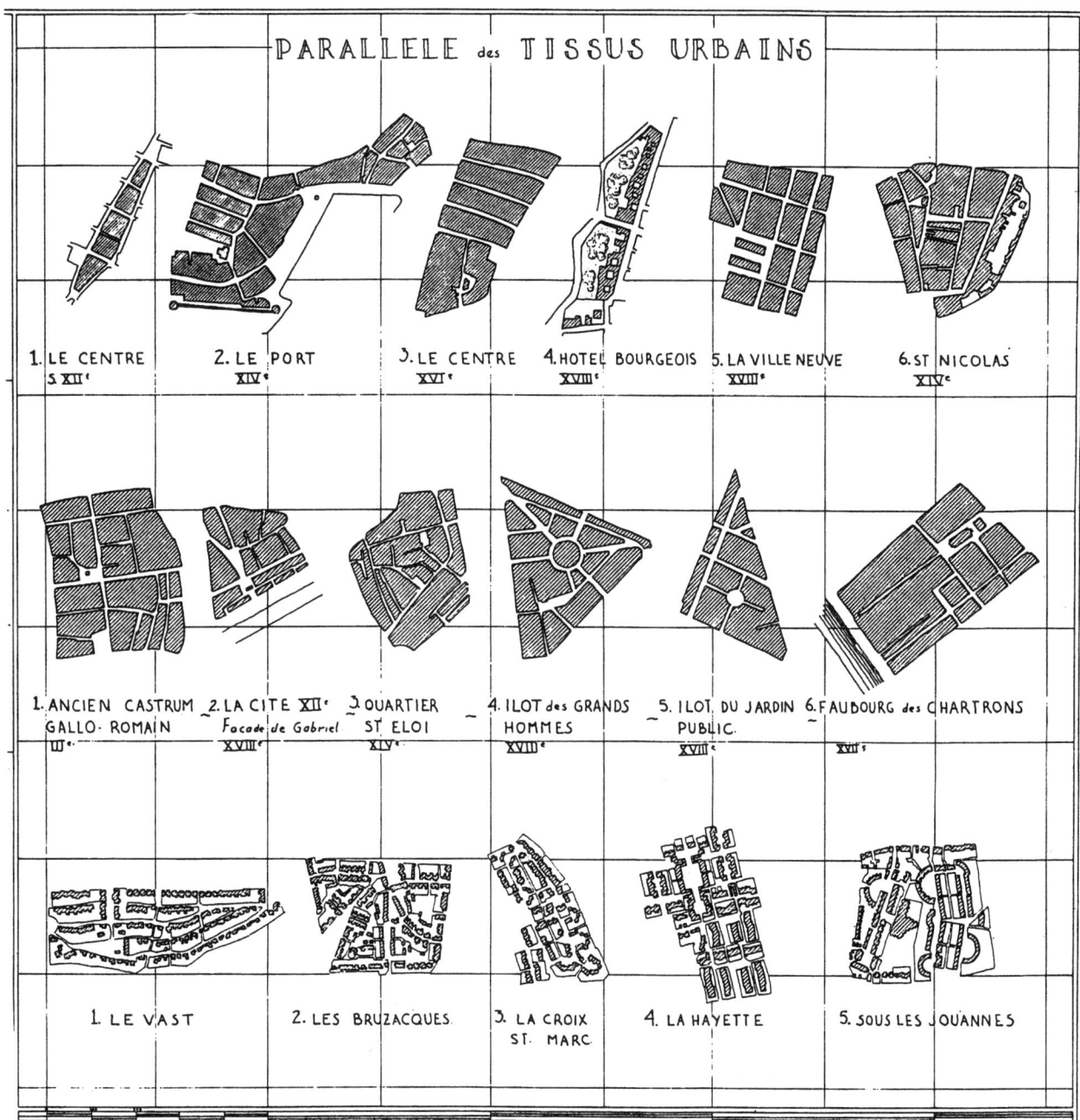

URBAN FABRIC PARALLEL.

FROM TOP TO BOTTOM:

- **La Rochelle:** an impression of regularity and sparing use of resources prevails.

- **Bordeaux:** instantly recognizable are the Roman castrum and the 18th-century improvements, with skilful compositions around circular squares and radiating streets.

- **Jouy-le-Moutier neighbourhood in Cergy-Pontoise:** despite the huge effort to diversify the urban fabric, what we have are clusters of houses, no blocks, no public spaces. Boredom, monotony, repetition and pseudo-variety prevail.

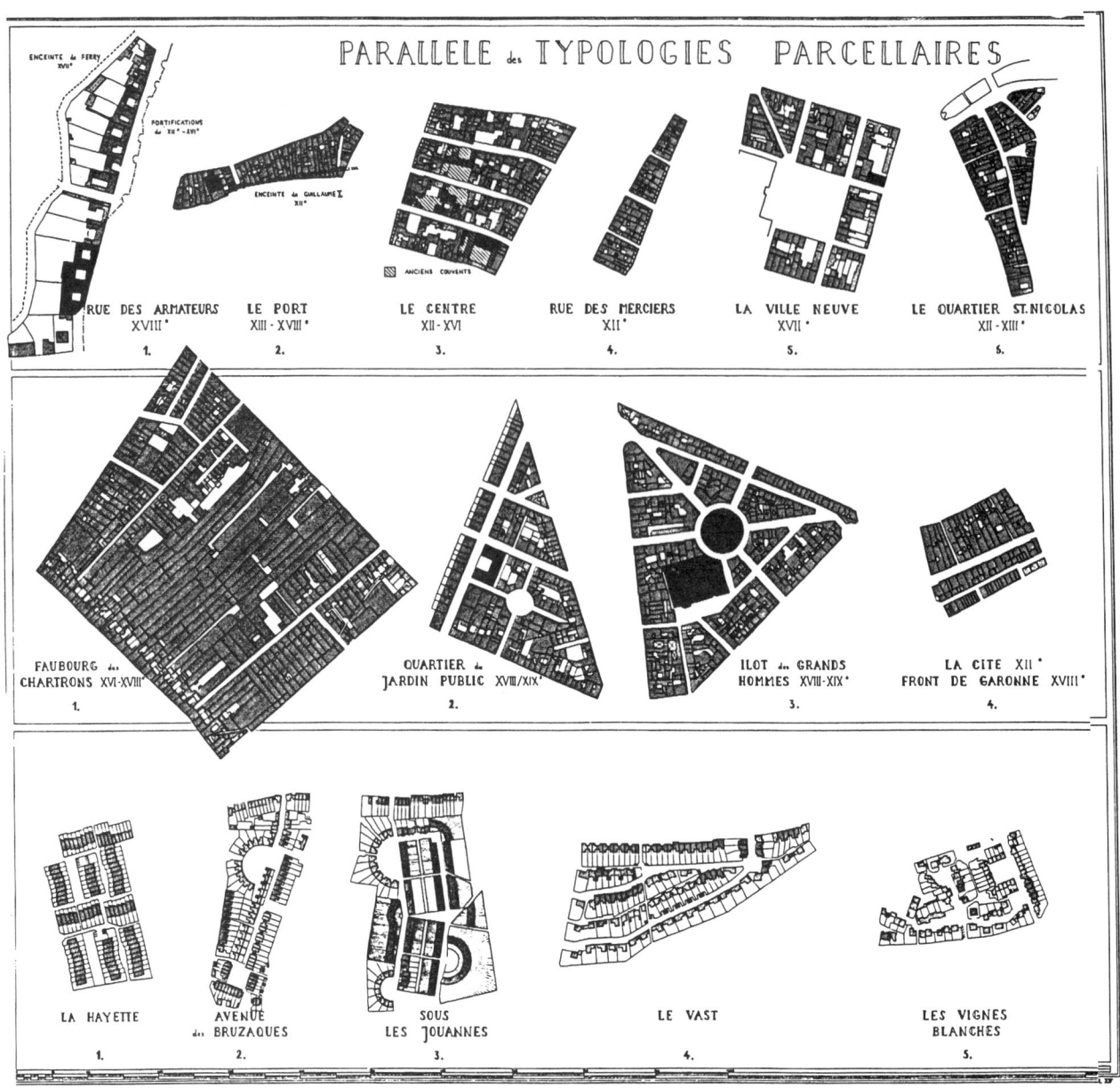

PLOT TYPOLOGY PARALLEL.

FROM TOP TO BOTTOM:

- **La Rochelle, left to right:** the rich merchants' mansions, with courtyards and gardens; the narrow-strip blocks facing the port (many of these share wharf space); the regular plots of the 18th-century new town.

- **Bordeaux, left to right**: the Chartrons strips, 200-metre-long plots housing the wine stores. The irregular plots of the new 18th- and 19th-century subdivisions. A typological diversity that only a rich bourgeois city with highly skilled craftsmen can afford.

- **Jouy-le-Moutier:** there is no justification for plot fantasy but to differ for the sake of differing. This is subdivision urbanism, not neighbourhood urbanism.

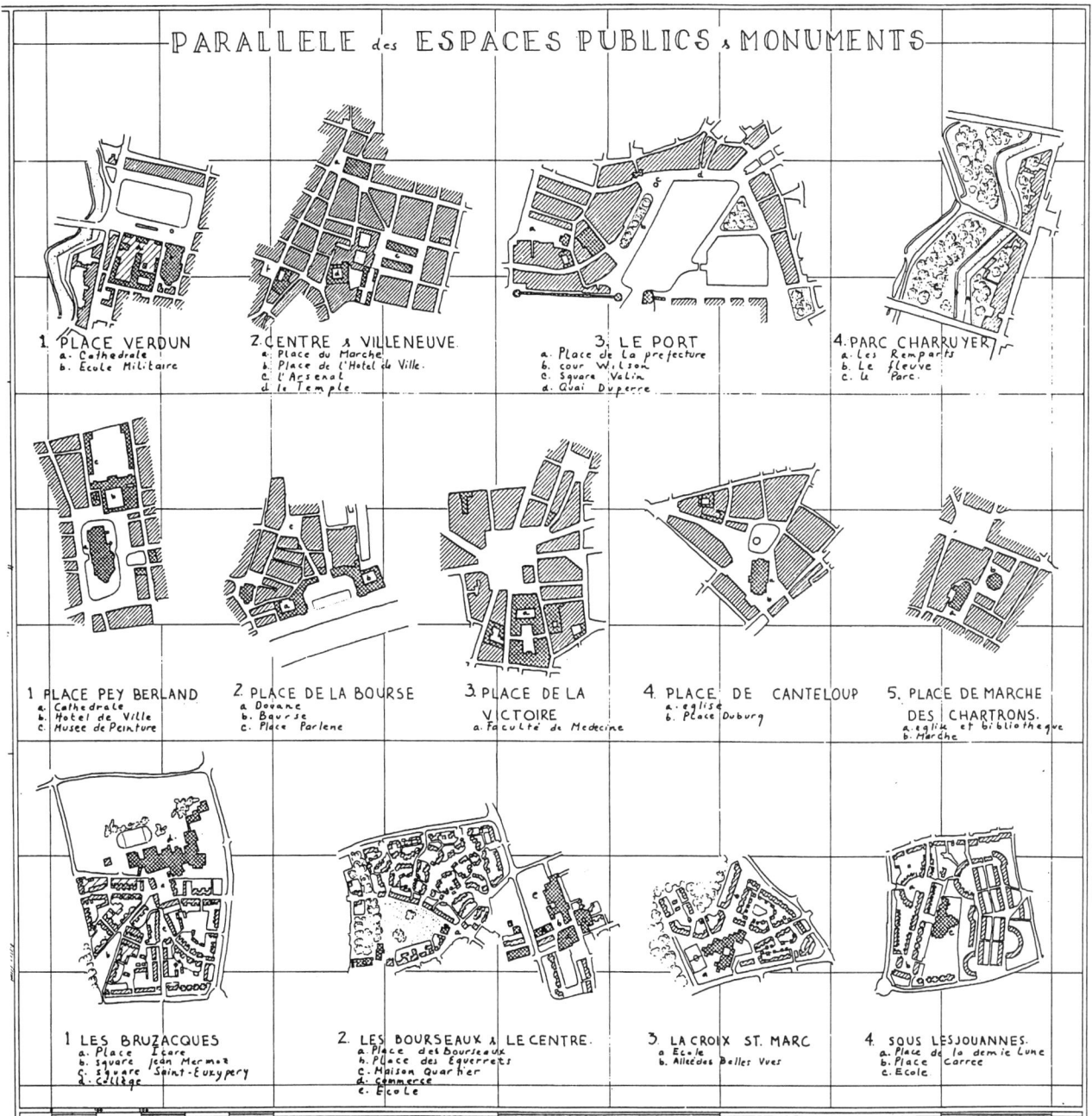

PUBLIC AREAS AND MONUMENTS PARALLEL.

FROM TOP TO BOTTOM:

- **La Rochelle:** virtually all the monuments are integrated into the urban fabric; very few monuments are apart or isolated. This is because the city was a fortress whose development was long confined within the walls.

- **Bordeaux:** isolated religious buildings, visible from all sides; a Place Royale integrated into the urban fabric and opening towards the river (typological complexity).

- **Jouy-le-Moutier:** all the public buildings are proliferating structures that fail to delineate any coherent, recognizable public space. Disorder, anarchy and monotony prevail. Architects given too much latitude. They all pursue their own ideas and the community derives no benefit.

AFTER THE ANALYSIS, THE PROJECT

The two plans below indicate:

- The present site of the Jouy-le-Moutier neighbourhood of Cergy-Pontoise, a new town of 10 000 inhabitants on 140 hectares. The urban form is incoherent and the distinction between the built-up zone and the countryside is blurred.

- The same site urbanized according to the constituent principles of the European city (neighbourhood, square, street). A population of 40 000 could live there in comfort, in neighbourhoods that include varied activities, many squares and streets of different character and fine urban perspectives. Nature and city are clearly differentiated.

The site lends itself to building a fine terrace looking out on Paris (as in St-Germain), under which large car parks can be provided.

Culot / Krier / Steil architects.

A PRESSING DESIRE FOR MEMORY

6. WARSAW

GREATNESS AND LIMITATIONS OF THE SYMBOL

A PRESSING DESIRE FOR MEMORY

6. WARSAW

GREATNESS AND LIMITATIONS OF THE SYMBOL

Human beings are often driven to action by symbols. What seems impossible then comes true. For good and for evil.

In the aftermath of World War II, the Poles rebuilt Warsaw's old town centre from old photographs, plans, drawings and paintings.

For them it was a matter of strongly asserting the permanence of their cultural and urban identity, which the Nazis had attempted to eradicate.

This reconstruction strategy is therefore more of a symbolic act than a rational method of rebuilding cities. This observation is confirmed by the fact that, around the centre of reconstructed Warsaw, suburbs of low-rise and tower blocks are springing up like anywhere else in Europe.

The reconstruction of Warsaw's historical centre as it was arouses admiration and deserves respect. The message conveyed by those new stones is that injustice and tyranny should be resisted. Resistance, however, is a moral code, not an end in itself. The Nazi ignominy is but a ghastly episode in Warsaw's history. Symbolic action is essential but not sufficient. It cannot replace rational thought or the city-reconstruction method. Otherwise we will end up by being content with symbols. Tourists will visit Warsaw's old reconstructed centre or the reconstructed *îlot Sacré* [Sacred Isle] (a name that speaks for itself!) of Brussels. There they will find restaurants, souvenir shops and hotels, but all around will be nothing but absurd suburbia.

Doc. I.F.A.

A DESIRE FOR METHOD

7. POUNDBURY MASTER PLAN

DORCHESTER, DORSET
1988-1991

In the aftermath of World War II the Athens Charter, drawn up on the initiative of a few modernist architects, emerged as the reference method for substitution projects in existing cities and for new neighbourhood designs and city extensions.
The Charter's principles were taught in architecture schools and cast as laws and directives for the development of towns that all favoured zoning, mechanical traffic flows and the absolute rejection of the traditional street and square systems.
In the late 1960s the validity of that model was being increasingly challenged in the light of the frequently disastrous developments and the incredible waste of energy, land and human resources caused by its implementation. The Athens Charter was then almost unanimously condemned, but it was not replaced by another town-planning method.

Each project manager, architect, developer, planner had their own personal ideas on what had to be done, and the results were often less convincing than those achieved by the Athens Charter which had the merit of functionalist rigour.

Nowadays more and more political leaders are aware of the need for a method that could be understood and applied by all, and would take into account the people's legitimate aspirations to live in urban atmospheres and architectural settings inspired by tradition and respectful of local features.

The rift between architecture and the people widened.
Private architecture is virtually always traditional, whereas the architecture of public buildings (schools and post offices for instance) is always abstract and modelled on successive architectural fashions. Modern architecture has now become the official architecture, pleasing no one but its originators and possibly its sponsors.

Léon Krier (1946) was the first, from the 1970s, to suggest a rational method of viewing urbanism, based on a knowledge and analysis of the constituent elements of European cities.

«Most of the debate of the 70s and 80s is powerfully suggested by the work of Léon Krier,» writes Demetri Porphyrios as an introduction to the monograph on this architect and theoretician published in 1992 (Academy Editions, London).

As early as 1978 Léon Krier published a reconstruction Charter for the European city. He argued for the study of master plans, which were dropped by the municipalities in the 1970s because they had not lived up to the planners' expectations.

«Yet,» Léon Krier writes, «the depressing monotony of the suburbs and the fairground chaos of new enterprise zones are timely reminders that large urban development can simply not happen in an intelligent and civilised way without a master plan».

According to Léon Krier, a «master plan» consists of 4 parts:

- The first is the master plan itself, defining the population, location, size and form of the urban community to be developed. It also defines «the formal relationship between each urban district and each district's individual centres and high streets; the use, form and extent of land contiguous to and between neighbouring quarters, the overall traffic concepts».

Within the master plan, a ground plan for each district «defines the precise shape, pattern and dimensions of streets and squares and individual plots on each block...».

- The second part of the master plan is «the urban code which describes the allowed position of buildings on plots, the plot-ratio and/or number of floors without metric height limitation finally uses per plot and floor».

- The third part of the master plan is: «the architectural code which describes the materials, configurations, techniques and proportions for external building walls, roofs, windows and doors, garden walls, chimneys and porches...».

- The fourth and last part of the master plan deals with the issue of public space: «the materials, configurations and techniques of hard and soft surfaces, furnishings, fences, lighting, planting, commercial and traffic signage as well as landscaping».

«To counter excessive vertical expansion in city centres and excessive horizontal expansion in the suburbs we must,» says Léon Krier, «reorganize the cities into neighbourhoods, ie redistribute all the functions of the city over a limited area and provide each area with its own centre. The right percentage of public space is in itself a factor of equilibrium. Within a city neighbourhood,» Léon Krier stresses, «the streets and squares together must not occupy more than 35% of the total area. Beyond this figure, the planning, maintenance, supervision and management of the [public] space becomes difficult at the level of quality required. Almost all council-housing neighbourhoods have 70 to 90% of public space. This is a false luxury.»

Léon Krier has had the opportunity to formulate several master plans for various European and

North American cities and neighbourhoods.

In particular, he is the designer of the Poundbury master plan, a series of neighbourhoods that will form the extension of the city of Dorchester.

The development programme, spread over 15 years, will be self-sufficient in terms of jobs, primary and secondary education, shops and leisure. The first streets and squares, built over the past two years, already reflect the urban atmosphere of traditional Dorset towns – from which Krier draws inspiration – and illustrate the realism and pragmatism of his theories. These have proved to be all the more operational since this project is proceeding without any public funding of the infrastructure, while Great Britain is in the throes of a property recession such as it has not experienced since World War II.

The extension of the city of Dorchester as viewed by Léon Krier is neither a series of subdivisions nor a Utopia. The urban foundation is modern (but not «modernistic»), with streets, squares and four autonomous neighbourhoods. One of the plan's original features is that it rejects the division of functions into separate zones, and that it offers a great variety of building plots (from 150 to 4 000 m2) in any neighbourhood, thereby providing a mix of urban functions (private or public) compatible with the surrounding area. This arrangement also guarantees the aesthetic harmony of a very contrasted functional complex. Beyond these theoretical and operational considerations, the new neighbourhoods aim to provide a quality product built with quality materials – not to revolutionize or reform the very nature of the urban English house. That is why the dimensions of the houses proposed are similar to those usually found on the English market. Krier has ruled out significant size differences as these would immediately lead to speculation that would cause the city to be deprived of a large part of its social and functional mix.

Dorchester has started to expand according to the instructions of Léon Krier's plan. Its present population of 15 000 should increase by 7 000 in the next 25 years. The new residents will be accommodated in some 2 500 houses and flats spread over the four new neighbourhoods.

The extension of Dorchester is a convincing example, a concrete application of this building conception of the European city according to a method directly inspired by an analysis of traditional cities and their constituent concepts (street, square, block, neighbourhood). This practical and operational method is based on numbers and dimensions derived straight from an analysis of the most accomplished and successful neighbourhoods in the traditional city. The basic yardstick is a person on foot. This physical limit (a 10-minute walk) indicates the ideal size of a neighbourhood: its area should not exceed 25 to 35 hectares and its population 5 000 to 10 000. Four neighbourhoods make up a district and five districts or more make up a town.

The ideal shape of a neighbourhood approximates a round or oval configuration that should not exceed 900 metres in any direction (the 10-minute-walk yardstick determines the maximum diameter).

The neighbourhood is structured according to a clearly visible hierarchy of streets and squares (dead-end roads must imperatively be banned). These streets and squares are laid out freely or geometrically, forming a network that fits and highlights the site's physical, topographical, natural and historical realities.

The boundaries of each neighbourhood are not only an administrative line. They are significant landscape features taking the form of a promenade, a boulevard, an avenue, a park, etc.

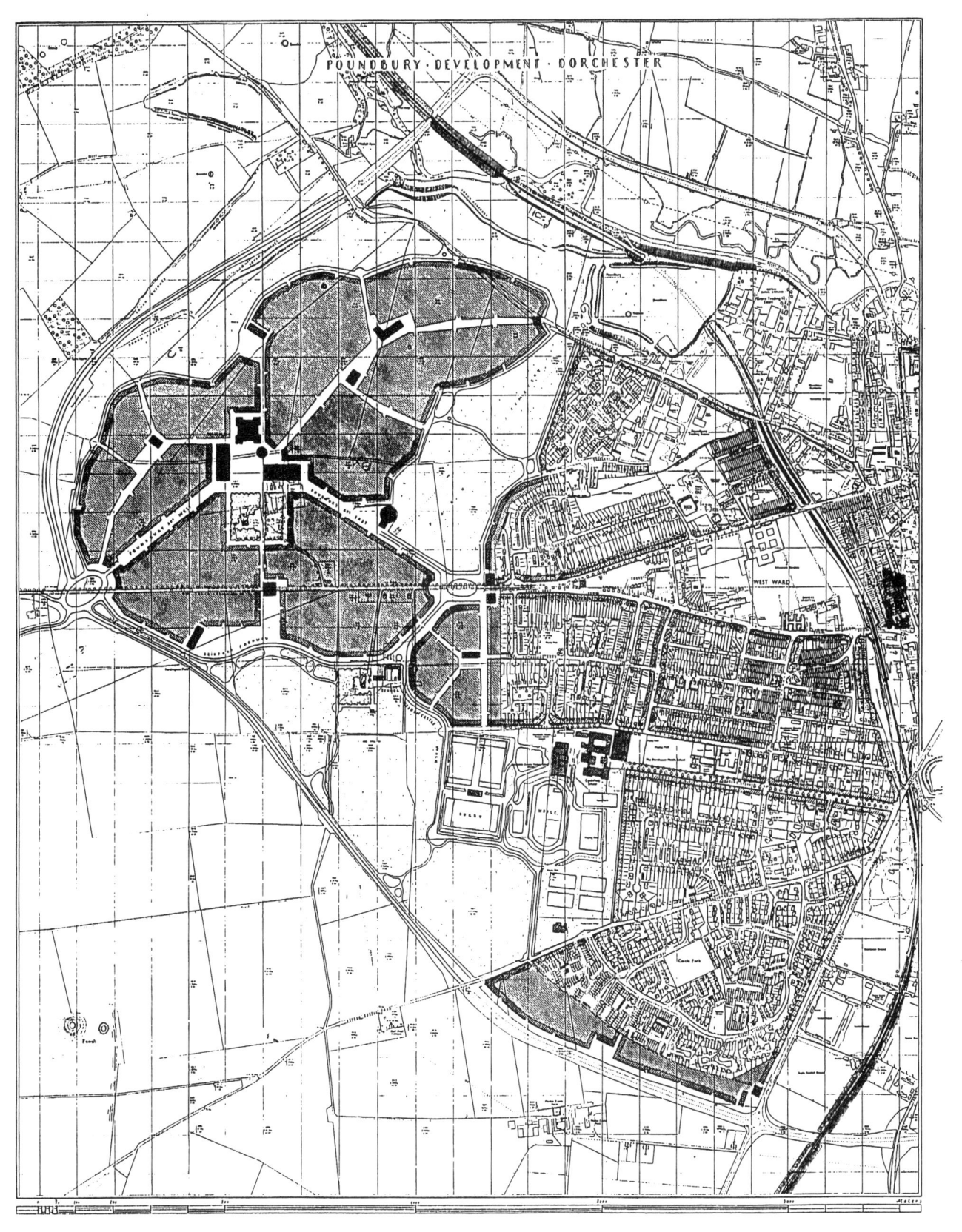

MASTER PLAN OF DORCHESTER BY LÉON KRIER.

Designed by Léon Krier.

AERIAL VIEW OF POUNDBURY, DORCHESTER'S NEW EXTENSION.

Léon Krier, architect.

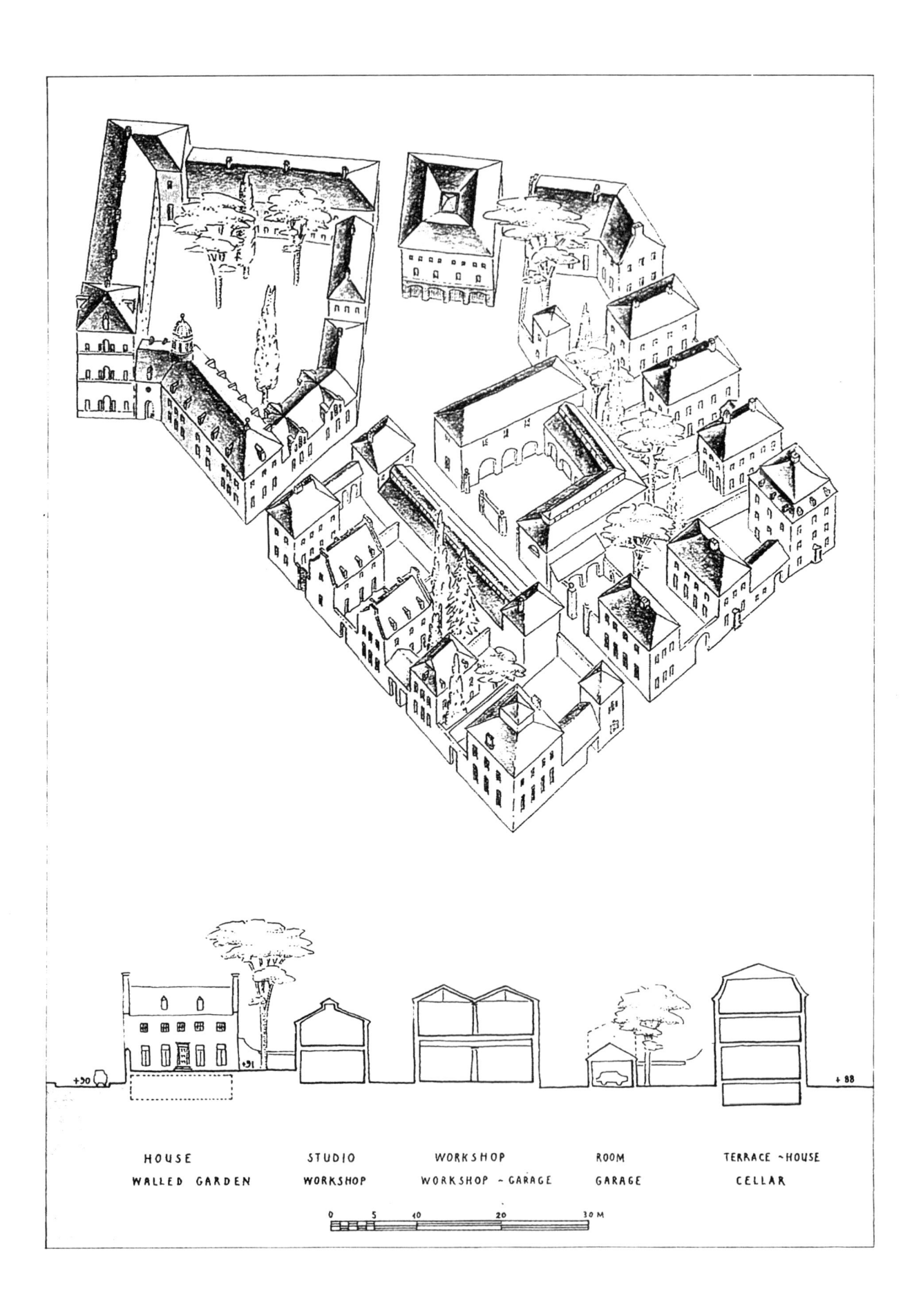

| HOUSE | STUDIO | WORKSHOP | ROOM | TERRACE-HOUSE |
| WALLED GARDEN | WORKSHOP | WORKSHOP - GARAGE | GARAGE | CELLAR |

THE BLOCKS AND PLOTS.

THE FRAMEWORK.

STAGE 1.

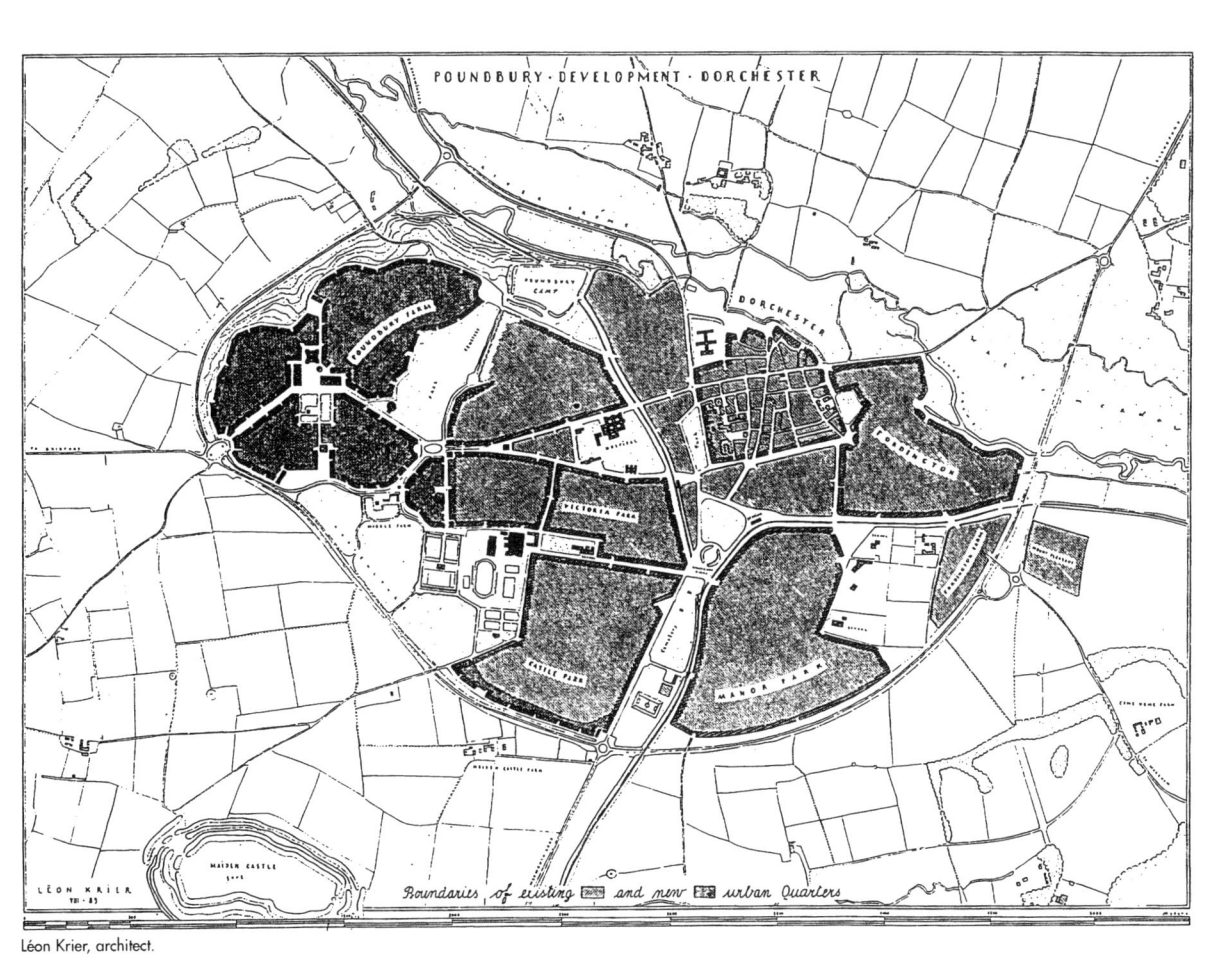

Léon Krier, architect.

DARKENED: STAGE 1.

125

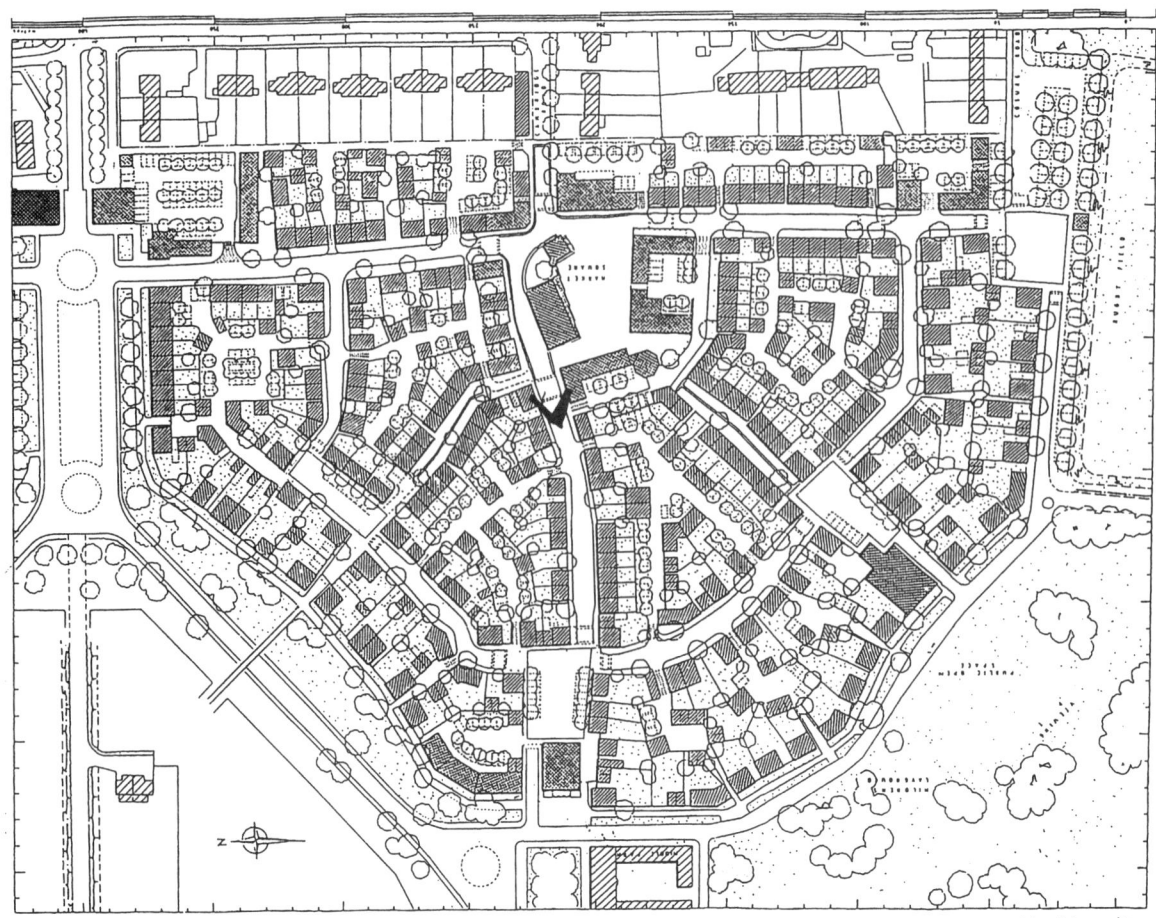

Léon Krier, architect.

PLAN OF STAGE 1.

Léon Krier, architect.
Drawing by Carl Laubin.

THE ARROW ON THE PLAN INDICATES THE OUT-LOOK.

VIEW OF POUNDBURY'S FIRST NEIGHBOURHOOD, 1995.

Doc. Léon Krier.

Doc. Léon Krier.

127

VIEW OF POUNDBURY'S FIRST NEIGHBOURHOOD, 1995.

Doc. Léon Krier.

Doc. Léon Krier.

128

A DESIRE FOR REFERENCES

8. NEW AMERICAN LESSONS OF VALUE TO EUROPE

A DESIRE FOR REFERENCES

8. NEW AMERICAN LESSONS OF VALUE TO EUROPE

The 20th century will have witnessed the loss of the city-building skill. Both the hallowing of historical centres and the conversion of the city into dull outskirts and suburbs have exacerbated the architects' desire for novelty at any price. Now that global references no longer exist, every one feels obliged to go one step further in an escalation of forms bordering on schizophrenia.

This quest for difference, and more often for extravagance, is not specific to architecture. It is apparent in the arts too, with the exception of music which is relatively unaffected.

This preference for originality at any price, this bulimia of new formal solutions for every occasion, are akin to a type of behaviour known as philandering. Don Juan is for ever seeking a new woman who will listen admiringly to the same story, the same trifle he tells all women. Being indicative of the troubles of our age, this behaviour has been analysed and presented by numerous writers and film makers.

In Les caprices de la jalousie [The quirks of jealousy], a novella published before the war, the French writer Pierre Drieu La Rochelle imagines a dialogue between Gilles, who leads a dissipated love life, and Bertrand who lives in a relationship. Both love women and «*had allocated them some time taken from work and pride, which they possibly resented; but such resentment did nothing but strengthen the bond*».

The following dialogue is taken from this novella and could apply to architecture and the concern of the modernist architect who feels constantly obliged to prefer the unknown to the familiar: «*For the hundredth time I complained of my inability to prefer the familiar to the unknown.*

- But what are you complaining about? he cried out suddenly with some bitterness. Since you are telling me about it, your attraction to women is primarily very strong; it is therefore pervasive and carries you along with it. Why then do you seem to believe that something of them escapes you? A sensitive intellect served by passion can reach the heart of a being in one single stroke. If we do not accept that, then we must question all gifts and all talents. If a skilful lover cannot divine his mistress from the first physical and intellectual embraces, can a doctor fathom out a patient at first sight, a politician his opponents, an artist his model? By giving you her all, a woman who loves you reveals everything of herself in no time.»

Pragmatists at all times, the Americans are now aware of the need to come out in favour of an urbanism generating less waste and violence, an American scourge caused mainly by the deterioration of the urban reality. A genuine urban renaissance movement and initiatives in support of an alternative to urban chaos are developing in the United States today.

In his preface to the recent book The New Urbanism, Toward an Architecture of Community (McGraw-Hill, 1994), which combines, under the titles Establishing the Urban Pattern and

Reconstructing the Urban Fabric, over 25 major projects throughout the United States, Peter Katz observes that:

«*By the summer of 1991*»... «*it seemed evident that a new urban design movement was taking shape. Publications as diverse as* The Atlantic, Travel & Leisure, People *and* Smithsonian *had all featured what was then being called 'Neo-traditional' planning.*

Several television networks had covered it as well. The architectural press was slower to come around; this story didn't fit neatly into their well-established celebrity system.

For me, an extensive article in Time Magazine *on the work of Andres Duany, Elizabeth Plater-Zyberk and Peter Calthorpe was the Clincher. A new architecture and urban design movement had already gone mainstream, yet few of the architects that I knew were even aware of it.*

The New Urbanism is a movement that I feel will be of great relevance to future planning efforts in this country. It addresses many of the ills of our current sprawl development pattern while returning to a cherished American icon: that of a compact, close-knit community.»

[Passage in English (in italics) transcribed verbatim - Transl.]

Among the founders of New Urbanism, the agency run by Andres Duany and Elizabeth Plater-Zyberk is the most active and famous. It formulates plans of towns and communities all over the world, using a method of urban codes and an accelerated sedimentation process. Planners and various specialists work in «charrettes», drafting plans that are then submitted to another team for criticism, correction and improvement, and so on in a short but intense period of time.

In this manner, the plan picks up different sensitivities, draws on new perspectives and the final plan benefits from an accelerated historical sedimentation.

This is in keeping with the American city-building tradition. Coral Gables, for instance, was established near Miami with the aim of creating the finest garden city in the world. It is just that, with its monumental stone gates, its fountains and its unique landscaped routes. The Mediterranean-style houses were given an artificial patina during the construction process (masonry struck with chains and façades whitewashed with a cow-dung solution promoting the growth of micro-organisms) so as to give an immediate impression of being lived in, of being steeped in time and history.

Very recently the Duany/Plater-Zyberk Agency did the planning specifications pages featured in the collection Architectural Graphic Standards published by the American Institute of Architects, a compulsory reference work in the event of a dispute. Planners are thus officially asked to follow recommendations in support of traditional urbanism (see Annex 1). America is therefore preparing to experience a real planning revolution, even though the concept of community tinged with segregationist connotations is mentioned more frequently than the concept of complex city as it is understood in Europe.

PROGRAMME OF THE THIRD NEW URBANISM CONFERENCE.
SAN FRANCISCO, 18-20 FEBRUARY 1995.

SESSIONS

1. OVERVIEW - THE NEW REGIONALISM

The questions of inner-city decay, environmental degradation, cultural disarray, and economic stress can be best articulated and resolved within a regional framework. Clearly the success of many New Urbanist principles are keyed to regional policies. National leaders in regional theory and practice will outline ways of understanding our environmental, social and economic conditions as fundamentally metropolitan in scale. From this perspective papers will be presented on metropolitan growth trends for the next generation; ecology and the region; land use/tax equity politics; metropolitan health and human services; regional growth management; and a history of the regional movement.

Speakers include: Neal Pierce, author *Citistates*; Tony Downs, author *New Visions for Metropolitan America*; Robert Fishman, author *Bourgeois Utopia*; Grantland Johnson, director of HHS Region 10; Henry Richmond, president of the National Growth Management Leadership Project; Myron Orfield, Representative, Minneapolis/St. Paul; Paul Hawken, author *Ecology of Commerce*; Chris Leinberger, economist and author.

2. REGIONAL PLANS - DESIGNS FOR THE 'CITISTATES' OF NORTH AMERICA

A range of regional plans for various metropolitan areas will be presented; some in process, some adopted, and some failed. Each uses New Urbanist principles as building blocks to produce a larger framework of growth and urban form. Areas to be covered include the metropolitan regions of: New York, Seattle, Portland, San Francisco, Philadelphia, San Diego, and South Walton County as well as historic regional plans of Chicago and TVA.

3. COALITION BUILDING - ENVIRONMENTAL AND INNER-CITY GROUPS JOIN THE CNU

Bridging the gaps among designers, environmentalists, and community group advocates is central to the philosophy of New Urbanism. New connections were initiated at a precongress meeting of thirty representatives of diverse groups concerned with different dimensions of the urban and suburban dilemma. Members representing these groups will each present a description of their organization's agenda and activities along with a notions of how we can collaborate to foster change for common interests. These groups include: National Civic League, Trust for Public Land; National Resource Defense Council; Environmental Defense Fund; Urban Edge; Energy Foundation; Local Governments Commission; National Downtown Association; Urban Ecology; and American Association of Retired Persons.

4. REGIONALISM IN ARCHITECTURE - FORM AND VOCABULARY FOR THE ARCHITECTURE OF NEW URBANISM

New Urbanism resists the world wide eradication of the distinctiveness of places. An important component of the particularity of place is an architecture grounded in local history, climate and building practice. The distinction between authentic regional architecture and kitsch marketing themes is often blurry and the subject of contention. It is in fact the ground upon which some have based their most vigorous criticism of New Urbanism. This panel will explore the dimensions of the debate about the architecture of regions and attempt to arrive at a common understanding of principle.

5. REGIONAL INFRASTRUCTURE - THE FRAMEWORK OF REGIONAL COOPERATION

Transit: A panel will review the state of the art of different transit systems and their applications. This group will update progress on the implementation of ISTEA, report on new research and its results, describe new transit systems and their performance, and review the basics of various transit options.

Environmental Systems: Regional open space systems and ecologies give each metropolitan area its unique qualities. They connect the diverse pieces of the metropolis with one of its most important unifying characteristics. Issues ranging from the location of growth in a region, to the water and waste systems which support individual neighborhoods will be discussed. Landscape and open space systems as urban connectors rather than suburban buffers will be illustrated.

Finance and Economy: Fundamental to the growth of New Urbanism is the economic environment; the availability of various types of financing, the prejudices of the banking system, the direction of job growth, and the

PROGRAMME OF THE THIRD NEW URBANISM CONFERENCE.
SAN FRANCISCO, 18-20 FEBRUARY 1995.

Market trends implicit in the new demographics. Regional policies of tax base distribution and finance structure effect the fundamental structure of growth. A panel will report on the latest thinking, research, and programs in this area.

REGIONAL POLICY : Central to balanced neighborhoods is the often unrecognized (and sometimes unused) influence of regional policies and guidelines. Urban Growth Boundaries, fair housing policies, tax base sharing, and land use/transit programs set the stage for local design and land use programs. Without strong, progressive regional policies the New Urbanism will face unrelenting difficulties on issues such as housing diversity, mixed use development, and traffic mitigation. Papers will cover land use laws, policy and politics, new growth management legislation, and recent policies in Australia and the UK.

5. CONCLUSION - General Discussion and Working Group Reports

Each of the Working Committees will report to the assembled Congress on their progress and direction. Comments and suggestions will be taken on the Committees efforts. The program and focus of CNU IV will be discussed. Concluding remarks will be delivered by John Norquist, Mayor of Milwaukee.

Working Committees

Each working committee will meet for two sessions during the congress and report back to the plenary session on Monday. It is expected that the groups will schedule work between the congresses and continue their work at CNU IV. The first three committees will begin to develop material for a publication, 'The Charter of the New Urbanism', which will contain a section on each of three areas: Principles and Policies, Nomenclature, and Case Studies. The Principles and Policies group will attempt to crystallize the fundamental postulates of New Urbanism into concise, usable statements. Nomenclature will define the elements of New Urbanism and develop a syntax for their relationships. The Case Studies will illustrate the Principles and Nomenclature with a variety of projects of differing

The subject of the third Congress in San Francisco on February 17-20 is the metropolitan region itself — the region as a physical entity and as the subject of governance. The third Congress will continue the process of coalition building, with emphasis on our common purpose with the environmental community and with inner city advocates. As a part of the third Congress members will assemble in working groups to begin drafting chapters for the 'New Urban Charter', the organization's comprehensive statement of principle and policy to be presented for adoption by the organization at a later Congress. In addition to these working sessions, the Congress will include presentation of papers and projects related to the task of coalition building and to the theme of the region — its architecture, its infrastructure and its political form.

Membership in the CNU is by invitation. Some 400 persons have been asked to join. They represent a national coalition of planners, architects, landscape designers, sociologists, historians, municipal administrators, elected officials, community organizers, traffic engineers, transportation specialists, and environmentalists. Additionally, the development and financial industries are represented. New coalition members have been invited from a variety of disciplines with a focus on environmental and local community groups. You have been invited to participate in the next two planned congresses and to help identify the future direction of the CNU. A membership and information card is enclosed. We look forward to your participation.

PETER CALTHORPE
DANIEL SOLOMON

CONFERENCE COORDINATORS

Doc. Culot / I.F.A.

Kentlands

Gaithersburg, Maryland, 1988

The town of Kentlands is the first application of the traditional neighborhood development (TND) principles to a real, year-round, working community. Unlike Seaside, which some critics dismiss as an isolated resort town and therefore not a true test of the TND concept, this community lies squarely in the path of suburban growth surrounded by housing subdivisions, shopping centers and office campuses.

Located within the city of Gaithersburg, just 23 miles northwest of Washington, D.C., in the heart of what some call the "I-270 technology corridor," Kentlands has been conceived as an authentic town made up of distinct neighborhoods, in the classic American tradition.

The master plan of the community, sited on the 356-acre Kent Farm tract, was the result of a widely publicized design charette led by town planners Andres Duany and Elizabeth Plater-Zyberk. It includes six neighborhoods, each combining elements of residential, office, civic, cultural and retail usage. To encourage diversity both in age and income level, a range of housing types and sizes is planned. For example, carriage houses, which may serve as retirement units, will exist next to single-family homes and townhouses, and rental apartments will be located above shops.

Kentlands includes a variety of civic facilities and public open spaces. A lake and wetland preserve, greenbelts and several small squares

Culot / I.F.A.

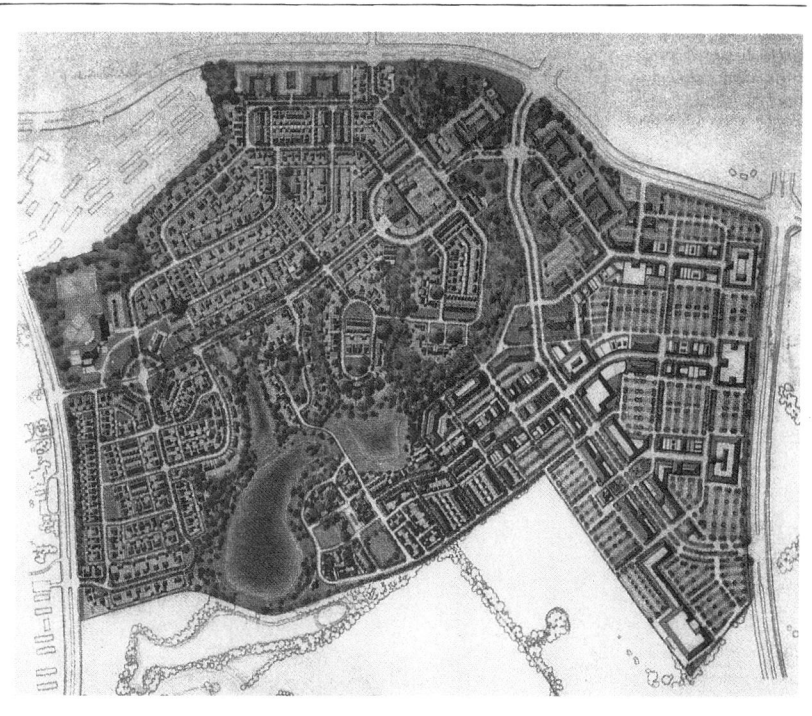

A stately 19th century house (left), originally the focus of the Kent Farm, has been retained on the site. Some of Kentlands' newer homes (opposite) employ similar architectural forms.

The community plan (above) includes six distinct neighborhoods and a large retail center. This version of the retail center (right in plan) has three main streets, each terminated by an anchor department store.

PLAN OF THE TOWN OF KENTLANDS.
EXTRACT FROM THE NEW URBANISM, TOWARD AN ARCHITECTURE OF COMMUNITY,
BY PETER KATZ, MCGRAW-HILL, 1994.

The buildings, gardens and landscape features of the original Kent Farm influenced the design of the Old Farm neighborhood (below).

An early plan proposed the restoration of the farm's ornamental garden (right and center of illustration, below). The site was ultimately used for Kentlands' town commons (page 40).

help to define individual neighborhoods. A school and health club are located in the community, providing additional recreation areas. Clustered at one end of the town commons, several original buildings from the Kent Farm house a new cultural center. This complex is the centerpiece of the Old Farm neighborhood.

The town's principal retail center fronts two major arterials. Though initially conceived as a regional mall with anchor stores connected at its center to the town's main street, the current plan follows a more conventional suburban model—what has become known among retail developers as a "power center."

The ultimate build-out of Kentlands includes 1,600 residential units with a population of over 5,000 total residents. Construction began in 1989, and since then, all roads, water mains, and sewer lines have been completed. The elementary school is now operating, and the town's first church will soon be in use. Several local home builders, along with Kentlands' founding developer, have sold more than 750 lots. At this writing over 300 units are occupied.

Harsh economic times, particularly in the retail sector, have led to a financial restructuring of the development. It is now controlled by the the principal lender to the project, a local savings bank. Despite this change of ownership, the design team's intent is being followed as Kentlands moves steadily toward completion.

Culot / I.F.A.

The provision of public buildings and open space within each of Kentlands' neighborhoods was an important priority for the town's design team.

The expansive town commons (opposite) is anchored by the existing Kent Farm house and barn (center and right, respectively in photo). Both buildings are slated for future use as Gaithersburg's cultural center.

A new house and outbuilding (left in photo) face across a street to the similarly scaled historic farm house.

The elementary school (below) was the first public building completed at Kentlands. The building's classical entry portico terminates the view from a nearby street.

Culot / I.F.A.

Wellington

Palm Beach County, Florida, 1989

An early plan for the Town of Wellington (below) was the result of a one-week design charette. During that session, the layout of each neighborhood was assigned to a different designer.

Though given a common set of rules to follow, all of the contributors' plans were unique. After the individual neighborhoods were first pieced together, some overall adjustments were required to achieve proper street connections between each.

This working method brings a sense of authentic variety to the larger composition that would not be possible with only one designer.

Planners of the new Town of Wellington proposed this 1,500-acre development as a way for Palm Beach County to "build its way out" of the acute growth-related problems it was experiencing. Approval required a controversial westward extension of the county's urban limit line. It was granted, ironically, because officials felt that this dense mixed-use project would help to both contain further sprawl and reverse a serious jobs/housing imbalance in the area.

Like much of Florida, Palm Beach County has seen tremendous low-density suburban growth in recent years. Residential subdivisions have pushed steadily inland from the desirable island community of Palm Beach and its "downtown" of West Palm Beach. Most of these new developments made little or no provision for shopping or workplaces. Offices and large stores then located on nearby arterials, turning those roads into congested "strips." As a result, east-west commuters who live in the newly developed areas suffer increasing traffic delays despite several recent road widenings.

The new Town of Wellington, at the western edge of the existing Wellington planned unit development (PUD), aims to ease the area's congestion by creating a community with a large workplace element to balance an abundance of housing in the adjacent PUD. Its planners, Andres Duany and Elizabeth Plater-Zyberk, proposed a town composed of nine

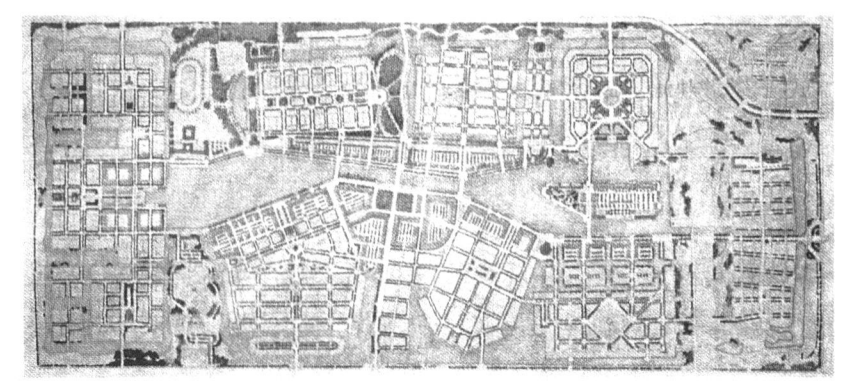

Like many Florida developments, a large percentage of the Town of Wellington's land area is required to be water for drainage purposes. Many such developments, like this one (left) in the present Wellington subdivision, completely surround bodies of water with private houses. While this strategy yields more waterfront homesites, it removes a key civic amenity from public use and enjoyment.

The proposed Town of Wellington (opposite) provides water views and public access to the lakefront from many points. Careful planning preserves the value of prime waterfront homesites and increases the appeal of properties in other parts of the development. The enhanced public realm thus creates a tangible benefit for the entire community.

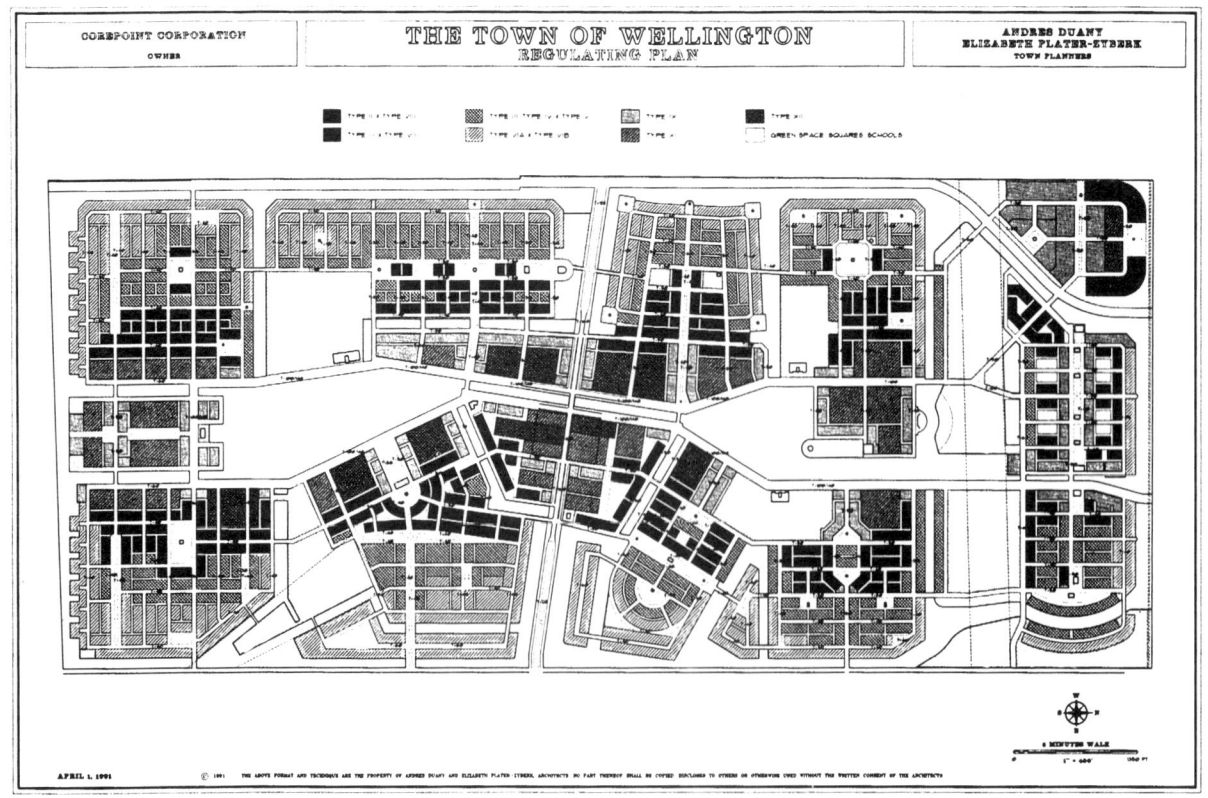

Culot / I.F.A.

138

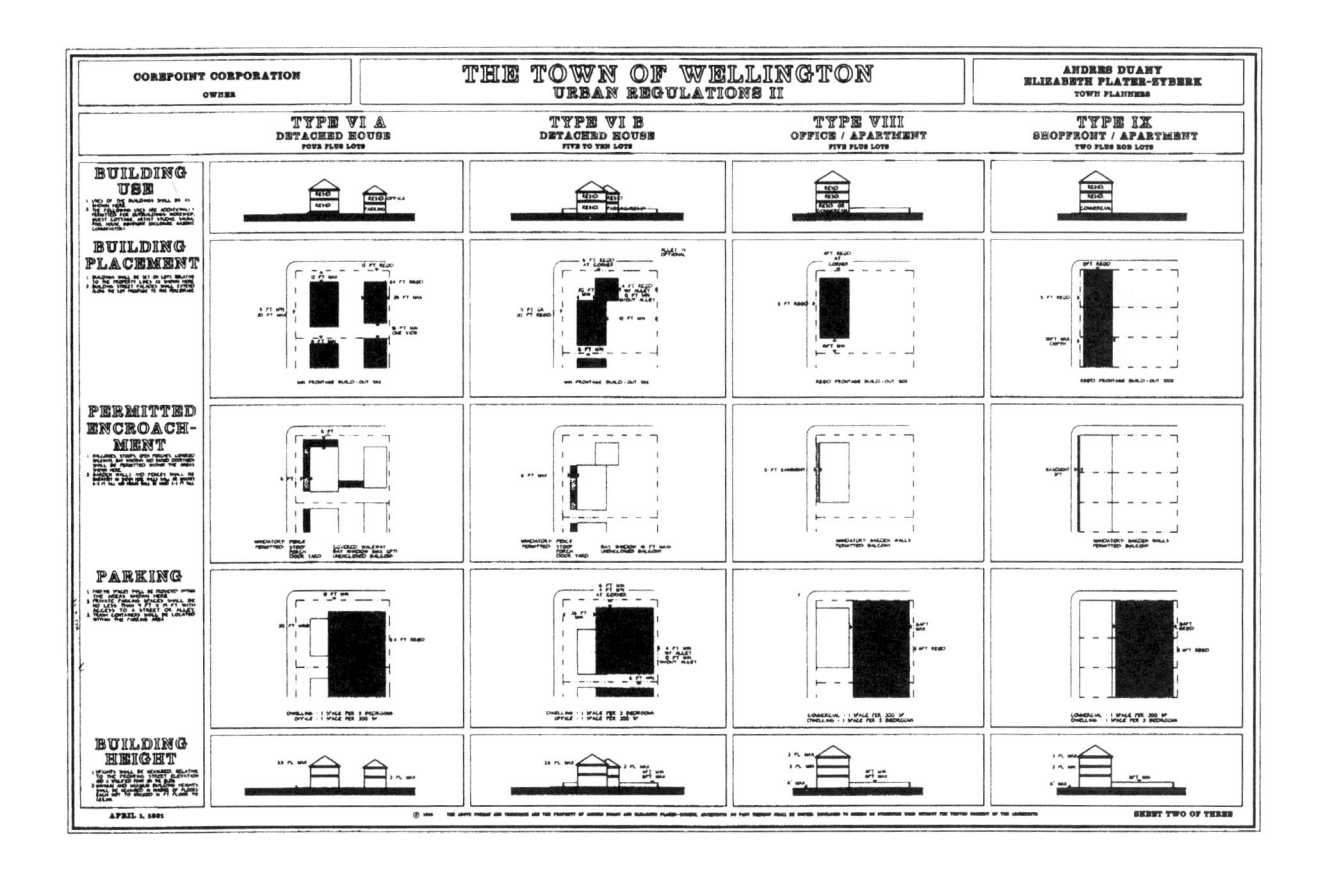

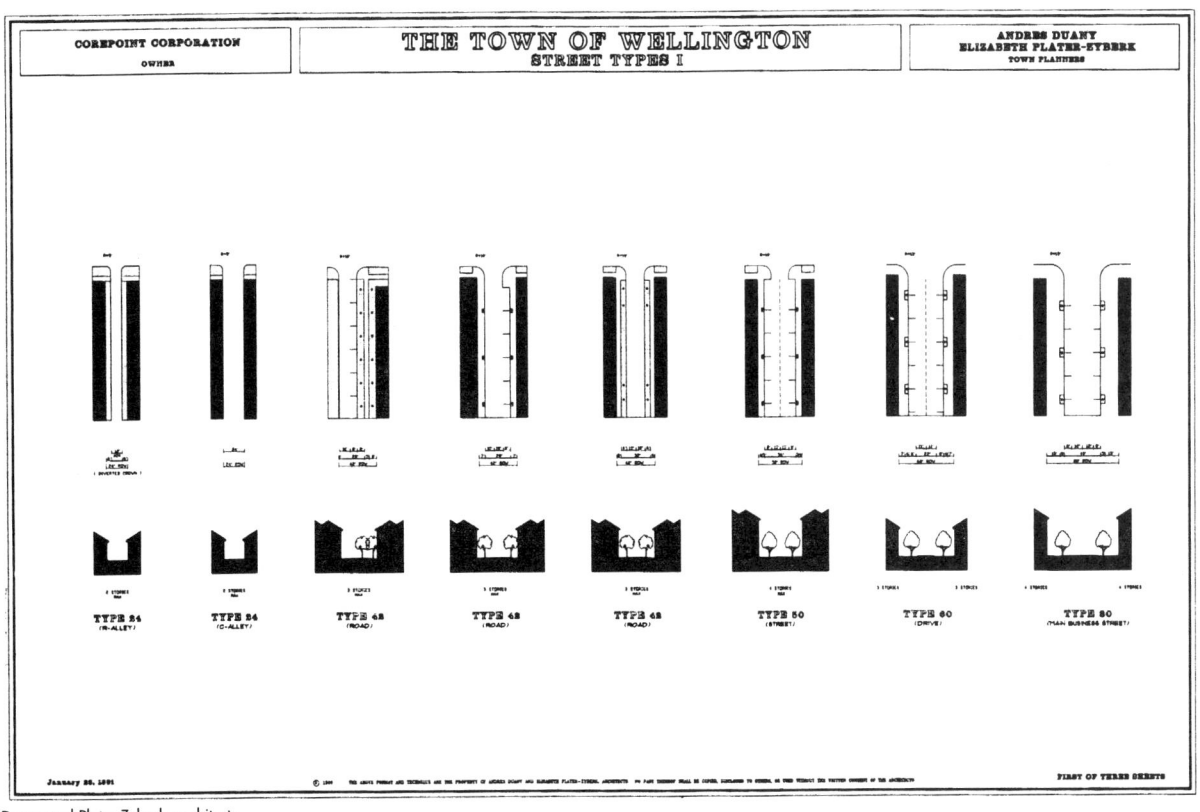

Duany and Plater-Zyberk, architects.
Culot / I.F.A.

GOUTTE D'OR

9. PARIS

HISTORY IS A MONUMENT
1988

*L'ASSOMMOIR, ÉMILE ZOLA'S GREAT REALIST NOVEL PUBLISHED IN 1877.
SET ENTIRELY IN GOUTTE D'OR.*

The Goutte d'Or neighbourhood of Paris has a bad reputation. For a long time it was a toll gate area (until it was joined to Paris in 1860, it stood outside the walls).
It had a population of humble folk – laundresses, coach drivers, small craftsmen.
Zola walked the streets of this neighbourhood in 1870 and decided to use it as a setting for his novel L'Assommoir, the first best-seller in French literature.

The novel describes the wretched life of Gervaise, a laundress. The Goutte d'Or neighbourhood echoes the fortunes of the heroine – bright and lively at the start when things are going well, dingy and sinister once Gervaise's downfall is sealed.

The neighbourhood, close to the Gare du Nord, has always played a part in the integration of provincial folk arriving in Paris. These were followed by aliens from Spain, Portugal, Italy and then by North Africans. Young men and women from the provinces settled there for a while and got the feel of Paris. Later, in the 1960s, it became one of the ill-fated foci of the Algerian resistance and its reputation grew worse.

In the early 1980s, anyone walking the streets of Goutte d'Or saw a lively, working-class area, free of violence, with a mixed, friendly population. The area was definitely in need of rehabilitation but conviviality and urbanity prevailed.

However, a political conjunction was to prove fatal to the neighbourhood that had lived through so much. In 1981 the Socialists came to power. Among other things, they had promised to build 20 000 new dwellings in Paris. Goutte d'Or was judged on its bad reputation, without any official taking the trouble to check whether it was justified. A large-scale renovation project was decided at once. The municipality of Paris, controlled by the Right, viewed this favourably. The renovation of the neighbourhood would provide an opportunity to drive back to the suburbs an undesirable Mediterranean-type population and to open the north of Paris to restoration.

That is how the Right and the Left found themselves in agreement to subject Goutte d'Or to a radical renovation project. An urbanist noted for his stark projects in the new towns was picked (whilst a specialist in old and working-class urban environments was needed). He drew up a plan that took no account of the area's reality and would lead to its near demolition.

The action of a courageous neighbourhood association failed to stop the renovators' steamrollers. Large tracts of the neighbourhood were demolished, then came the recession and the big reconstruction projects could not proceed due to lack of funds. Now, ten years after the works began, the area is still half in ruins.

What happened in Goutte d'Or is being repeated in all the working-class neighbourhoods of Paris. These are vulnerable areas that do not enjoy the legal protection extended to the historical neighbourhoods of the centre.

Yet all those areas, like Goutte d'Or, have their own history which is worthy of respect and attention. The case of Goutte d'Or in Paris illustrates how difficult it is to bring about a change of attitudes. This neighbourhood had remained intact, spared by Haussmann's works and hit by only a few bombs in 1944. On the whole, its streets and many of its buildings were those that Zola had seen and described.

Goutte d'Or is part and parcel of the history of Paris. Zola immortalized it and on that count alone it should be covered by a preservation plan. The history of Goutte d'Or is tantamount to a national monument; tens of millions of French people have read L'Assommoir, discovering the neighbourhood through the novel.

Back in 1981, as the threat loomed, a group comprising historians, sociologists, architects and the lecturers of two schools of architecture answered the association's call and carried out a survey of the neighbourhood, recounting its history, its urban development, the character of buildings, the unique morphology featuring crossroads with tapered corner buildings.

Then a team of students supervised by the lecturers and the leaders of the association made a criticism of the renovation project and designed a counter-project with diagrams and perspectives showing that there was an alternative to destruction: a gentle renovation, building by building, carried out with the desire to preserve and reinforce the neighbourhood's character. The architecture of the buildings is simple: plastered façades highlighted by fasciae, etc. Here and there a decorative element.

The proposals were incorporated into a book and representations were made to the municipality of Paris. The residents, however, were unable to have the decision overturned and the renovation plan was implemented bluntly.

Although the resistance campaign failed on the streets, it nevertheless helped to make the Parisians and the elected representatives aware of the need for a different approach to the capital's working-class neighbourhoods. The press conferences, the book and its counter-projects created a considerable stir in the press; other districts were warned of the danger and organized themselves. The working-class neighbourhood of Belleville, for instance, joined battle against the bulldozers and, this time, defeated them. Many lessons can be drawn from the battle of Goutte d'Or. First, it is essential to fight for ordinary architecture – the routine architecture of the streets – to be taken into account. Those repetitive buildings, devoid of ornamental pretension, give the working-class neighbourhoods their own character. They must be protected, rehabilitated, or rebuilt identically wherever demolition is necessary.

More steps should be taken and the European authorities should be asked to initiate programmes for the protection of working-class urban complexes, which are part and parcel of a city's history.

Ignorance and indifference are not necessarily where we expect them to be. The residents of the Goutte d'Or neighbourhood fought to retain their environment and for its intelligent rehabilitation. The intellectuals who supported them illustrated the relevance of typologies and urban plans, recalled the neighbourhood's history and stated its significance as the main protagonist of one of the 19th century's essential novels. They were not heeded on that occasion. Lack of education prevailed, bureaucracy triumphed and the desire to bridge the generation and history gap could not be satisfied. The Goutte d'Or neighbourhood, with its new council blocks, may be more functional but it has lost its soul, its singing, its future. This is a tragedy, an irretrievable loss for Paris and an operation not to be repeated.

However, the demonstration that things can be done differently remains valid and can be repeated. In this respect Goutte d'Or lives on and bears a message of hope.

The documents illustrating this chapter are taken from the book La Goutte-d'Or, faubourg de Paris [Goutte d'Or, a suburb of Paris], edited by Maurice Culot and Marc Breitman, with an introduction by Louis Chevalier, Éditions AAM/Hazan, 1988.

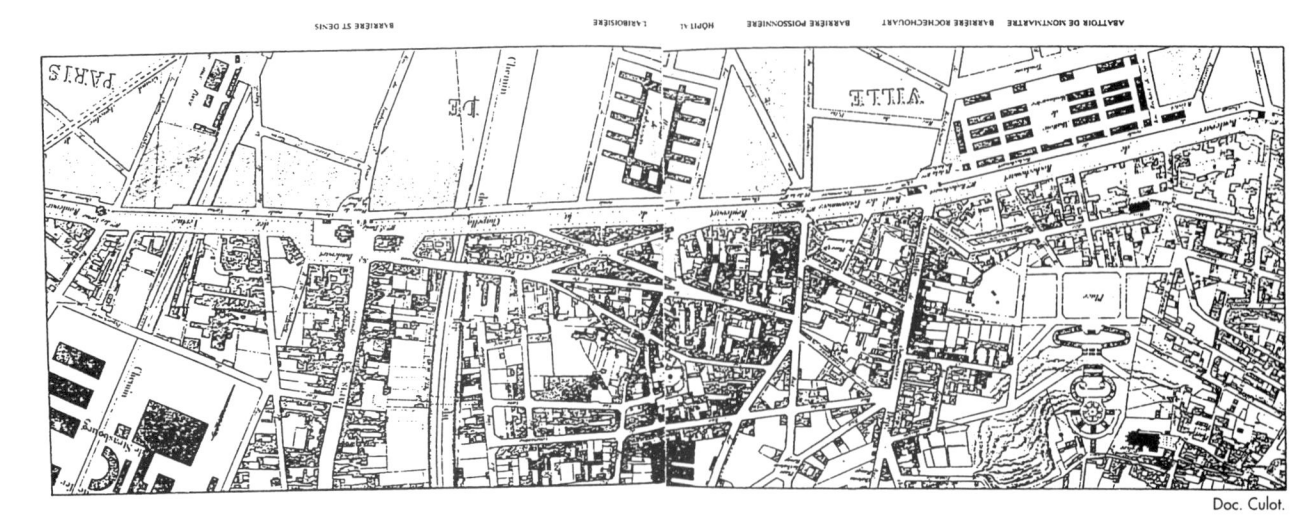

ÉMILE ZOLA'S GOUTTE D'OR.

In 1859 (see map above) the district was outside Paris. It was joined to Paris in 1860 and the toll gates were removed.

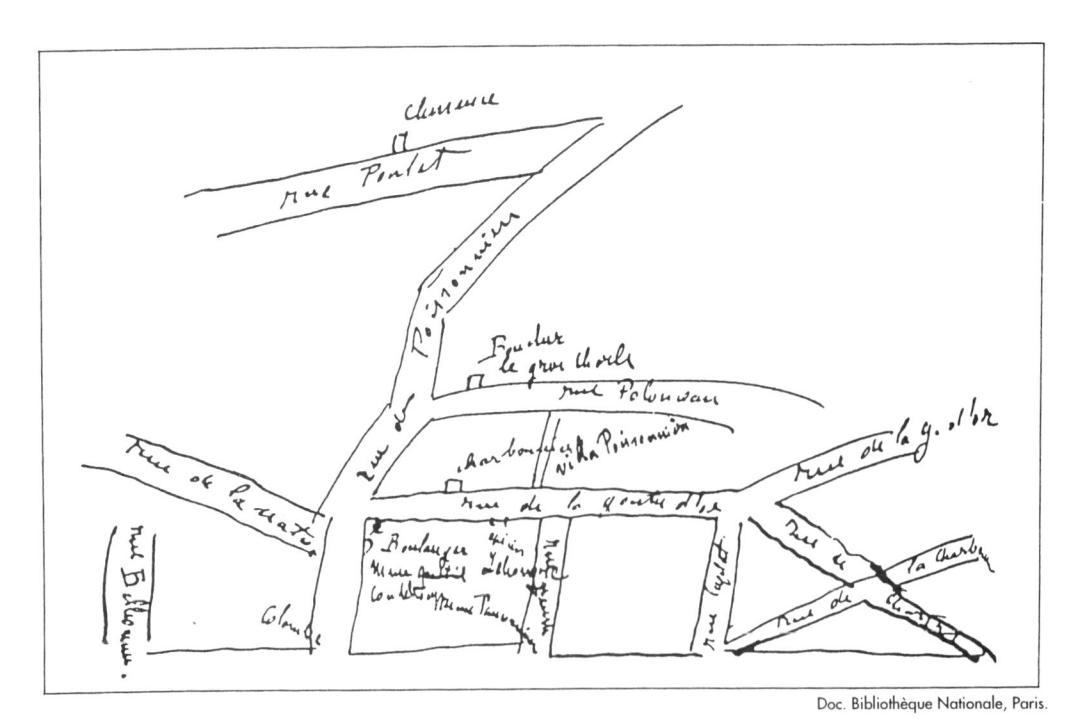

MAP OF THE GOUTTE D'OR NEIGHBOURHOOD BY ZOLA.

RUE DE LA GOUTTE D'OR AT THE END OF THE XIXᵉ CENTURY.

1985 : DEMOLITION BEGINS...

TOP PART OF THE VILLA-POISSONNIÈRE.

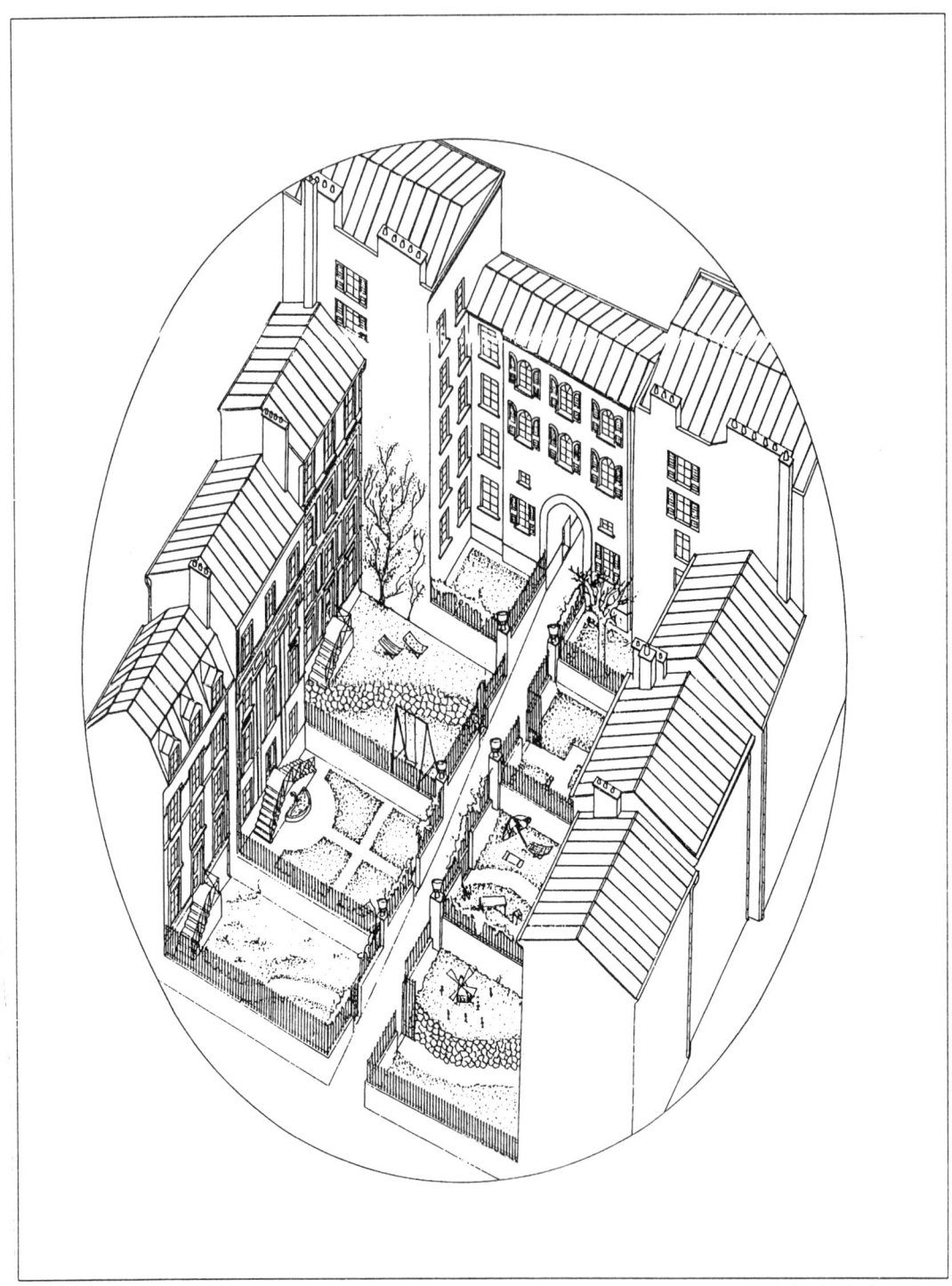

Doc. Culot, drawing by M. Zanin.

GOUTTE D'OR TYPOLOGY.
VILLA-POISSONNIÈRE, A PEDESTRIAN WALKWAY LINKING THE TOP AND BOTTOM PARTS OF THE NEIGHBOURHOOD.

GOUTTE D'OR TYPOLOGY.

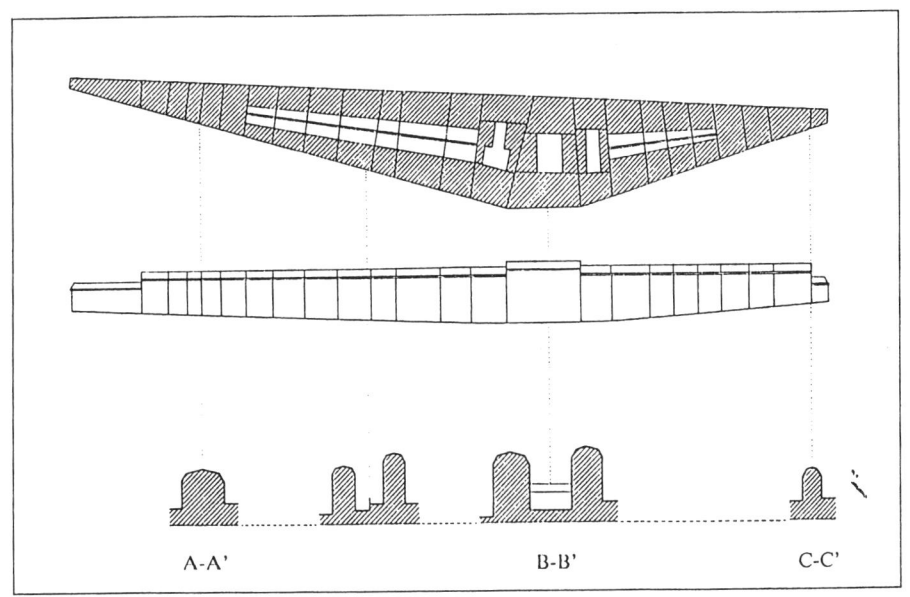

A-A'   B-B'   C-C'

Doc. Culot.

Doc. Culot.

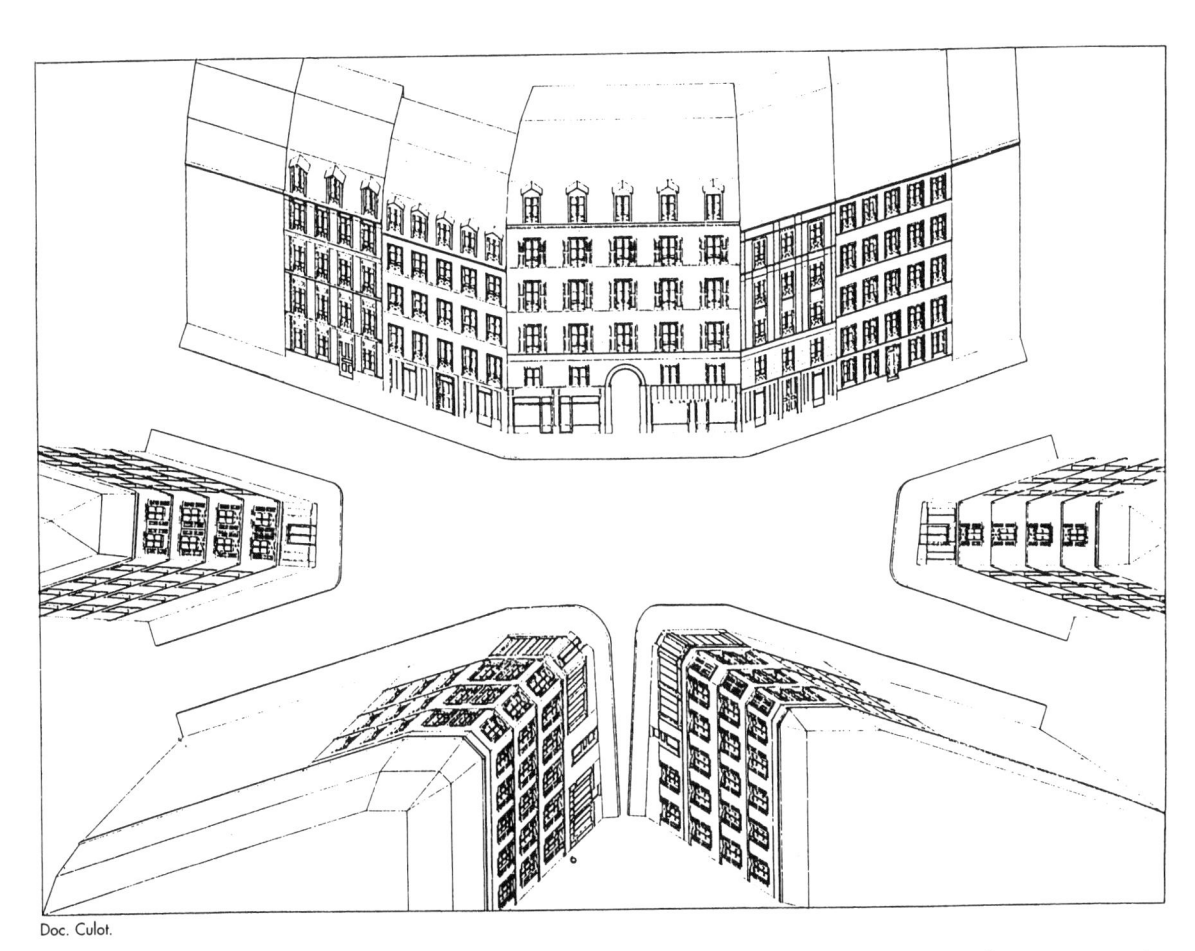

St Andrew's cross: located in the heart of the neighbourhood, it delineates sloping streets and tapered street corners that give character to this neighbourhood devoid of monuments.
The municipality of the Paris renovation plan provided for all the corners to be demolished!

GOUTTE D'OR TYPOLOGY.

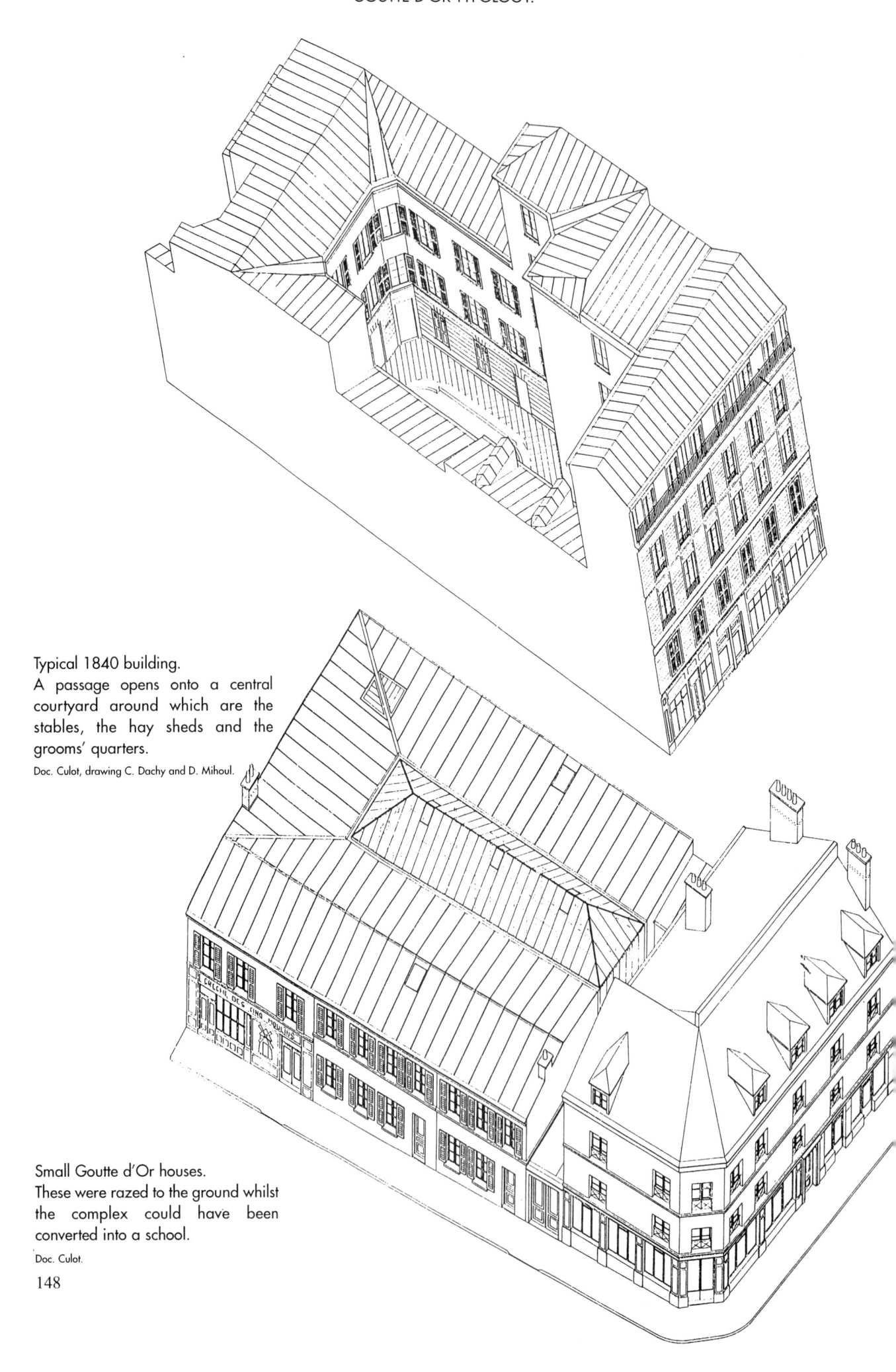

Typical 1840 building.
A passage opens onto a central courtyard around which are the stables, the hay sheds and the grooms' quarters.
Doc. Culot, drawing C. Dachy and D. Mihoul.

Small Goutte d'Or houses.
These were razed to the ground whilst the complex could have been converted into a school.
Doc. Culot.

GOUTTE D'OR PROJECTS.

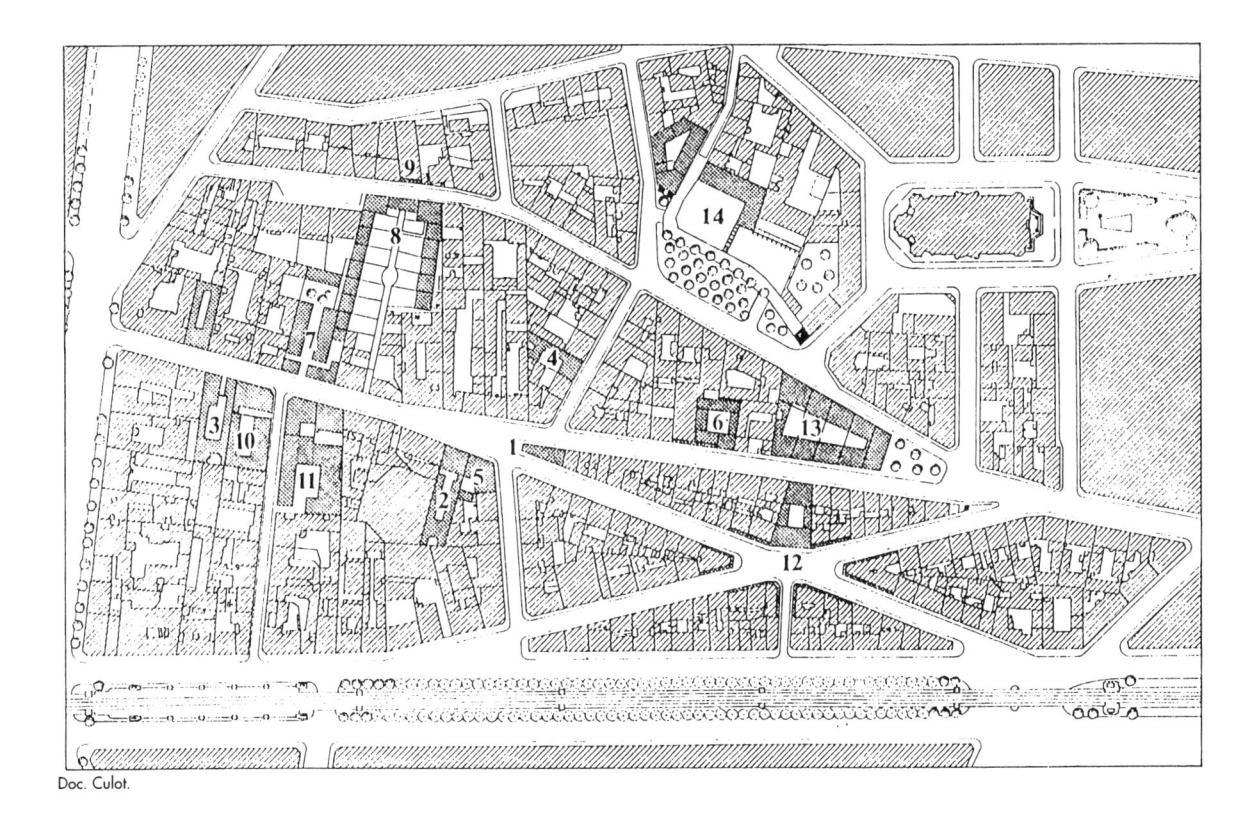

Doc. Culot.

These various projects were designed as part of the campaign conducted by the neighbourhood association for its preservation. They show that the neighbourhood could have been rehabilitated in keeping with the context.

RECONSTRUCTION PROJECT FOR THE CORNER OF THE RUE DE LA GOUTTE D'OR.

The tapered building is the result of the flat St Andrew's cross layout, a unique morphology that exists nowhere else in Paris.

These tapered buildings looked like ships' prows and gave the neighbourhood a very specific urban atmosphere.

Doc. Culot, drawing by J. Altuna.

RECONSTRUCTION PROJECT FOR THE CORNER CAFÉ.

Cafés play an important part in the life of working-class neighbourhoods. This is where people meet, discuss business, celebrate family occasions, catch up with gossip, leave messages, etc.

The café was pulled down in 1989 and nothing has been rebuilt in its place.

DEVELOPMENT PROJECT FOR A PLACE DE LA GOUTTE D'OR.

LA PLACE À L'ANGLE DES RUES DE LA GOUTTE D'OR ET POLONCEAU TELLE QU'ELLE AURAIT PU ÊTRE

Doc. Culot, drawing by J. Altuna.

THE SQUARE AT THE CORNER OF THE RUE DE LA GOUTTE D'OR AND THE RUE POLONCEAU AS IT COULD HAVE LOOKED.

Today the blind wall of a multi-storey car park runs alongside the site...

A DESIRE FOR IMITATION

10. TOULOUSE

THE DELIGHTS OF IMITATION
1984-1986

A DESIRE FOR IMITATION

10. TOULOUSE

THE DELIGHTS OF IMITATION
1984-1986

It is not unusual to come across houses in the form of Swiss chalets all over Europe, irrespective of the climate. These arise from a desire to imitate an aesthetic quality admired during a trip or holiday, or even at an international event such as the 1889 Paris Exposition where a whole Swiss village was on display. The cinema is not indifferent to the spreading of fashions, and it was the film The Thief of Baghdad that decided Curtiss, the American aircraft manufacturer, to build the town of Opa Locka, near Miami, in a style imitating the architecture of Arab cities.

Imitation is an inborn reflex and it conditions life's learning process. Up to the pre-industrial era, artists and craftsmen began by copying, the best then imitating, ie they produced new works from an ideal type. *«To imitate,»* wrote the theoretician Quatremère de Quincy, *«is to produce the likeness of an object in another»*. The concept of imitation was neglected by the industrial revolutions that gave priority to creations *ex nihilo* and developed a taste for originality for its own sake.
The creative outburst generated by this change in attitudes was contained by the traditional urban form. Art Nouveau, Modern Style and Art Deco, which laid an absolute claim to originality, wove their most unbridled works into the urban fabric of Barcelona, Brussels and Prague.
After World War II things changed and urbanism no longer acted as a safeguard. But even though it was ignored by the architects, imitation as a concept has retained its popularity with the public. Evidence of this can be found in an unfailing taste for regional architecture which is prevalent in private construction.

In order to show that the concept of imitation had lost none of its relevance and that it was most capable of coping with today's urban problems, the Institut Français d'Architecture carried out a survey from 1984 to 1986 of the city of Toulouse in France. The survey was then incorporated into a book (Toulouse, les délices de l'imitation, IFA/Mardaga publishers, 1986).
This survey analyses the city's urban and architectural development and proposes reconstruction projects for buildings or neighbourhoods. The criterion used for assessing the quality of these projects is as follows: a genuine *Toulousain*, who knows his city best, asks himself whether the projects or developments have eluded his daily vigilance. The young architects who designed the projects were guided not by fantasy, creative intuition or the quest for originality but, on the contrary, by a desire to imitate the best the town had ever produced in terms of buildings and public spaces. The emphasis was placed on all that partakes of the

Toulouse myth: first the brick, then an urban structure dominated by narrow streets lined with buildings opening onto internal courtyards and gardens, triangular squares and ubiquitous fountains. To train their hand, their eye and their memory to the specific context of Toulouse, the young architects sketched, measured, and produced accurate drawings for a hundred or so buildings.

Toulouse, an exceptionally coherent city, has perfectly assimilated the various periods of its history, from the great fire of 1463 – a dramatic reference point – to the building of the rue Ozenne at the turn of the century. Toulouse has managed to preserve its integrity. Today's beating heart is the reward of yesterday's painful denial, of a deliberate decision not to sacrifice the city to the industrialist ardour of the 19th century. Later, in the second half of the 20th century, the growth problem was solved by the construction of a separate town: Toulouse-le-Mirail. It is regrettable that inspiration was not drawn from the former to design the latter, whose dominant dormitory-town character causes deleterious traffic flows. However, this initiative has probably saved the existing city from stark internal remodelling. The surveys of Toulouse carried out by the IFA are part of a global reflection postulating an equilibrium between the various urban functions, without any of these (eg motorized traffic) overriding the others excessively. If, for instance, the suitability of building a road along the banks of the Garonne – a question that was raised a few years ago – is not mentioned, the restructuring projects for the downstream and upstream neighbourhoods provide an indirect answer. Indeed the presence of such an expressway at this location is as incompatible with sound local planning as it is with the smooth operation of the city's various neighbourhoods.

The choice and diversity of the *improvement* projects for Toulouse can still be explained by their ability to provide a framework for discussions on architecture, construction and town planning, and also for theoretical refinements. Each project therefore attempts to challenge operational concepts that modern architecture deliberately forwent: the didactic and creative principle of imitation as well as the debate on the picturesque, the issues of copying and identical reconstruction, the dialectics of monuments and urban fabric, the separate fields of Architecture and Construction, the organization of the city into complex neighbourhoods, etc.

What form should city imitation take to be just that? Which ancients should one turn to for consistent and convergent advice? The question, which was relevant in relation to the Fine Arts, should be formulated differently when dealing with the city. How can one define what is proper and useful to imitate today, how can one determine what is best in each city, each neighbourhood, each square, each street? In the unpredictable arena of the Fine Arts, Quatremère failed in his methodical and vigorous effort to establish a classical aesthetics. The city provides a firmer foundation, reinforced by an urban organization, public spaces, habits, a consensus, a collective pride, etc.

Are we not experiencing precisely this episodic impulse that compels a generation, at a given time, to gather its strength and knowledge in order to take a loftier stand rather than assert its dominance? Over the past few years the demanding nature of industry has softened. Production – if not yet the products – is becoming increasingly compatible with the complexity of the urban structure. The smooth machinist cycle of Le Corbusier's dreams can at last find a place in the traditional city without destroying it.

No more than the history of man does the history of cities provide ready-made recipes for the future. It does, however, illustrate the merits of being different, of belonging and even possibly of being rooted in a culture. Today's western and cosmopolitan society claims, and is supposed to be prepared to assume the contradictions inherent in any process bringing the citizens closer to the decision-makers. Yet this yearning for identity, hence for difference – that haunts our times, that is claimed by countries, peoples, races, regions, minorities – stumbles over the issues of architecture, urbanism, town and country planning. The modern obsession with being oneself is echoed by an unprecedented standardization of the built-up space. It will be said – with arguments in support – that pursuing architectural and urban continuity is an illusion in a modern world where man has been freed from so many recent constraints. And yet, when I step outside my home, I see a metropolis – fashioned mostly in the 19th century – which is present, alive, being used. Its qualities and defects never cease to seek our attention, even though most of us – deliberately and by force of circumstance – live on the drab fringes of suburbs and zones devoid of any sense of drama other than the violence generated by despair.

By opening out, by assuming a dialectic of order and disorder, by aiming to create knowledge loops rather than following a predetermined direction, modern history has given itself new avenues to explore. But at the same time, as though in fear of its own boldness, it has become impervious to synthesis and taken over from the critique of ideologies (which has done it so much harm) by rejecting any form of all-embracing thought. However, in the absence of synoptic works accessible to the general public, the biases relentlessly tracked down by historians then reappear elsewhere, elusive as will-o'-the wisp.

The projects presented in the following pages illustrate the operational nature of the imitation concept implemented within the scope of a global reflection on Toulouse.

TOULOUSE.
AGGRESSION OR INTEGRATION?

Dominique Delaunay / I.F.A.

VIEW OF THE PRESENT-DAY BUILDING ON THE PLACE DE LA TRINITÉ.

Barthélémy Dumons, architect / I.F.A.

NEW FAÇADE PROJECT FOR THE PLACE DE LA TRINITÉ.

The architect who designed the Place de la Trinité's modern façade believes that he has created something bold, that he has impressed the bourgeois. In fact he has ruined Toulouse's finest square with a façade admired by no one but himself.
And once we allow an architect to act in this way, what argument can be opposed to the requests of others? If all the buildings in the square were replaced by modern facades, it would lose its character.
Urbanism and architecture are very closely related, and the context must take precedence over aesthetics, otherwise there are no more rules and arbitrariness prevails - as it does here on what was once Toulouse's finest triangular square.

TOULOUSE.
ÎLOT DE LA DALBADE - RECONSTRUCTION PROPOSAL.

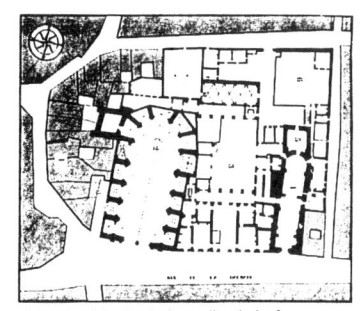

Map of the îlot [block] de la Dalbade before 1813.
1. La Dalbade Church. 2. Hôtel St-Jean.
3. St-Rémy's Chapel. 4. Archives Tower.
5. Les Hospitaliers cemetery.

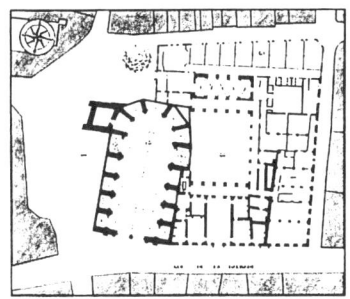

Current map of the îlot de la Dalbade.

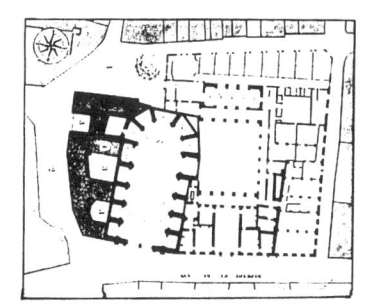

Reconstruction proposal for the block.

Jean-Philippe Garric, architect / I.F.A.

THE NEW SQUARE CREATED BY THE CHEVET OF LA DALBADE CHURCH.

PRESENT SITUATION.

THIS PROJECT ILLUSTRATES PERFECTLY THE CONCEPT OF IMITATION.

La Dalbade Church has always been surrounded by houses. In 1922 the steeple was hit by lightning and collapsed. The municipality then decided to knock down the houses at the northern end of the church.

This has created an amorphous public space, lined by the blind façade of the church (which was never designed to be seen). A green area of sorts was laid out. Beyond the intent to restore what was there, the project provides a different solution. Although the side of the church alongside the nave has been rebuilt with apartment blocks, the open space on the chevet side will not be rebuilt on in order to preserve a lovely tree and an existing façade. It is therefore proposed to design a triangular square in the Toulouse tradition, and to line it with a cupboard building backing onto the church tower. This building facing the new square has a monumental façade. This new façade is plausible though it had never existed in Toulouse. Its architecture is inspired by developments seen in the city. The material used is brick highlighted by terracotta ornaments.

A convincing illustration of Quatremère de Quincy's definition that «to imitate is to produce the likeness of one object in another».

TOULOUSE.
HOW TO INTEGRATE THE AGGRESSIVE ARCHITECTURE OF A MULTI-STOREY CAR PARK INTO THE URBAN FABRIC.

Present view of the car park from the rue des Filatiers.

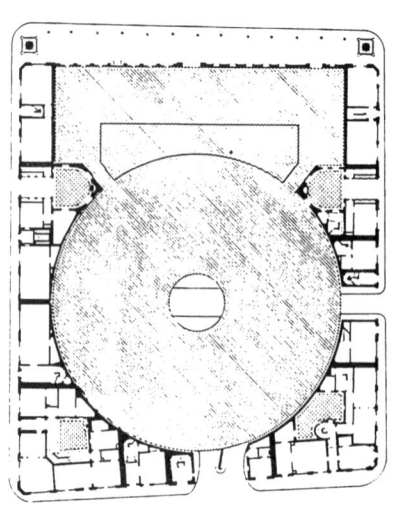

Car-park dressing-up project using residential dwellings and shops.

Philippe Gisclar, architect / I.F.A.

VIEW OF THE CAR PARK DRESSED BY APARTMENT BLOCKS.

In the 1960s/1970s many municipalities succumbed to the proposals of car-park manufacturers offering multi-storey models to be erected in the city centres.
Later, the municipalities were to regret those buildings that disfigured the neighbourhoods, and some simply decided to have them pulled down. This is what happened to the central Marseilles car park that was demolished a few years ago and replaced by a pleasant square. In 1995 the municipality of Bayonne replaced the car park that defaced the city centre with a small, covered market and a square admired by all. Though most of these car parks should be destroyed, some could be preserved and remodelled.
This is the case of the Parking des Carmes in Toulouse. Designed as a concrete drum on a rectangular plot, it leaves enough unused space on its perimeter to put up blocks of flats, thereby concealing the unattractive bulk and re-establishing street continuity.

TOULOUSE: APROPOS THE PLACE ST-ÉTIENNE.

Up to 1933 the triangular Place St-Étienne was enclosed on three sides.
In 1933 the houses abutting on the church façade were demolished to isolate the religious building and provide it with a side façade.

The project was not completed and a public garden was laid out on the site of the old houses. This was unsatisfactory in terms of urban art as the triangular square has been ripped open and cannot be brought to life.

The imitation process provides a solution for the various development problems. Although the ideal would be to rebuild the block that framed the church, the present context points to an alternative. The garden trees have grown and no one wants them to be cut down. The solution is therefore to propose a loggia building, for public purposes, that can be built with a slight overhang on the church façade to create a public space. This building encloses the square while the garden is spared.

Jean-Philippe Garric, architecte / I.F.A.

ABOVE:

Preliminary sketches for the building project next to the façade of St-Étienne Church.

A search for the picturesque showing how much skill and knowledge is demanded by tradition. In this case, it was a matter of coming up with a picturesque solution matching the church's monumental and eclectic façade.

«There is also room for the picturesque in architecture, through the use of different materials by the artist to create pleasant contrasts between the walls and the pilasters decorating them, between the piers and the window frames. The most skilful architects have made very tasteful use of these means of diversifying the elevation and massive structure aspects of their buildings.»

Quatremère de Quincy
ENCYCLOPÉDIE MÉTHODIQUE
Dictionnaire d'architecture
Volume 3, Paris, 1825

TOULOUSE.
REDEVELOPMENT OF THE PLACE ST-ÉTIENNE.

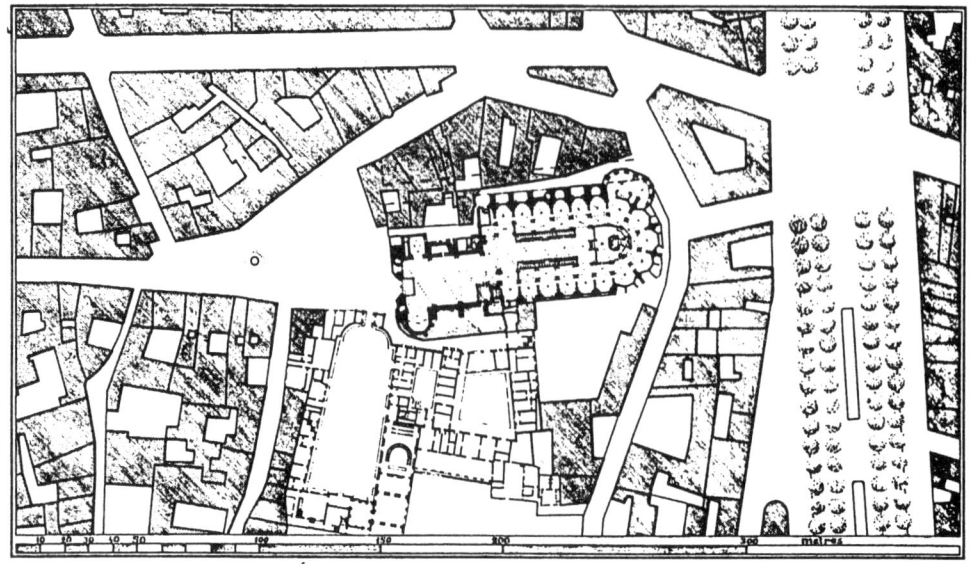

The place St-Étienne and the church before the 1933 clearance.

The place today.

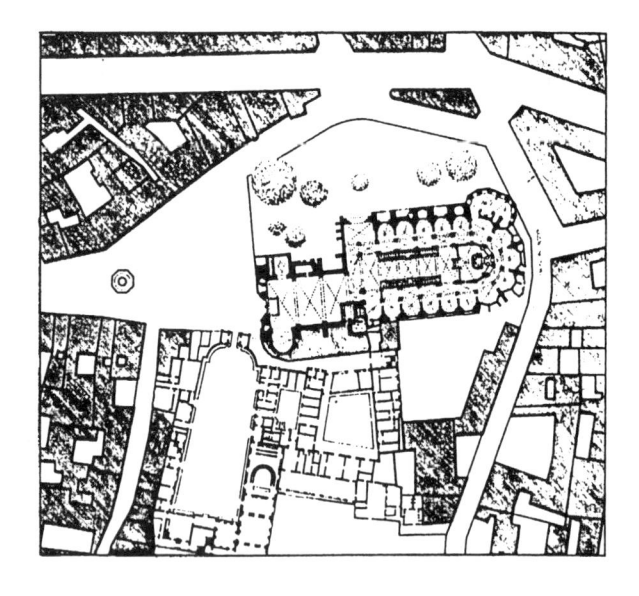

Re-enclosure project for the place.

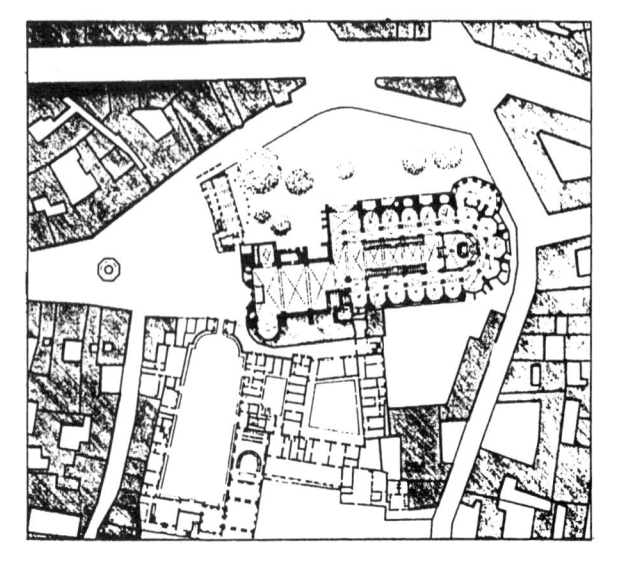

TOULOUSE.
REDEVELOPMENT OF THE PLACE ST-ÉTIENNE.

Doc. I.F.A.

THE PLACE ST-ÉTIENNE AT THE BEGINNING OF THE XXe CENTURY AND UP TO 1933.

Rez-de-chaussée de la grande salle publique.

Jean-Philippe Garric, architect / I.F.A.

CONSTRUCTION PROJECT FOR A LOGGIA ENCLOSING THE PLACE ST-ÉTIENNE.

PART THREE

Conclusion and recommendations

CONCLUSION

Despite broad criticism going back to the late 1960s, functionalist theory is still being followed for lack of an operational alternative.

The quasi-universal condemnation of the Athens Charter has reinforced the feeling of rejection and suspicion experienced by architects and planners for any reference, rule or planning discipline.

In doing so, they have left the field clear for the technicians and specialists. Despite being competent in their own respective areas, they are incapable of apprehending the city in its comprehensiveness.

Although in most cases the architects and planners deplore this situation, they are doing nothing to remedy it and, in the final analysis, they seem content to put up with it.

Some see this as an unexpected opportunity to indulge in the mostly extravagant creations commissioned by anonymous clients, eg multinationals, States, administrations, housing councils, property speculators, etc.
Most architects and planners, however, pay dearly for the additional latitude such laxness in urban organization seems to allow them. They are subjected to the tyranny of standards, to fussy bureaucracies and to clients seeking nothing but short-term profitability. The end result is often disenchantment, frustration and acquiescence.

The professional associations have been unable to reach a consensus and define a series of demands for a European alternative to functionalism.
And it is not exaggerating to say that there are today as many opinions as there are architects and planners. One should therefore not expect the practitioners to initiate any campaign for architectural and planning pluralism.

It is up to the public, to the citizens, to the associations, to the elected representatives to demonstrate their willingness to play the part of clients who are well-versed in architecture and urbanism.

The collapse of the ideologies and of the antagonisms they sustained for their self-perpetuation urges public opinion to reclaim its entire freedom of judgement.
It is no longer necessary to obey slogans, to accept absurd projects and to support evil deeds on the pretence that it is for the defence of the European civilization threatened by Soviet imperialism or neo-bourgeois revisionism.
The analysis of environmental disasters in Russia and the countries of the former Eastern Bloc shows that ownership of the ground by the authorities is in no way a universal panacea for the proper

resolution of urban and environmental problems. On the contrary, one might be tempted to say in the light of the results.

Public opinion should therefore mobilize and organize, especially by taking an active part in community associations. In the private arena, the public always prefers solutions along the lines of continuity, tradition, environmental harmony. In the public arena, where decisions are entirely controlled by functionalism, the reverse happens and the public is forced to accept discontinuity solutions, without any regard for the context or its most legitimate aspirations.

To say that the public has no taste and needs educating falls short of the mark. Many architecture-lovers show more discernment, more architectural culture and more taste than some experienced practitioners.

The conditions are now ripe for reversing a situation deplored by many and justified by some as the ransom or inevitability of progress.

Functional urbanism, standards, legislation, bureaucratic procedures, professional habits supporting the former: all that can be replaced by simple rules accessible to all - the same rules that governed the foundation and development of the European civilization, subject to the kind of adjustment made by each successive period.

All over Europe now there are citizens, elected representatives, professionals, craftsmen, shopkeepers, industrialists, teachers, etc, who wish to apply themselves to the European city-reconstruction project.

In addition to the projects, more and more developments show that an alternative to functionalism does exist.
This study and the recommendations that follow are aimed at all those who are anxious to share and experience this alternative. The recommendations provide a framework for the maintenance and repair of the city while ensuring that its identity and specificity are preserved. And let us remember that advice is ineffective without a global vision, a willingness to learn, to see and to experience personally the modern developments that epitomize the European genius for building cities.

RECOMMENDATIONS

Many of these recommendations are derived from the experience accumulated and the work carried out over a number of years by the Archives d'Architecture Moderne and the Atelier de Recherche et d'Action Urbaines run by René Schoonbrodt in Brussels; the studies carried out by Gabriele Tagliaventi at Bologna University's Faculty of Architecture; the developments and the city-building methods designed by the architects Andres Duany and Elizabeth Plater-Zyberk in Miami; the architectural achievements of Demetri Porphirios, winner of the European Urban Reconstruction Award set up by the architect Philippe Rotthier; and many others it would be impossible to acknowledge here.

The main source of reference is provided by the writings and theoretical works of the Luxembourg architect Léon Krier, who is also an esteemed friend. Krier was the first to come up with an operational, non-Utopian alternative to functionalism. He is at the origin of the urban reconstruction movement whose nature and constituent elements he has stated and clarified. He is our inspiration.

Desire and desirability: Desire for a city is something most of us have experienced at one time or another. It is a complex blend of nostalgia and longing, of projection into the future.

City desire is always associated with good times, with moments of intense joy, sometimes also of sadness and grief. The city is also a desire for change, for achieving a different status, a desire for speaking out, for access to political decision-making.

City desire has long been curbed and censored by functionalism.

To encourage the return of desire and allow it new freedom of expression, the first decision to take is to reject censorship.

Censorship begins with terminology. Let us therefore begin by reinstating, in bulk and in a positive manner, the terms and concepts of coexistence, cohabitation, mix, charm, picturesque, architectural styles, copy, imitation, pastiche, beauty, generosity, curiosity, taste, pleasure, patina, etc, into the terminology of architecture.

This list is far from being exhaustive and anyone may add to it by recalling memories of good times. For all those words conceal atmospheres and these atmospheres are the product of considered decisions, knowledge, composition methods, comparisons between things, etc.

Building a picturesque neighbourhood, for instance, is not the result of chance or an architect's whim. There are rules to be observed for road layout, width and building, for plant arrangements, building composition, gradient and type of roofing, etc.

Europe, regions, cities: Although regional realities are indisputable and constitute one of the main foundations of the European structure, most Europeans nevertheless refer to cities when it comes to clarifying an identity or membership of an historically founded society; talking about everyday life, treasured public spaces and symbolic buildings; recalling the context of local, social and political history. If the regions are a means of reinforcing the European identity, then the cities are the dynamic, personalized element. For the citizens and most of the elected representatives, they are the operational European norm.

In architecture the concept of regionalism is associated with constructive traditions, specific materials, a way of grouping and arranging buildings, with colours, ways of living, etc. It is essential that the authorities and the regional and local administrations keep the public as well as the primary and secondary schools continuously supplied with accurate information on the history and characteristics of regional architectural identities in order to prevent questionable interpretations and a slide into kitsch.

European city: Its primary feature is to be lived in. It is made up of neighbourhoods, and the constituent elements of these neighbourhoods are the streets, the squares and their derivatives (avenues, boulevards, galleries, porticoes, alleyways, etc), and their specific local forms. [regional terms for the above - Transl.].

City boundaries: Cities must have a clear boundary with the countryside. In many cases, that boundary could be re-established by reclaiming space from the suburbs.

Neighbourhoods: The size of European city neighbourhoods is determined by walking. In no circumstances should these exceed 35 hectares. A neighbourhood comprises all the activities of traditional neighbourhood life (tradesmen, small-scale industry, local administration, housing, schools, etc).
Activities relating to several neighbourhoods are located at their junction or at the city boundary.

Mix: This is essential – the prerequisite for the European city. Activities are distributed among the neighbourhoods, but the mix must also feature in the buildings. The top floors must always be set aside for housing.

Zoning: To be banned. Zoning is functionalism's battle horse, a *de facto* obstacle to the city. Small business zones, industrial zones, housing (council or middle-class) zones, commercial zones are to be banned.
Only those activities that are incompatible with urban life can be located outside the city, eg airports, nuclear power stations, polluting factories, cemeteries, etc.

Public spaces: The concept of public space has been thoroughly researched by Léon Krier, who found that in the most successful and pleasant European cities, public space never exceeds 35% of the urban area, while this figure rises to between 70 and 90% in the new towns and high-density estates. This makes them unmanageable, leading to neglect and vandalism. On the whole, these huge public spaces are not recognizable as such, and generate nothing but slums and outcasts.

Plot: This is the smallest urban unit. Several plots make up a block.

Functionalism has rejected plot subdivision in favour of isolated construction units on a piece of land.

The plot system is the only one that makes city-building possible. Experience has shown that promoting only large projects means running the risk of economic recessions and bankruptcies. In Europe, we have lost count of the number of abandoned large projects. These decaying areas cause the ruin of cities. The centre of Liège, in Belgium, has been a huge waste ground for the past thirty years, due to the collapse of successive megalomaniac projects.

A return to the subdivision of blocks into different-sized plots would attract investors (urban middle-class, shopkeepers, small industrialists, tradesmen, professionals, etc) who have the varied financial means to reinvest into the city.

Suburb, new town, high-density housing: All these land-use concepts and the typologies underlying them are based on a waste of land, energy and human resources. They are in contradiction with the formation, the durability and the continuity of the European city.

They can be corrected and improved if we draw inspiration from the traditional cities. This can be achieved on the one hand by increasing building density and reducing public space, introducing a mix of activities and restructuring the space into neighbourhoods; on the other hand by converting land into parcels of real countryside, parks, public gardens and youth recreation areas.

Context: This is an essential element. Context is ever present, making fundamental decisions possible: block and plot size, street types, architectural styles, etc. Functionalism favours a break with context, retaining only the sunlight and wind-direction aspects.

Density: A city's density depends on its size, population and character. Having studied hundreds of European cities, Léon Krier observed that the most successful featured buildings between 3 and 4 storeys high. It is the difference in the floor-to-ceiling height in each of the buildings that creates street variety and colourfulness. Blocks of more than four storeys should be avoided and skyscrapers banned.

Architecture and planning competitions: Competitions can be interesting and productive only if they are organized stringently and have a preset, clearly defined objective. At present, almost all the competitions are controlled by the advocates of discontinuity and formal originality. Not a single competition in France has selected a tradition-inspired project.

Under the guise of democracy, competitions have become instruments to force the people into accepting architectures and urban developments they do not want.

If competitions are to be truly pluralistic in their outlook, the rules must be laid down from the outset. Either a competition is aimed at architects and planners who reject tradition and that competition is then set up and judged by modernists, or it is aimed at those who work within the European city-building tradition and the jury is then made up of persons who are competent in the subject. Otherwise it would be preferable not to resort to architecture and planning competitions, as these are partly responsible for some of the fiercest attacks on the European city.

Master plan: Functionalism has drawn up numerous master plans. All have been designed from the viewpoint of ad lib urban expansion, assigning huge tracts of countryside to the extension of residential zones. Land-use plans generally provide for excessive densities in the centres and insufficient densities elsewhere. Many of these plans are now under review or have been abandoned. They must imperatively be replaced by other master plans that provide support and a reliable framework for the European urban reconstruction strategies based on the historical concepts of neighbourhoods, streets and squares.

These new master plans should be initiated as a matter of urgency, for in today's climate of laxity, no plan could have the same dramatic effect as the implementation of functionalist master plans.

Planning permission: With this tool, the city can be managed on a daily, case-by-case basis. Outside the so-called «historical» areas, planning permission is usually assessed in a mainly bureaucratic manner. In many cases insufficient attention is paid to the context, the heritage and history.

In France's historical centres, the preserved areas and protection zones are subject to the opinion of the official architect for French buildings. This advisory function should be extended to all planning permissions.

Engineering departments: Small towns that have no architecture and planning divisions readily entrust many town-planning assignments to their engineering departments. Although these are competent, their involvement in the field of urbanism very frequently leads to the installation of unsuitable urban furniture (inappropriate plant tubs, lamp-posts, etc), intricate or gaudy floor coverings, car parks on the site of demolished houses, incongruous conversions of public monuments and buildings.

Even the small towns should have permanent access to an architect for advice on, and supervision of, the architectural and urban development work carried out by the engineering departments.

Involvement, consultation and dialogue: Getting the citizens to contribute to a dialogue is essential in an increasingly complex and specialized society. One person cannot know everything.

Through involvement, consultation and dialogue, programmes can be clarified, wishes considered and suggestions listened to.

It is then up to the elected representatives and administrations to act as responsible project managers and specify not only the quantitative aspects (square metres), but also the qualitative ones, eg architectural style, context integration, choice of urban furniture, materials, etc.

Involvement, consultation and dialogue must take place before the final decision is made.

The architect and planner are then responsible for carrying out the project in accordance with the programme approved.

Discontinuity and tradition: Discontinuity advocates indifference to the context, basing itself on zoning and framework discontinuity. It encourages originality of forms at any price (the never-seen). Tradition, on the contrary, is a rational approach in keeping with the spirit of the European city-building continuum. It attempts to highlight the identity and specificity of every neighbourhood of every city. Its concern is for original thinking and solutions, not for the invention of never-seen forms.

Vernacular and classical: According to the definition given by Léon Krier: *«Vernacular construction is the material culture of building while classical architecture – which has nothing to do with classical style – is the artistic and intellectual culture of vernacular construction, raised to the status of a symbolic language.»*

Imitation: This is the creative process *par excellence*. It was defined by Quatremère de Quincy as the operation *«producing the likeness of one object in another»*.
The European city reproduces itself and reinforces its identity through this process. To imitate is to choose the most relevant examples and imitate them, either to correct unsatisfactory existing solutions or to create new complexes. Imitation is a creative process in its own right, requiring a genuine architectural and building culture.

Copying: This is the creative process that analyses a work to reconstruct it as faithfully as possible, with the option of adapting it to the context and incorporating the modern elements of comfort and technique.

Pluralism: This is not a blank cheque for anyone. It means that complexes reflecting different theories of the city can be built and must be consistent in character so that they may be compared. In other words, pluralism is not a patchwork of modernist and traditional buildings.

Styles: The architectural styles fashion the look of a city and its neighbourhoods.
Functionalism has banned all the styles except modernism and its derivatives in the form of successive fashions.
The public is always concerned about the quality of complexes with homogeneous stylistic features, whether these are based on imitation of vernacular architecture as in Port-Grimaud or Poundbury, or on the Art Deco architecture of Miami Beach or the Art Nouveau and Eclectic architecture of the Cogels Osylei neighbourhood of Antwerp. Residents readily identify with a stylistic complex and are prepared to organize themselves to maintain it and safeguard its identity.
There can be no desirable architecture if the client does not specify the style he wants or if he is not given the opportunity to choose between several styles.

Calling things by their name: It is important to call things by their name and to discard the functionalist designations. For instance we must plan alleys, gardens, parks and squares (each of these terms relates to a specific type) and dismiss the green areas, the buffer zones, the green runs which are abstractions not recognized by the public.

Architectural quality: A development is a success when the residents of a neighbourhood ask themselves whether what has just been built has always been there or is truly recent, and if they approve of it without seeking clarification or justification.

Lighting of public spaces: Uniform sheet lighting should be avoided in the streets and coloured lighting (yellow, orange, green) should be banned.
«Lighting plans» – which are as essential as the «master plans» – should be drawn up by architects and scenographers who are competent in this field.

EPILOGUE

A DESIRE TO FORGE IN ORDER TO LOOK REAL
THE INSTITUT FRANÇAIS D'ARCHITECTURE'S PROJECT-BOOKS

EPILOGUE

A DESIRE TO FORGE IN ORDER TO LOOK REAL
THE INSTITUT FRANÇAIS D'ARCHITECTURE'S PROJECT-BOOKS

The Institut Français d'Architecture is located in one of the finest streets of Paris, in an 18th-century mansion with courtyard and garden, just round the corner from the Jardin du Luxembourg.

No visitor can remain insensitive to the beauty of the architecture and the poetry of the falsely derelict-looking garden. It is one of those rare buildings that have a reflected effect on the men and women entering them, even though institutional solemnity has not yet crossed the porch of 6 rue de Tournon. The Institut Français d'Architecture occupies these prestigious premises with a discretion – as recommended by the writer Jacques Chardonne – that befits those who have a sense of the ephemeral. Regular visitors are no longer surprised that this house in the heart of the publishers' quarter is the source of a flow of books enhancing the cities of France, Europe and even America: historical cities, capital cities, harbour cities, 19th-century cities, rough industrial towns, mining towns, towns rebuilt after the war, seaside and health resorts. Neither history books nor tourist guides, these works have in common the power to evoke virtual charms, those very charms anticipated by the subconscious at the mere mention of Marseilles (a whiff of household soap); Toulouse-the-Pink; Biarritz-the-imperial; Boulogne, the Mecca of the film industry, etc. All these books build up the reader's expectations and confirm that reality does not necessarily fall short of fiction when it is sought with acute inquisitiveness.

These books are the product of a guided, selective vision deliberately discarding whatever may stand in the way of the obvious, of coherence, of the clear interpretation of the modern myths that sustain every city. Photographers and cameramen operate like the human eye, automatically centring and cutting out parasites, eg the ugliness of a modern structure, overhead wires, posts, ludicrous urban furniture, etc. Not wanting to be outdone, the authors ignore historiography and concentrate on the sole facts, persons and events that have had a direct impact on the face of the city and contributed to its individuality. A mention of soap conjures up the industrial Marseilles, bristling with chimney stacks and factories. An aperitif of the inter-war years (Suze) recalls the figure of Fernand Moureaux, also known as the <u>Haussmann of Trouville</u>. A mythical car recalls the changing street pattern of Boulogne-Billancourt. A book is just a book, a few hundred grams of paper, but today the lifespan of reference books is expanding continuously into the vacuum of over-communication and over-information, reaching into the fringes of our reading hours. Books can be either a starting point for further research, or an effective weapon for questioning some mediocre architecture or planning project, or again they can bring about improvements, classifications, etc.

As works of fiction, keener than portraits, they focus on the virtual image – more akin to a composition than an inventory. These are project-books, designed to move and mobilize the readers, to compel interest in the ordinary, non-classifiable heritage. They use the lever of desire to raise the level of standards. Their starting points and roots are not so much the sublime monuments of civil and religious architecture as the commonplace: tough guys (Marseilles), a patron-mayor (Trouville), film studios (Boulogne), false wood panels (Basque Country), Art Deco (Miami Beach), mountain chalets (Megève), a ruling and deposed emperor (Biarritz), the *lost generation* and France seen from England (Le Touquet), the realm of brick (Toulouse), healing air and the city of doctors (Arcachon), a great French novel and a neighbourhood of toll gates (Goutte d'Or), etc.

Every city is an adventure in which the passing flow of platitudes gradually uncovers a city, neighbourhoods, streets in all their character. The *raison d'Ître* of such a publishing venture is merely to please in order to arouse a desire for the city. These are books that play on the imagination – powerful aphrodisiacs containing what anyone can see when they take the trouble to look. Finally, these are books worthy of the closing lines of the Great Gatsby, «*And so we beat on, boats against the current, borne back ceaselessly into the past.*»

The planning of these books recalls a proven method that artists and theatre people are familiar with: forging in order to be plausible. The knowing reader is not fooled and feels invigorated by such an unexpected introspective gaze. These books are apolitical by vocation, critical *a contrario*, outrageously nostalgic: hence they are genuine action books since they are bearers of hope even in the midst of desperate situations.

LE NOUVEL
AMIENS

SOUS LA DIRECTION DE MARC BREITMAN ET ROB KRIER
PHOTOGRAPHIES DE DOMINIQUE DELAUNAY

COLLECTION VILLES

MARDAGA

Doc. I.F.A.

Culot / A.A.M.

I.F.A. / NORMAL

179

ANNEXES

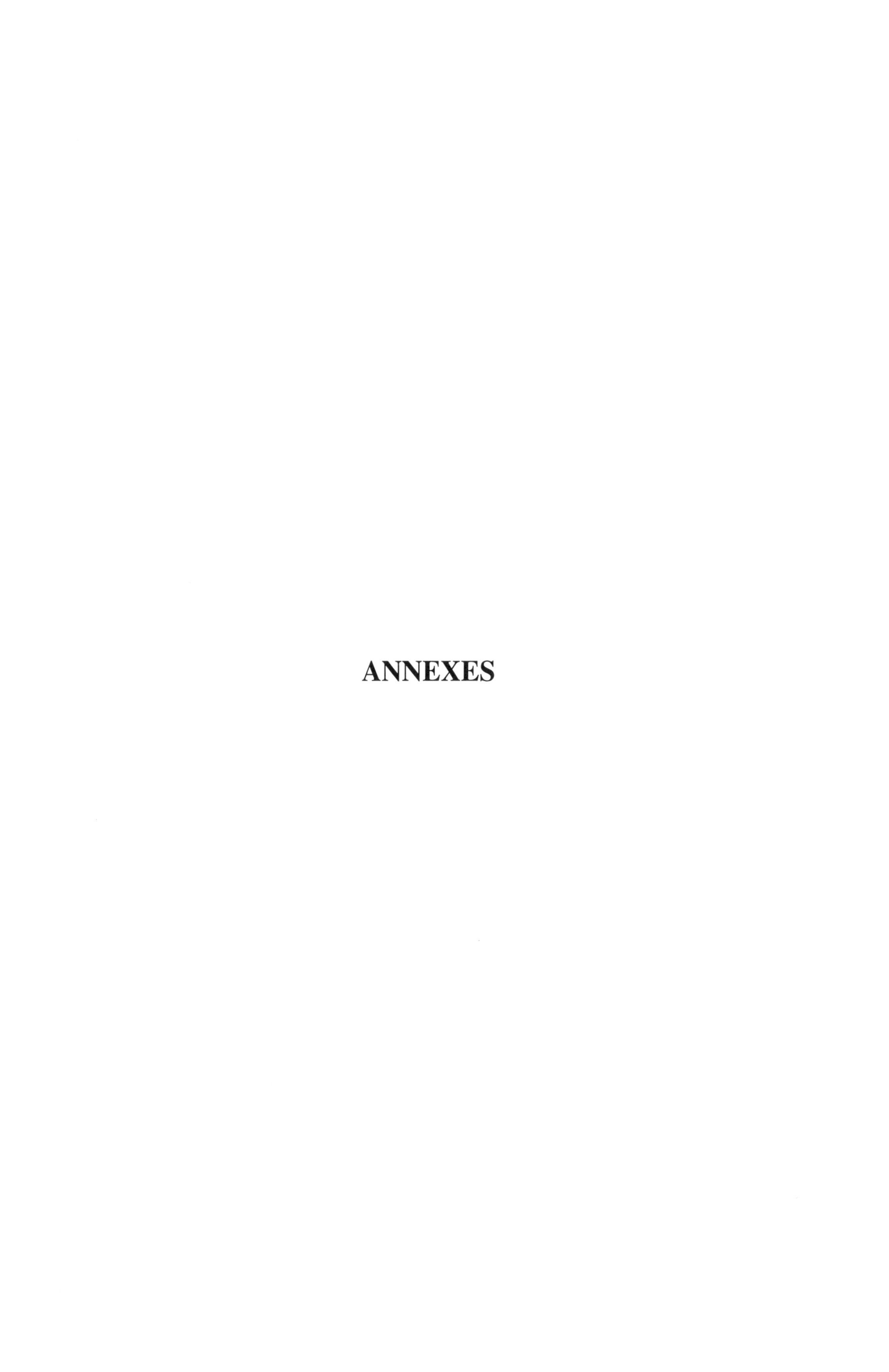

ANNEX

Pages taken from Architectural Graphic Standards, 9th Edition, 1994, published by the American Institute of Architects.

The recommendations included in this document are for information only. However, in the event of a dispute or lawsuit, the solicitors shall refer to them, thereby giving them quasi-legal force. It is significant that, from 1994, the planning recommendations of the Architectural Graphic Standards have been drafted by the Duany/Plater-Zyberk Agency of Miami, the originators of many city plans inspired chiefly by traditional American and European examples.

This marks a significant change in the approach to urban problems and a genuine volte-face in the way in which urban problems are viewed in the United States.

As concepts developed in the United States always have an impact in Europe, there are grounds for believing that this new approach to cities will greatly contribute to a redefinition of European planning practices.

RAMSEY/SLEEPER
Architectural GRAPHIC Standards

Ninth Edition

JOHN RAY HOKE, JR., FAIA
EDITOR IN CHIEF

THE AMERICAN INSTITUTE OF ARCHITECTS

Elements of Urbanism

THE NEIGHBORHOOD, THE DISTRICT, AND THE CORRIDOR

The fundamental elements of urbanism are the neighborhood, the district, and the corridor. Neighborhoods are urbanized areas with a full and balanced range of human activity. Districts are urbanized areas organized around a predominant activity. Neighborhoods and districts are connected and isolated by corridors of transportation or open space.

Neighborhoods, districts, and corridors are complex urban elements. Suburbia, in contrast, is the result of simplistic zoning concepts that separate activities into residential subdivisions, shopping centers, office parks, and open space.

THE NEIGHBORHOOD

Cities and towns are made up of multiple neighborhoods. A neighborhood isolated in the landscape is a village.

The nomenclature may vary, but there is general agreement regarding the physical composition of a neighborhood. The neighborhood unit of the 1929 New York Regional Plan, the *quartier* identified by Leon Krier, traditional neighborhood design (TND), and transit-oriented development (TOD) share similar attributes. The population, configuration, and scale may vary, but all of these models propose the following:

1. The neighborhood has a center and an edge. This combination of a focus and a limit contributes to the social identity of the community. The center is a necessity, the edge less so. The center is always a public space–a square, a green, or an important street intersection–located near the center of the urbanized area, unless compelled by geography to be elsewhere. Eccentric locations are justified by a shoreline, a transportation corridor, or a promontory with a compelling view.

   The center is the locus of the neighborhood's public buildings. Shops and workplaces are usually here, especially in a village. In the aggregations of neighborhoods that create towns and cities, retail buildings and workplaces are often at the edge, where they can combine with others to draw customers.

   The edges of a neighborhood vary in character. In villages, the edge is usually defined by land designated for cultivation or conservation of its natural state. In urban areas, the edge is often defined by rail lines and boulevards, which best remain outside the neighborhood.

2. The neighborhood has a balanced mix of activities: shops, work, school, recreation, and dwellings of all types. This is particularly useful for young, old, and low-income populations who, in an automobile-based environment, depend on others for mobility.

   The neighborhood provides housing for residents with a variety of incomes. Affordable housing types include backyard apartments, apartments above shops, and apartment buildings adjacent to workplaces.

3. The optimal size of a neighborhood is $1/4$ mile from center to edge, a distance equal to a five-minute walk at an easy pace. Its limited area gathers the population within walking distance of many of its daily needs.

   The location of a transit stop within walking distance of most homes increases the likelihood of its use. Transit-oriented neighborhoods create a regional network of villages, towns, and cities accessible to a population unable to rely on cars. Such a system can provide the major cultural and social institutions, variety of shopping, and broad job base that can only be supported by the larger population of an aggregation of neighborhoods.

4. The neighborhood consists of blocks on a network of small thoroughfares. Streets are laid out to create blocks of appropriate building sites and to shorten pedestrian routes. An interconnecting street pattern provides multiple routes, diffusing traffic. This pattern keeps local traffic off regional roads and through traffic off local streets. Neighborhood streets of varying types are detailed to provide equitably for pedestrian comfort and automobile movement. Slowing the automobile and increasing pedestrian activity encourage the casual meetings that form the bonds of community.

5. The neighborhood gives priority to public space and to appropriate location of civic buildings. Public spaces and public buildings enhance community identity and foster civic pride. The neighborhood plan creates a hierarchy of useful public spaces: a formal square, an informal park, and many playgrounds.

THE DISTRICT

The district is an urbanized area that is functionally specialized. Although districts preclude the full range of activities of a neighborhood, they are not the single-activity zones of suburbia. Rather, multiple activities support its primary identity. Typically complex examples are theater districts, capital areas, and college campuses. Other districts accommodate large-scale transportation or manufacturing uses, such as airports, container terminals, and refineries.

The structure of the district parallels that of the neighborhood. An identifiable focus encourages orientation and identity. Clear boundaries facilitate the formation of special taxing or management organizations. As in the neighborhood, the character of the public spaces creates a community of users, even if they reside elsewhere. Interconnected circulation encourages pedestrians, supports transit viability, and ensures security. Districts benefit from transit systems and should be located within the regional network.

THE CORRIDOR

The corridor is the connector and the separator of neighborhoods and districts. Corridors include natural and technical components ranging from wildlife trails to rail lines. The between is not the haphazardly residual space remaining outside subdivisions and shopping centers in suburbia. It is a civic element characterized by its visible continuity and bounded by neighborhoods and districts, to which it provides entry.

The transportation corridor's trajectory is determined by its intensity. Heavy rail corridors should remain tangent to towns and enter only the industrial districts of cities. Light rail and trolley corridors may occur as boulevards at the edges of neighborhoods. As such, they are detailed for pedestrian use and to accommodate building sites. Bus corridors may pass into neighborhood centers on conventional streets.

The corridor may also be a continuous parkway, providing long-distance walking and bicycling trails and natural habitat. Parkway corridors can be formed by the systematic accretion of recreational open spaces, such as parks, schoolyards, and golf courses. These continuous spaces can be part of a larger network, connecting urban open space with rural surroundings.

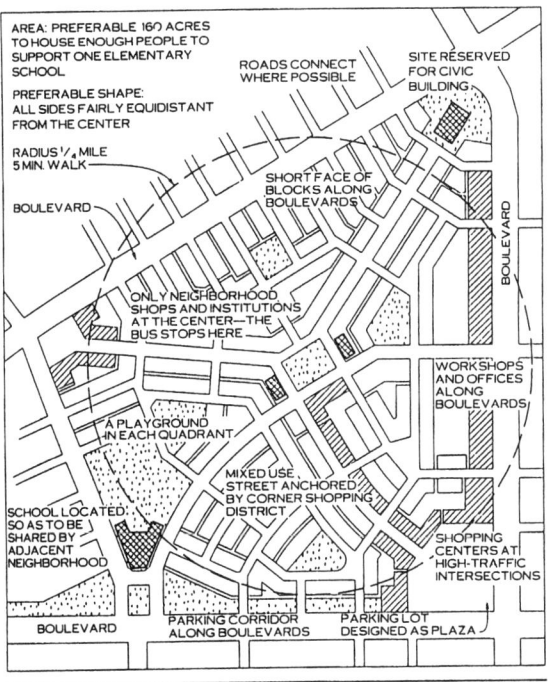

AN URBAN NEIGHBORHOOD (PART OF A TOWN)

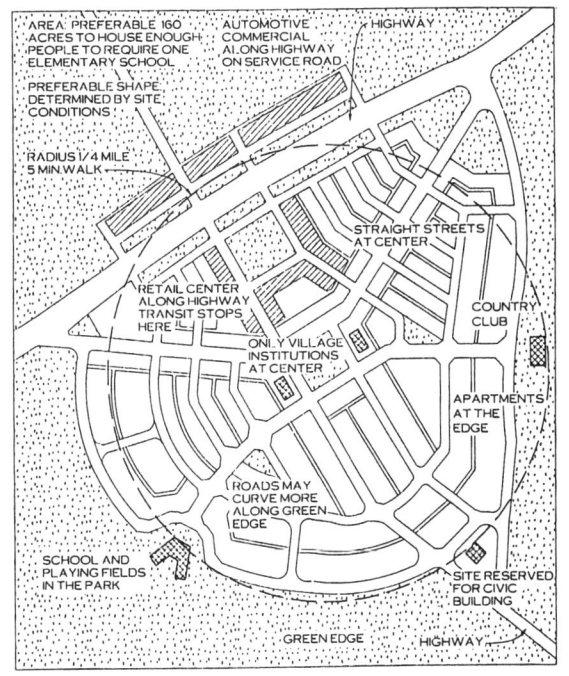

A RURAL NEIGHBORHOOD (A VILLAGE)

Gary Greenan, Andres Duany, Elizabeth Plater-Zyberk, Kamal Zaharin, Iskandar Shafie; Miami, Florida
The Cintas Foundation

SITE, COMMUNITY, AND URBAN PLANNING

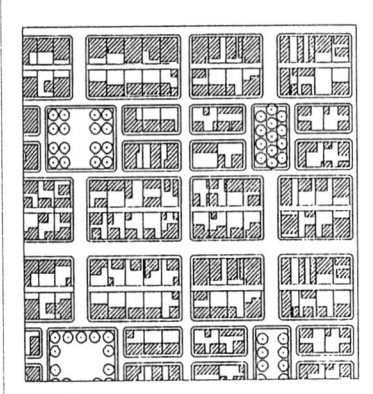

Plan Types

SAVANNAH

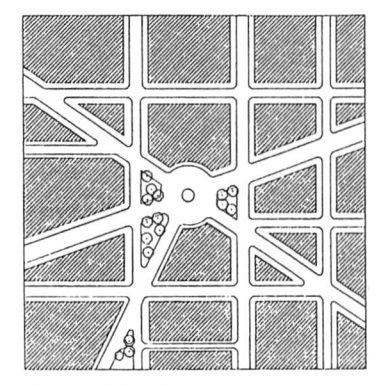

ADVANTAGES
1. Excellent directional orientation
2. Lot shape controllable
3. Street hierarchy with end blocks for through traffic
4. Even dispersal of traffic through the grid
5. Straight lines enhance rolling terrain
6. Efficient double-loading of alleys and utilities

DISADVANTAGES
1. Monotonous unless periodically interrupted
2. Does not accommodate environmental interruptions
3. Unresponsive to steep terrain

ORTHOGONAL GRID

WASHINGTON, D.C.

ADVANTAGES
1. Street hierarchy with diagonals for through traffic
2. Even dispersal of traffic through the grid
3. Diagonals respond to the terrain
4. Diagonals interrupt monotony of the grid

DISADVANTAGES
1. Uncontrollable variety of blocks and lots
2. High number of awkward lot shapes
3. Diagonal intersections spatially ill defined

GRID WITH DIAGONALS

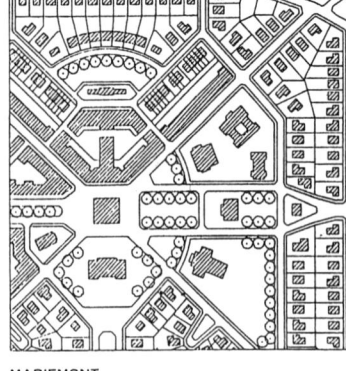

MARIEMONT

ADVANTAGES
1. Street hierarchy with diagonals for through traffic
2. Even dispersal of traffic through the network
3. Diagonals respond to terrain
4. Intrinsically interesting by geometric variety
5. Controllable shape of blocks and lots
6. Efficient double-loading of alleys for utilities
7. Diagonal intersections spatially well defined

DISADVANTAGES
1. Tends to be disorienting

DIAGONAL NETWORK

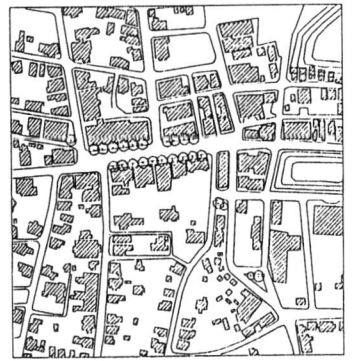

NANTUCKET

ADVANTAGES
1. Street hierarchy with long routes for through traffic
2. Even dispersal of traffic through network
3. Intrinsically interesting by geometric variety
4. Responsive to terrain
5. Easily accommodates environmental interruptions
6. Short streets, terminated vistas

DISADVANTAGES
1. None

ORGANIC NETWORK

RIVERSIDE

ADVANTAGES
1. Intrinsically interesting by deflecting vistas
2. Easily accommodates environmental interruptions
3. Highly responsive to terrain
4. Even dispersal of traffic through the network

DISADVANTAGES
1. Little directional orientation
2. Uncontrollable variety of lots
3. No natural hierarchy of streets

CURVILINEAR NETWORK

RADBURN

ADVANTAGES
1. Street hierarchy with collectors for through traffic
2. Controllable variety of blocks and lots
3. Easily accommodates environmental interruptions
4. Highly responsive to p terrain

DISADVANTAGES
1. Concentration of traffic by absence of network

DISCONTINUOUS NETWORK

Gary Greenan, Andres Duany, Elizabeth Plater-Zyberk, Kamal Zaharin, Iskandar Shafie, Rafael Diaz; Miami, Florida
The Cintas Fountain

SITE, COMMUNITY, AND URBAN PLANNING

Block Types

GENERAL
The urban plan must be assembled of blocks before building frontage and landscape types are assigned. The disposition of blocks has distinct socioeconomic implications.

THE SQUARE BLOCK
This type was an early model for planned settlements in America, particularly in Spanish colonies. It was sometimes associated with agricultural communities, providing four large lots per block, each lot with a house at its center. When the growth of the community produced additional subdivision, replatting created irregular lots (Fig. 1). While this may provide a useful variety, it is more often regarded as a nuisance by a society accustomed to standardized products. A further disadvantage is that discontinuous rear lot lines make alleys and rear-access utilities impractical. Despite these shortcomings, the square block is useful as a specialized type. When platted only at its perimeter, with the center left open, it can accommodate the high parking requirements of certain buildings. The open center, well insulated from traffic, may also be used as a common garden or a playground (Fig. 2).

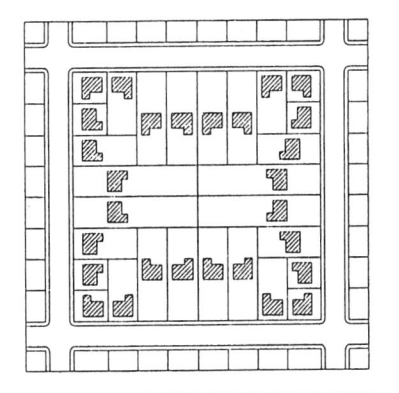

1. SQUARE BLOCK

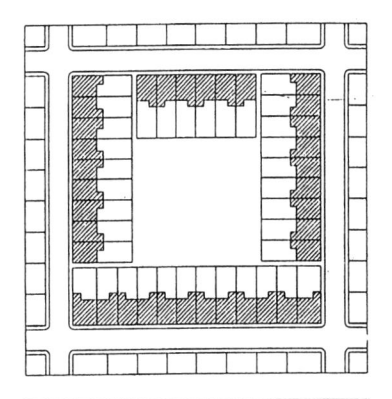

2. SQUARE BLOCK

THE ORGANIC BLOCK
This type is characterized by its irregularity; its variations are unlimited. The original organic block was the subdivision of residual land between well-worn paths (Fig. 3). It was later rationalized by Olmsted and Unwin to achieve a controllable, picturesque effect and to negotiate sloping terrain gracefully. The naturalistic block, despite its variety, generates certain recurring conditions that must be resolved by sophisticated platting. At shallow curves, it is desirable to have the facades follow the frontage smoothly. This is achieved by keeping the side lot lines perpendicular to the frontage line (Fig. 4-1). At the same time it is important for the rear lot line to be wide enough to permit vehicular access (Fig. 4-2). At sharper curves, it is desirable to have the axis of a single lot bisect the acute angle (Fig. 4-3). In the event of excessive block depth, it is possible to colonize the interior of the block by means of a close (Fig. 4-4).

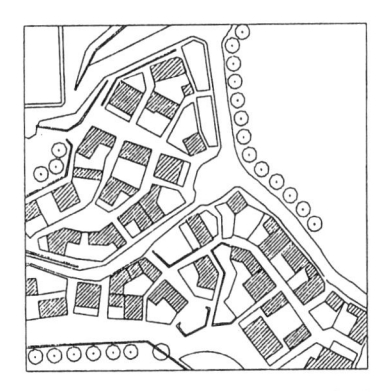

3. ORGANIC BLOCK

4. ORGANIC BLOCK

THE ELONGATED BLOCK
The elongated block overcomes some of the drawbacks of the square block. More efficient and more standardized, elongated blocks provide economical double-loaded alleys, with short utility runs, to eliminate the uncontrollable variable of lot depth and maintain the option of altering lot width. By adjusting the block length, it is possible to reduce cross streets toward rural edges or to add them at urban centers. This adjustment alters the pedestrian permeability of the grid and controls the ratio of street parking to building capacity. The elongated block can "bend" somewhat along its length, giving it a limited ability to shape space and negotiate slopes (Fig. 6).

Unlike the square block, the elongated block provides two distinct types of frontage. Residential buildings are placed on the quieter sides of the block (Fig. 5-1). Commercial buildings can be set on the short end of the block, platted to face the busy street; the amount of parking behind these properties is controlled by the variable depth (Fig. 5-2).

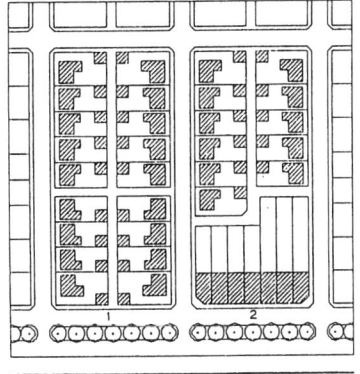

5. ELONGATED BLOCK

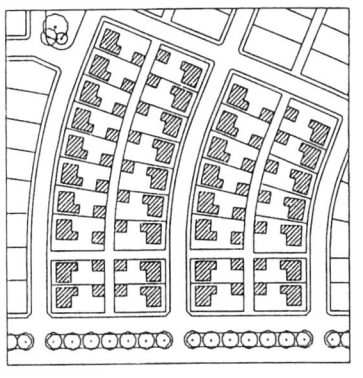

6. ELONGATED BLOCK

Gary Greenan, Andres Duany, Elizabeth Plater-Zyberk, Kamal Zaharin, Iskandar Shafie; Miami, Florida
The Cintas Foundation

1 SITE, COMMUNITY, AND URBAN PLANNING

Open Space Types I

GENERAL
Public open space provides orientation, hierarchy, and communal structure to a neighborhood. The specialized open spaces shown here are derived from the elongated block types. They can also be adjusted to fit both square and organic block types.

LANE
Children often make lanes behind houses into informal playgrounds. The paved surface in front of garages is convenient for ball games. Lanes are particularly successful when they are designed to eliminate through traffic (right). Garage apartments provide supervision.

PLAYGROUND
Playgrounds can be easily extracted from any block by assigning one or several lots to this use. There should be a playground within 500 ft of every residence. The playground should provide both sunny and shaded play areas, as well as an open shelter with benches for parents. Playgrounds must be fenced, lockable, and lit, if they are not to become a nuisance at night.

NURSERY
A nursery can be inserted in the middle of a block, away from major thoroughfares. It requires a limited amount of parking but substantial vehicular drop-off space. The attached playground should be securely fenced and have both sunny and shaded areas. Children's games may be noisy, so it is advisable to locate nurseries where adjacent houses are buffered by outbuildings.

CLOSE
A close is a space shared by buildings inside the block. It may be pedestrian, or it may have a roadway loop around a green area. Its minimum width must coincide with emergency vehicle turning standards. The close is a superior alternative to the cul-de-sac, as the focus is a green rather than pavement. It is especially recommended for communal subgroups such as cohousing or assisted-living cottages. The close provides additional frontage for deep square and organic blocks.

ATTACHED SQUARES
Squares are green spaces that provide settings for civic buildings and monuments, which are located at the center or edge of the square. Buildings play a part, but the space is largely defined by formal tree planting. Squares should be maintained to a higher standard than playgrounds and parks.

DETACHED SQUARES
Squares detached on all sides by roads are particularly formal. Since adjacent buildings provide much of the population that uses a public space, detached squares are less likely to be used than other types. This separation also limits the amount of natural security provided by adjacent windows. The detached square remains appropriate as a means to symbolically enhance important places or institutions.

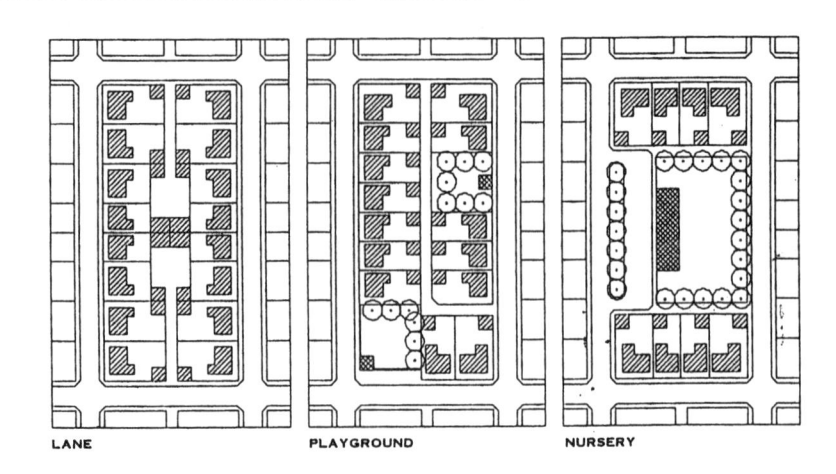

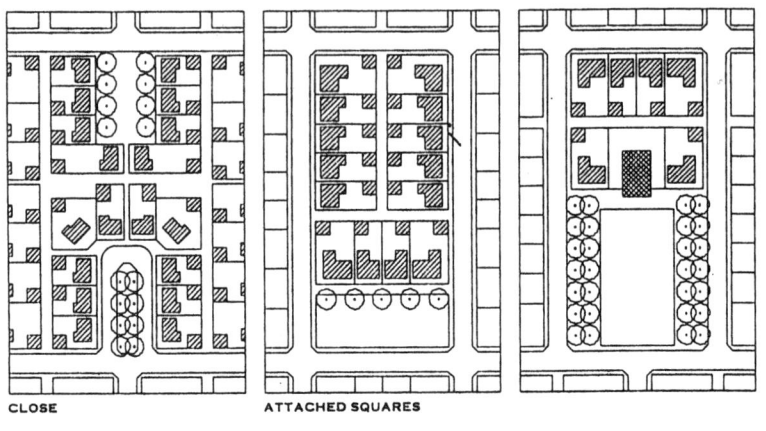

LANE PLAYGROUND NURSERY

CLOSE ATTACHED SQUARES

OPEN SPACE TYPES

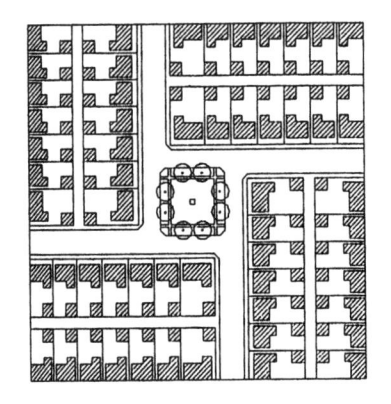

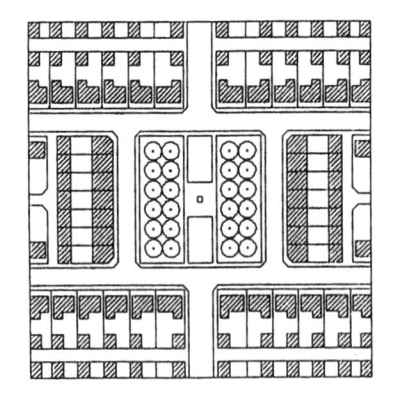

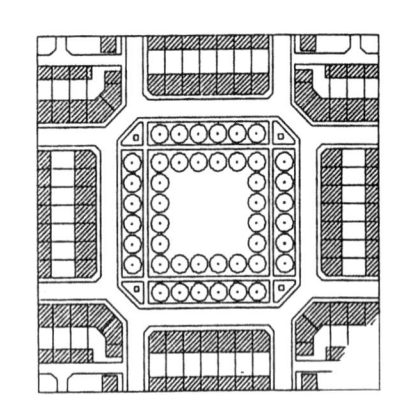

OPEN SPACE TYPES—DETACHED SQUARES

Gary Greenan, Andres Duany, Elizabeth Plater-Zyberk, Kámal Zaharin, Iskandar Shafie; Miami, Florida
The Cintas Foundation

SITE, COMMUNITY, AND URBAN PLAN

84 Open Space Types II

MARKET PLAZA
Plazas are public spaces that are primarily paved rather than green. They can sustain very intense use by crowds and even by vehicles. Parking lots should be designed as plazas that happen to have cars on them, rather than as single-purpose areas. A smaller shopping center can be transformed into a town center if it has been designed so it can be seamlessly attached to the block system and detailed as a plaza.

CIVIC PLAZA
Civic buildings are often no larger than the private ones that surround them, and their legibility as more important buildings cannot depend solely on architectural expression. Their setting within the block system must communicate their elevated status. Sites on squares or at the terminations of avenues are ideal but not always available. Thus the most dependable technique is to organize and detail the parking areas of civic buildings as plazas.

GREEN
The green is an urban, naturalistic open space. Like the square, it is small, civic, and surrounded by buildings. Unlike the square, it is informally planted and may have an irregular topography. Greens are usually landscaped with trees at the edges and sunny lawns at the center. Greens should contain no structures other than benches, pavilions, and memorials; paths are optional.

PARK
Parks are naturalistic open spaces, like greens, but larger and less tended. They are most successful when created from virgin woodland. Parks have grassy areas only periodically. A knoll or a pond can be used as an important organizing feature. Parks exist within the urban fabric of large cities, but their inherent size usually puts them at the edges of towns and villages. Parks may be edged by public drives or by houses on very large lots, as long as connections to public paths occur at every block.

BUFFER
The buffer has the basic elements of a green, with the added purpose of buffering the impact of traffic from a highway or boulevard. Shown is a small lot development fronting a green. On the opposite side are larger lots on which houses are placed further back from the roadway edge as another buffer technique.

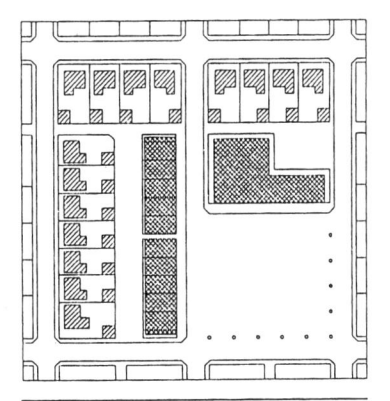

MARKET PLAZA

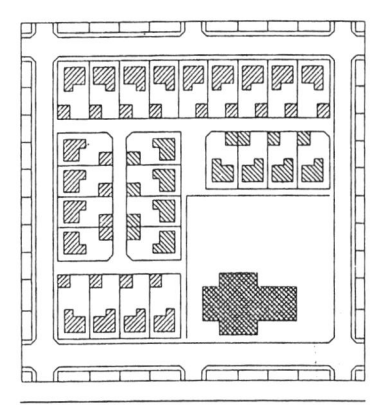

CIVIC PLAZA

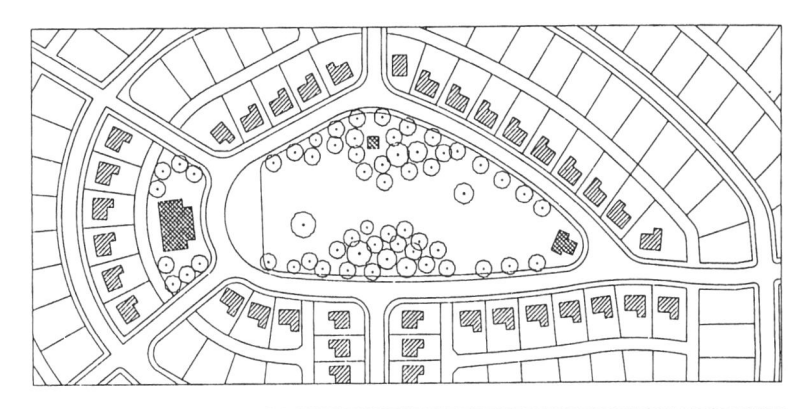

GREEN

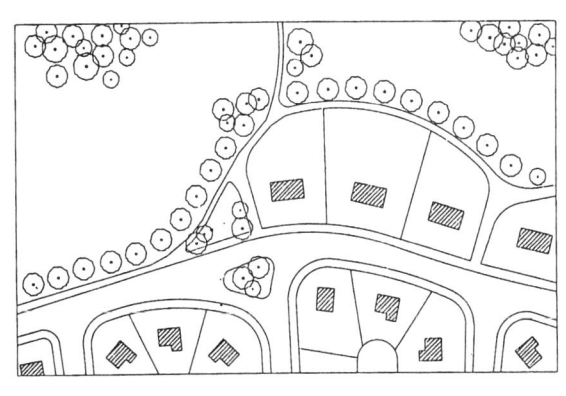

PARK

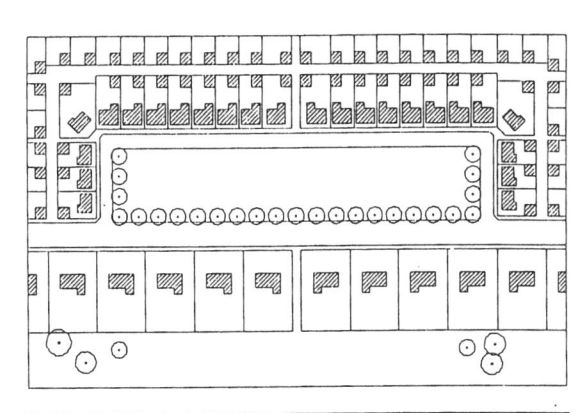

BUFFER

Gary Greenan, Andres Duany, Elizabeth Plater-Zyberk, Kamal Zaharin, Iskandar Shafie; Miami, Florida
The Cintas Foundation

1 SITE, COMMUNITY, AND URBAN PLANNING

Building Types

GENERAL

The traditional increment for platting lots in North America has been the 50-ft width. This subdivision dimension was efficient for many years, creating 25-ft rowhouse and shopfront lots, as well as 50-, 75-, and 100-ft lots suitable for houses. However, the advent of the automobile added a set of dimensional constraints that required new platting standards. The 50-ft width is wasteful, since the basic increment of efficient parking is the double row at 64 ft.

The 64-ft increment, when divided by four, provides the absolute minimum rowhouse lot of 16 ft, which allows one car to be parked with additional room for pedestrian passage. The minimum side yard lot is 32 ft. The minimum perimeter yard lot is 48 ft. The 64-ft lot efficiently provides for the high parking requirement of shopfronts, apartments, and office buildings.

The platting module of 16 ft corresponds to the traditional measure of the rod. Platting in rods, without knowing what building types will occupy the lots, maintains flexibility and ensures maximum density through parking efficiency.

Four building types accommodate the common residential, retail, and workplace uses of urban life. Some buildings, however, cannot be categorized typologically. Buildings dedicated to manufacturing and transportation may be distorted by large-scale mechanical trajectories. Civic buildings, which must express the aspirations of the institutions they embody, should also be exempt from the discipline of type.

COURTYARD BUILDING

This type of building occupies all or most of the edges of its lot and defines one or more private spaces internally. This is the most urban of types as it is able to completely shield the private realm from the public realm. It is common in hot climates, but its attributes are useful everywhere. Because of its ability to accommodate incompatible activities in close proximity, it is recommended for workshops, hotels, and schools. The high security the boundary provides is useful for recolonizing crime-prone urban cores.

SIDE YARD BUILDING

This type of building occupies one side of the lot, with the primary open space on the other side. The view of the side yard on the street front makes this building type appear freestanding, so it may be interspersed with perimeter yard buildings in less urban locations. If the adjacent building is also a side yard type with a blank party wall, the open space can be quite private. This type permits systematic climatic orientation, with the long side yard elevation facing the sun or the breeze.

REAR YARD BUILDING

This type of building occupies the front of its lot, full width, leaving the rear portion as a private space. This is a relatively urban type appropriate for neighborhood and town centers. The building facade defines the edge of the public space, while the rear elevation may reflect different functional purposes. In its residential form, this type is represented by the rowhouse with a rear garden and outbuilding. In its commercial form, the depth of the rear yard can contain substantial parking for retail and office uses.

PERIMETER YARD BUILDING

This building stands free on its lot, with substantial front and rear yards and smaller side yards. It is the least urban of the types, so it is usually assigned to areas away from neighborhood and town centers. This building type is usually residential, but when parking is contained within the rear yard it lends itself to limited office and boarding uses. The rear yard can be secured for privacy by fences and a well-placed outbuilding. The front yard is intended to be semipublic and visually continuous with the yards of neighbors. The illusion of continuity is usually degraded when garage fronts are aligned with the facades, as cars seldom pull in beyond the driveway. To avoid a landscape of parked cars, garages should be set back a minimum of one car's length from the facade or entered sideways through a walled forecourt.

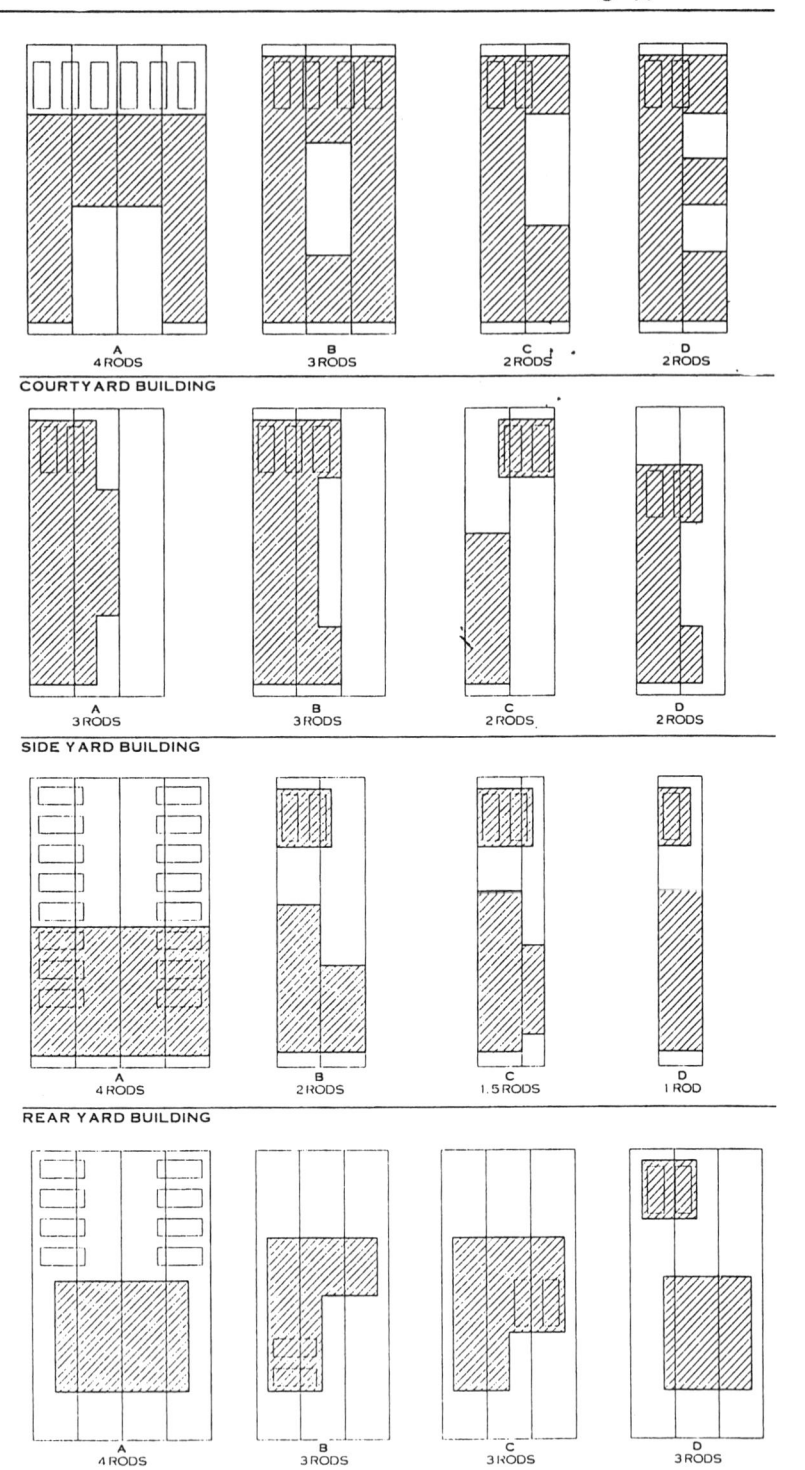

COURTYARD BUILDING
A 4 RODS | B 3 RODS | C 2 RODS | D 2 RODS

SIDE YARD BUILDING
A 3 RODS | B 3 RODS | C 2 RODS | D 2 RODS

REAR YARD BUILDING
A 4 RODS | B 2 RODS | C 1.5 RODS | D 1 ROD

PERIMETER YARD BUILDING
A 4 RODS | B 3 RODS | C 3 RODS | D 3 RODS

Gary Greenan, Andres Duany, Elizabeth Plater-Zyberk, Kamal Zaharin, Iskandar Shafie; Miami, Florida
The Cintas Foundation

SITE, COMMUNITY, AND URBAN PLANNING

86 Spatial Definition

GENERAL

Building delineates public space in an urban setting. Successful spatial definition is achieved when bounding buildings are aligned in a disciplined manner and the defined space does not exceed a certain height-to-width ratio.

Alignment occurs when building facades cooperate to delineate the public space, as walls form a room. Urban building articulation takes place primarily in the vertical plane or facade. If appendages such as porches, balconies, bay windows, and loggias do not obliterate the primary surface of the facade, they do not destroy alignment.

The height-to-width ratio of the space generates spatial enclosure, which is related to the physiology of the human eye. If the width of a public space is such that the cone of vision encompasses less street wall than sky opening, the degree of spatial enclosure is slight. The ratio of 1 increment of height to 6 of width is the absolute minimum, with 1 to 3 being an effective minimum if a sense of spatial enclosure is to result. As a general rule, the tighter the ratio, the stronger the sense of place and, often, the higher the real estate value. Spatial enclosure is particularly important for shopping streets that must compete with shopping malls, which provide very effective spatial definition. In the absence of spatial definition by facades, disciplined tree planting is an alternative. Trees aligned for spatial enclosure are necessary on thoroughfares that have substantial front yards.

NOMENCLATURE

THE FRONTAGE LINE

The lot boundary that coincides with a public thoroughfare or public space. The frontage line may be designed independently of the thoroughfare, to create a specific sense of place.

FACADE

The vertical surface of a building set along a frontage line. The elevation is the vertical surface set along any other boundary line. Facades are subject to control by building height, setback lines, recess lines, and transition lines. Elevations are only subject to building height and setback lines.

SETBACK

The mandatory distance between a frontage line and a facade or a lot line and an elevation

BUILDING HEIGHT

The defined limit to the vertical extent of a building. The building height should be stated as a number of stories, rather than a prescribed dimension. This prevents the compression of internal ceiling heights. Height may be determined by density and view and not by the requirements of spatial definition, which are addressed by the recess line.

RECESS LINE

A line prescribed for the full width of the facade, above which the facade is set back. The recess line effectively defines the enclosure of public space. Its location is determined by the desired height-to-width ratio of that space, compatibility with the average height of existing buildings, or provision for daylighting at the street level.

TRANSITION LINE

A line prescribed for the full width of the facade, expressed by a variation of material or by a limited projection such as a cornice or a balcony. The transition line divides the facade, permitting shopfronts and signage to vary over time without destroying the overall composition.

RATIO 1:1

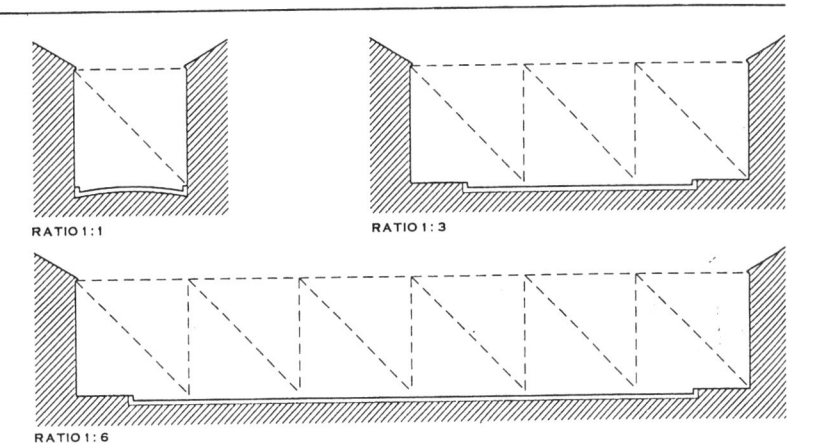

RATIO 1:3

RATIO 1:6

PROPORTIONS OF BUILDING HEIGHT TO PUBLIC SPACE

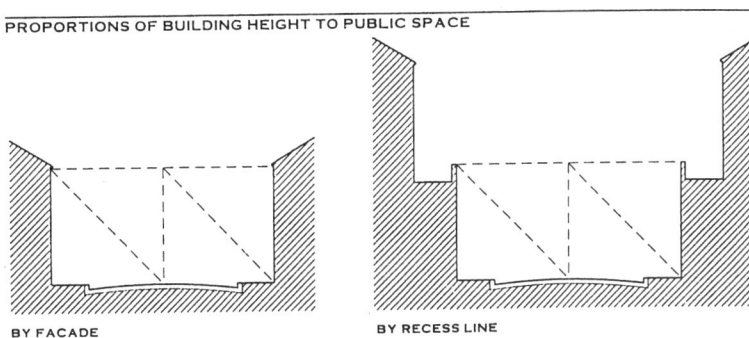

BY FACADE

BY RECESS LINE

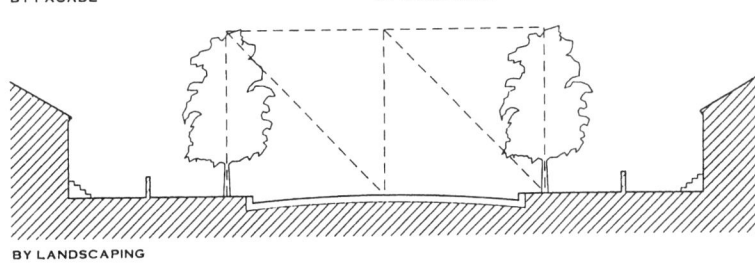

BY LANDSCAPING

TECHNIQUES OF DELINEATING PUBLIC SPACE

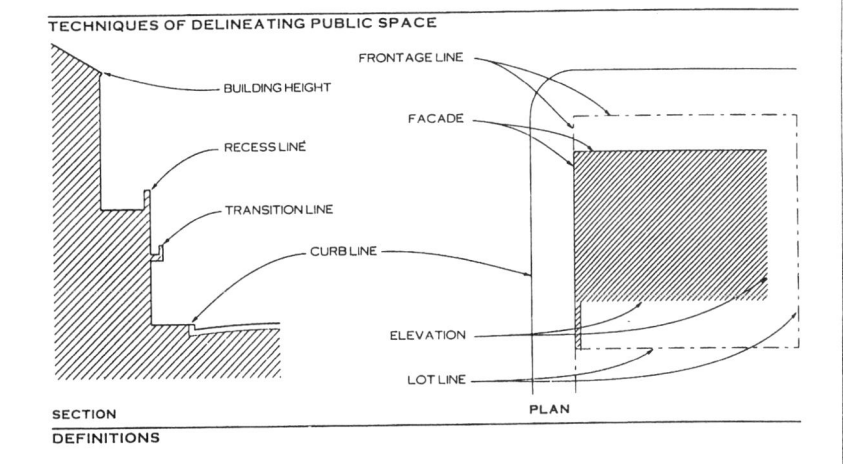

BUILDING HEIGHT
RECESS LINE
TRANSITION LINE
CURB LINE
FRONTAGE LINE
FACADE
ELEVATION
LOT LINE

SECTION   PLAN

DEFINITIONS

Gary Greenan, Andres Duany, Elizabeth Plater-Zyberk, Kamal Zaharin, Iskandar Shafie; Miami, Florida
The Cintas Foundation

1 SITE, COMMUNITY, AND URBAN PLANNING

Frontage Types

GENERAL
Building type is independent of frontage type. For example, a courtyard building may have an arcade, a shopfront, a stoop, or a porch as its frontage type. Frontages can be ranked from most urban to most rural.

ARCADE
The facade overlaps the sidewalk, while the storefront remains set back. This type is excellent for retail use, but only when the sidewalk is fully absorbed so the pedestrian cannot bypass the arcade. An easement for public use of private property is required.

SHOPFRONT
The facade is aligned directly on the frontage line, with the entrance at grade. This type is conventional for sidewalk retail. It is often equipped with an awning or a porch. A transition line should separate the signage from the facade above. The absence of a setback and elevation from the sidewalk prevents residential use on the ground floor, although it is appropriate above.

STOOP
The facade is aligned directly on the frontage line, with the first floor elevated to achieve some privacy for the windows. This type is suitable for residential uses such as rowhouses and apartment buildings. An easement may be necessary to accommodate the encroaching stoop. This type may be interspersed with the shopfront.

FORECOURT
The facade is set back and replaced by a low wall at the frontage line. The forecourt thus created is suitable for gardens, vehicular drop-offs, and workshop loading and storage. It should be used sparingly and in conjunction with the shopfront and stoop types, as a continuous blind wall is boring and unsafe for pedestrians. Tree canopies within the forecourt should overhang the sidewalk.

DOORYARD
The facade is set back from the frontage line, with an elevated garden or terrace between. This type can effectively buffer residential quarters from the sidewalk, while removing the yard from public use. The terrace, when roofed, is suitable for restaurants and cafes, as the eye level of the sitter is level with that of passersby.

PORCH AND FENCE
With an encroaching habitable porch, the facade is set back substantially from the frontage line. The porch should be within a conversational distance of the sidewalk. A fence at the frontage line marks the boundary of the yard.

FRONT LAWN
The facade is set back substantially from the frontage line. The front lawn this creates should be unfenced and visually continuous with adjacent yards. The ideal is to simulate buildings sitting in a rural landscape. A front porch is usually not appropriate, since no social interaction with the street is possible at such a distance. The large setback can provide a buffer from heavy traffic, so this type is sometimes found on boulevards.

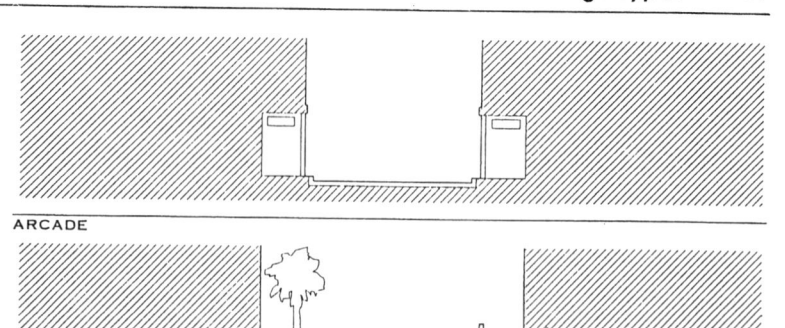

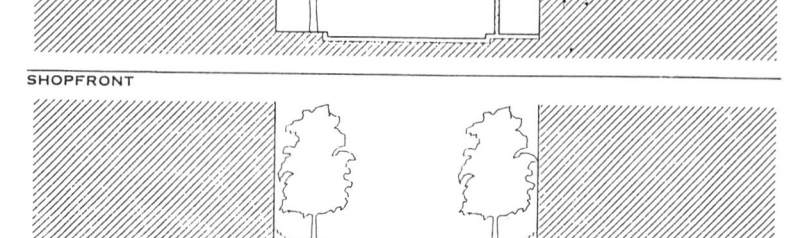

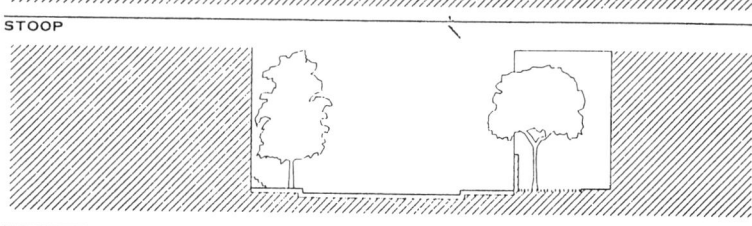

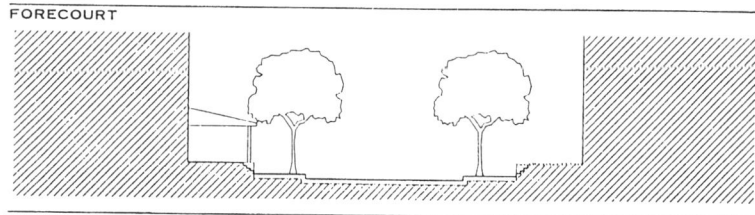

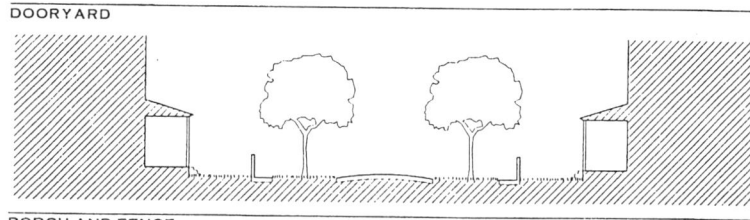

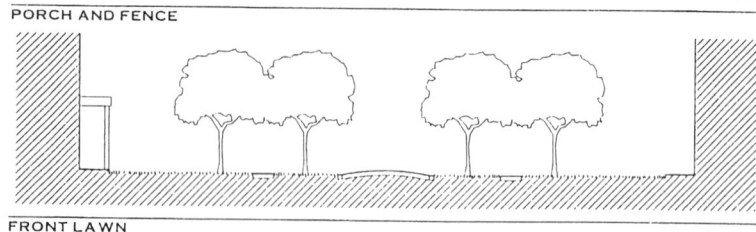

ARCADE

SHOPFRONT

STOOP

FORECOURT

DOORYARD

PORCH AND FENCE

FRONT LAWN

Gary Greenan, Andres Duany, Elizabeth Plater-Zyberk, Kamal Zaharin, Iskandar Shafie, Miami, Florida
The Cintas Foundation

SITE, COMMUNITY, AND URBAN PLANNING

88 Landscape Types

GENERAL
The urban landscape is a set of interdependent elements that creates a controlled sense of place. It includes thoroughfare type, building type, frontage type, and the form and disposition of landscape.

Public landscaping plays many roles above and beyond that of ornamentation:

1. To correct inadequacies of spatial definition caused by building frontages. Planting steady rows of trees at the edges usually reduces the height-to-width ratio of the street space. Grids of trees are used to fill gaps left by unbuilt lots and surface parking.
2. To adjust the microclimate by providing the appropriate level of shade or sun for buildings and sidewalks. For thoroughfares running east-west, this may involve the use of asymmetrical planting.
3. To support the intended urban or rural character of the public space. Selecting appropriate species and varying the species planted, as well as the regularity of their disposition, can alter the landscape significantly.
4. To create a pleasing visual composition, being careful to mask the aesthetic failure of certain buildings as well as to reveal the successes. Consider seasonal changes of each species.
5. To create a harmonious whole of specific character by coordinating public and private plantings. Selection should vary, to ensure resistance to pests, but not result in an incoherent collection of specimens. Native species should predominate to reduce maintenance, with an emphasis on species that support wildlife compatible with human settlement.

RURAL ROAD
This type is appropriate for buildings at the edges of the neighborhood and along parks and greenbelts. There is no public planting line. The tree species should be episodic, but in coherent clusters. There are no curbs; the drainage is by open swale. Bicycle paths may be paved in asphalt.

RESIDENTIAL ROAD
This type is appropriate for houses outside of neighborhood centers. Since the frontage usually includes a substantial setback, the tree canopy may be quite wide. The rural aspect may be supported by planting several species in imperfect alignment. Roads are detailed with open swales, and, where possible, drainage is through percolation.

RESIDENTIAL STREET
This type is appropriate for residential buildings at neighborhood and town centers. Trees are in continuous planting strips, since the sidewalk does not require unusual width. Plant a single species of tree in steady alignment. A thin, vertical canopy is necessary to avoid nearby building facades. This type is dimensionally interchangeable with the commercial street type and may alternate in correspondence to the building facade. Streets are detailed with raised curbs and closed storm drainage.

COMMERCIAL STREET
This type is appropriate for commercial buildings at neighborhood and town centers. Trees are confined by individual planting areas, creating a sidewalk of maximum width with areas accommodating street furniture. Plant a single species of tree in steady alignment. Clear trunks and high canopies are necessary to avoid interference with shopfront signage and awnings. Streets are detailed with raised curbs with closed storm drainage.

AVENUE
This type is appropriate for approaches to civic buildings. The general principle is a thoroughfare of limited length, with a substantial planted median. At town centers, the median may be wide enough to hold monuments and even buildings. In residential areas, the median may be planted naturalistically to become a parkway or green.

BOULEVARD
This type is appropriate for high-capacity thoroughfares at neighborhood edges. The detailing is similar to that of a commercial street. The effect of the medians is to segregate the slower traffic and parking activity, at the edges, from through traffic, at the center.

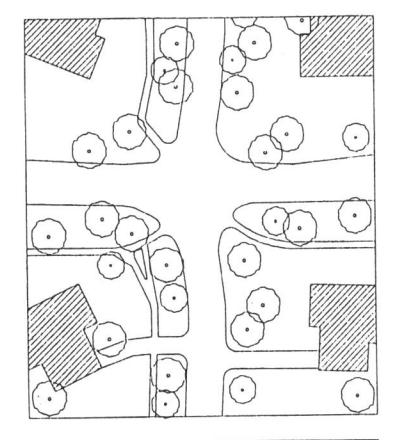

RURAL ROAD

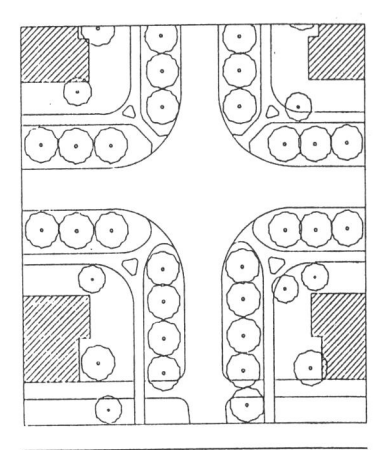

RESIDENTIAL ROAD

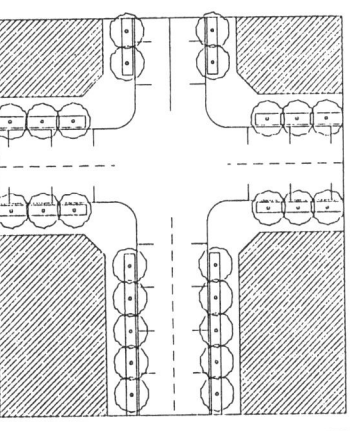

RESIDENTIAL STREET

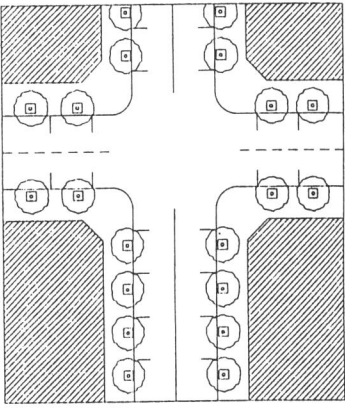

COMMERCIAL STREET

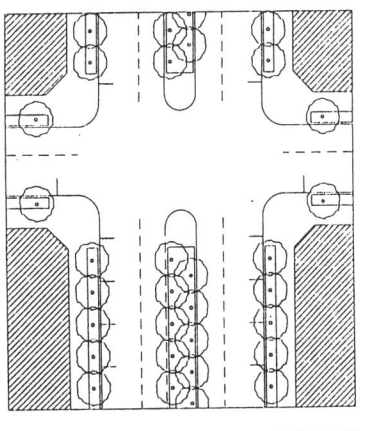

AVENUE

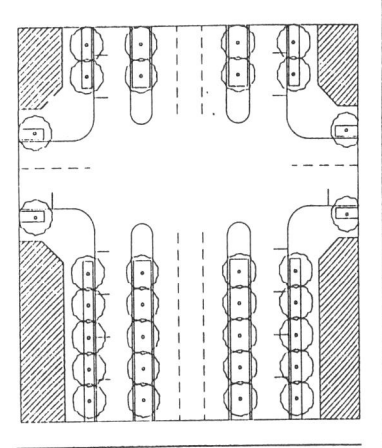

BOULEVARD

Gary Greenan, Andres Duany, Elizabeth Plater-Zyberk, Kamal Zaharin, Iskandar Shafie; Miami, Florida
The Cintas Foundation

1 SITE, COMMUNITY, AND URBAN PLANNING

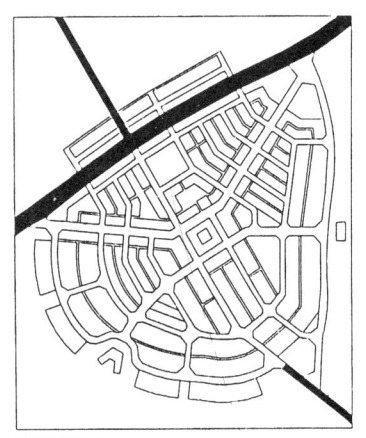

Thoroughfare Nomenclature

GENERAL
Thoroughfares are endowed with two attributes: capacity and character. Capacity refers to the number of vehicles that can move safely through a segment within a given time. It is physically manifested by the number of lanes and their width and by the centerline radius, the curb radius, and the super elevation of the pavement. Character refers to a thoroughfare's suitability for pedestrian activities and a variety of building types. Character is physically manifested by the thoroughfare's associated building, frontage, and landscape types and sidewalk width.

Conventional traffic engineering practice uses terms such as "collector" and "arterial," which denote only capacity. This is too simplistic and tends to create an environment inhospitable for pedestrians. The following nomenclature more adequately describes the combination of capacity and character necessary to create true urbanism.

NOMENCLATURE
HIGHWAY: A long-distance, medium speed vehicular corridor that traverses open country. A highway should be relatively free of intersections, driveways, and adjacent buildings; otherwise it becomes a strip, which interferes with traffic flow. (Related terms include expressway, a high speed highway with intersections replaced by grade separation, and parkway, a highway designed with naturalistic landscaping, partially accommodated within a wide and varying median.

BOULEVARD: A long-distance, medium speed vehicular corridor that traverses an urbanized area. It is usually lined by parallel parking, wide sidewalks, or side medians planted with trees. Buildings uniformly line the edges.

AVENUE: A short-distance, medium speed connector that traverses an urban area. Unlike a boulevard, its axis is terminated by a civic building or monument. An avenue may be conceived as an extremely elongated square. (A related term is allée, a rural avenue spatially defined by trees aligned on either side but devoid of buildings except at the terminus.)

DRIVE: An edge between an urban and a natural condition, usually along a waterfront, park, or promontory. One side of the drive has the urban character of a boulevard, with sidewalk and buildings, while the other has the qualities of a parkway, with naturalistic planting and rural detailing.

STREET: A small-scale, low speed local connector. Streets provide frontage for high-density buildings such as offices, shops, apartment buildings, and rowhouses. A street is urban in character, with raised curbs, closed drainage, wide sidewalks, parallel parking, trees in individual planting areas, and buildings aligned on short setbacks.

ROAD: A small-scale, low speed connector. Roads provide frontage for low-density buildings such as houses. A road tends to be rural in character with open curbs, optional parking, continuous planting, narrow sidewalks, and buildings set well back. The rural road has no curbs and is lined by pathways, irregular tree planting, and uncoordinated building setbacks.

ALLEY: A narrow access route servicing the rear of buildings on a street. Alleys have no sidewalks, landscaping, or building setbacks. Alleys are used by trucks and must accommodate dumpsters. They are usually paved to their edges, with center drainage via an inverted crown.

LANE: A narrow access route behind houses on a road. Lanes are rural in character, with a narrow strip of paving at the center or no paving. While lanes may not be necessary with front-loaded garages, they are still useful for accommodating utility runs, enhancing the privacy of rear yards, and providing play areas for children.

PASSAGE: A very narrow, pedestrian-only connector cutting between buildings. Passages provide shortcuts through long blocks or connect rear parking areas with street frontages. Passages may be roofed over and lined by shopfronts.

PATH: A very narrow pedestrian and bicycle connector traversing a park or the open country. Paths should emerge from the sidewalk network. Bicycle paths are necessary along highways but are not required to supplement boulevards, streets, and roads, where slower traffic allows sharing of the vehicular lanes.

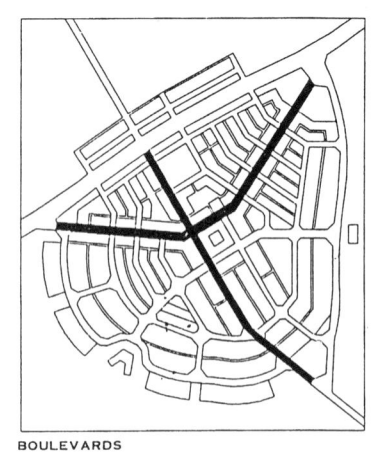

HIGHWAYS

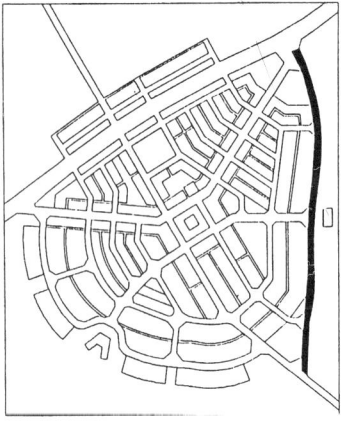

DRIVES

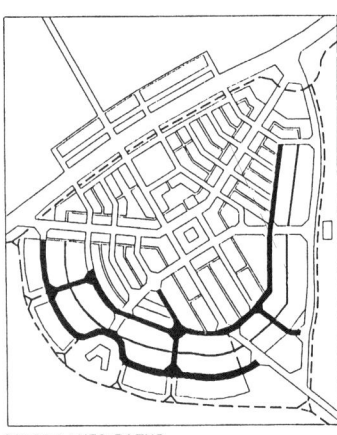

ROADS, LANES, PATHS
MORE RURAL

BOULEVARDS

AVENUES

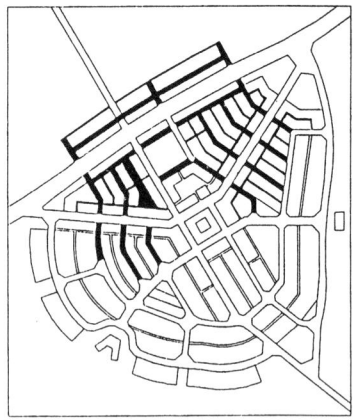

STREETS, ALLEYS, PASSAGES
MORE URBAN

Gary Greenan, Andres Duany, Elizabeth Plater-Zyberk, Kamal Zaharin, Iskandar Shafie; Miami, Florida
The Cintas Foundation

SITE, COMMUNITY, AND URBAN PLANNING

Thoroughfare Types

GENERAL
Capacity and character are combined and adjusted to achieve a complete series of useful thoroughfare types. The series is best regarded in pairs: keeping the right-of-way width (R.O.W) constant, each pair illustrates one type suitable in two ways, one for a relatively rural condition and another suitable for a more urban condition.

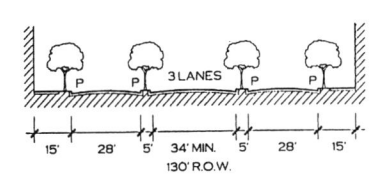

BOULEVARD — 15' | 28' | 5' | 34' MIN. | 5' | 28' | 15' — 130' R.O.W. (3 LANES)

MAIN STREET — 20' | 40' MIN. | 20' — 80' MIN. R.O.W. (2 LANES)

STREET — 10' | 40' | 10' — 60' R.O.W. (2 LANES)

MINOR STREET — 10' | 30' | 10' — 50' R.O.W. (2 LANES)

ALLEY — 24' R.O.W.

PASSAGE — 12' R.O.W.

MORE URBAN

BOULEVARD / HIGHWAY

BOULEVARD		HIGHWAY
25-50 MPH	DESIGN SPEED	35-55 MPH
90 FT	MIN. CENTERLINE RADIUS	165-800 FT
15 FT	CURB RETURN RADIUS	35 FT
30 SEC	PEDESTRIAN CROSS TIME	N/A
ALWAYS	ON-STREET PARKING	NEVER
CLOSED	DRAINAGE	OPEN

MAIN STREET / AVENUE

MAIN STREET		AVENUE
20-25 MPH	DESIGN SPEED	25-35 MPH
90 FT	MIN. CENTERLINE RADIUS	165 FT
15 FT	CURB RETURN RADIUS	25 FT
12 SEC	PEDESTRIAN CROSS TIME	15 SEC
ALWAYS	ON-STREET PARKING	ALWAYS*
CLOSED	DRAINAGE	OPEN/CLOSED

STREET / ROAD

STREET		ROAD
20-25 MPH	DESIGN SPEED	25-35 MPH
90 FT	MIN. CENTERLINE RADIUS	165 FT
15 FT	CURB RETURN RADIUS	25 FT
12 SEC	PEDESTRIAN CROSS TIME	8.5 SEC
ALWAYS	ON-STREET PARKING	USUALLY*
CLOSED	DRAINAGE	OPEN/CLOSED

MINOR STREET / RURAL ROAD

MINOR STREET		RURAL ROAD
20-25 MPH	DESIGN SPEED	25-35 MPH
90 FT	MIN. CENTERLINE RADIUS	165 FT
15 FT	CURB RETURN RADIUS	20 FT
8.5 SEC	PEDESTRIAN CROSS TIME	13 SEC
ALWAYS*	ON-STREET PARKING	NEVER
CLOSED	DRAINAGE	OPEN

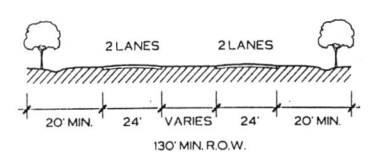

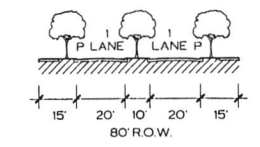

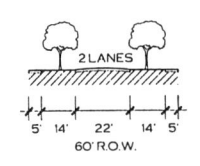

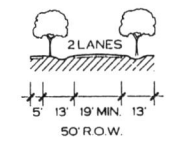

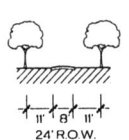

ALLEY / LANE

ALLEY		LANE
N/A	DESIGN SPEED	N/A
N/A	MIN. CENTERLINE RADIUS	N/A
5 FT	CURB RETURN RADIUS	20 FT
6.5 SEC	PEDESTRIAN CROSS TIME	3.5 SEC
USUALLY*	ON-STREET PARKING	USUALLY
CLOSED	DRAINAGE	OPEN

PASSAGE / PATH

PASSAGE		PATH
N/A	DESIGN SPEED	N/A
N/A	MIN. CENTERLINE RADIUS	40 FT
N/A	CURB RETURN RADIUS	5 FT
4.5 SEC	PEDESTRIAN CROSS TIME	4.5 SEC
NEVER	ON-STREET PARKING	NEVER
CLOSED	DRAINAGE	OPEN

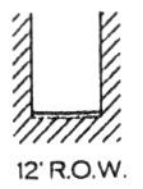

* Not striped

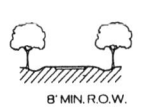

HIGHWAY — 20' MIN. | 24' | VARIES | 24' | 20' MIN. — 130' MIN. R.O.W. (2 LANES, 2 LANES)

AVENUE — 15' | 20' | 10' | 20' | 15' — 80' R.O.W. (1 P LANE, 1 LANE P)

ROAD — 5' | 14' | 22' | 14' | 5' — 60' R.O.W. (2 LANES)

RURAL ROAD — 5' | 13' | 19' MIN. | 13' — 50' R.O.W. (2 LANES)

LANE — 11' | 8' | 11' — 24' R.O.W.

PATH — 8' MIN. R.O.W.

MORE RURAL

Chester Chellman, P.E.; Ossipee, New Hampshire
Gary Greenan, Andres Duany, Elizabeth Plater-Zyberk, Kamal Zaharin, Iskandar Shafie; Miami, Florida
The Cintas Foundation

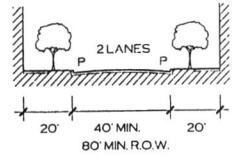

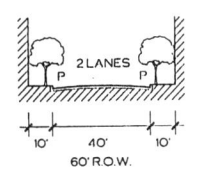

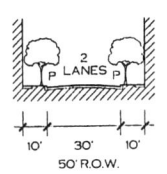

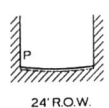

1 SITE, COMMUNITY, AND URBAN PLANNING

Traditional Neighborhood Design

INTRODUCTION

The traditional neighborhood development (TND) ordinance produces compact, mixed-use, pedestrian friendly communities. It can be incorporated in municipal zoning ordinances as an overlay or as a separate district. It is intended to ensure the following conventions:

Traditional neighborhoods share the following characteristics:

1. The neighborhood's area is limited to what can be traversed in a 10-minute walk.
2. Residences, shops, workplaces, and civic buildings are located in close proximity.
3. A hierarchy of streets serves the pedestrian and the automobile equitably.
4. Physically defined squares and parks provide places for formal social activity and recreation.
5. Private buildings form a clear edge, delineating the street space.
6. Civic buildings reinforce the identity of the neighborhood, providing places of assembly for social, cultural, and religious activities.

Traditional neighborhoods pursue certain social objectives:

1. To provide the elderly and the young with independence of movement by locating most daily activities within walking distance
2. To minimize traffic congestion and limit road construction by reducing the number and length of automobile trips
3. To make public transit a viable alternative to the automobile by organizing appropriate building densities
4. To help citizens come to know each other and to watch over their collective security by providing public spaces such as streets and squares
5. To integrate age and economic classes and form the bonds of an authentic community by providing a full range of housing types and workplaces
6. To encourage communal initiatives and support the balanced evolution of society by providing suitable civic buildings

SPECIAL DEFINITIONS

Terms used in a TND ordinance may differ in meaning from their use in conventional zoning ordinances.

ARTISANAL USE: Premises used for the manufacture and sale of items that are made employing only handwork and/or table-mounted electrical tools and creating no adverse impact beyond its lot.

BLOCK: The aggregate of lots and alleys circumscribed by public use tracts, generally streets.

BUILDING HEIGHT: The height measured in stories. Attics and raised basements do not count against building height limitations.

CITIZENS' ASSOCIATION: The organization of owners of lots and buildings associated under articles. The articles shall reference an approved master plan; set standards for building location, construction, and maintenance; provide for maintenance on public tracts; and provide for the construction of new civic buildings by an ongoing special assessment.

FACADE: The building wall parallel to a frontage line.

FRONTAGE LINE: The lot line that coincides with a street tract.

GREEN EDGE: A continuous open area surrounding the neighborhood proper. The area shall be preserved in perpetuity as a natural area, golf course, or growing or playing fields, or it shall be subdivided into house lots no smaller than 20 acres each.

LIMITED LODGING: Residential premises providing no more than eight rooms for short-term letting and food services before noon only.

LIMITED OFFICE: Residential premises used for business or professional services, employing no more than four full-time employees, one of whom must be the owner.

LOT: A separately platted portion of land held privately.

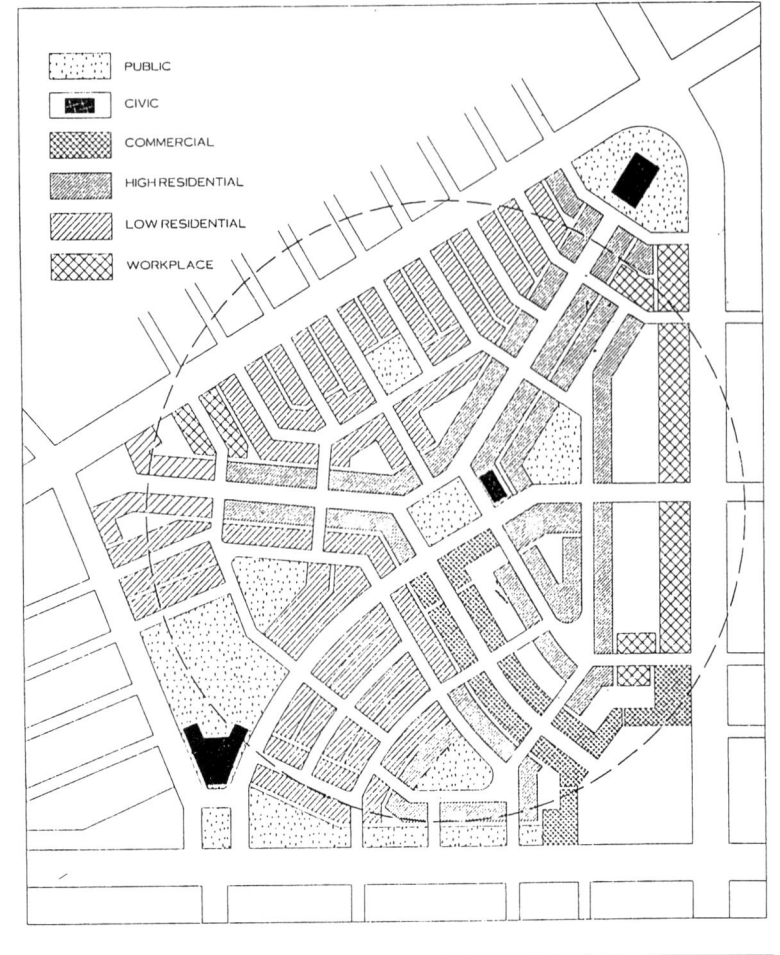

TND LAND ALLOCATION

Legend:
- PUBLIC
- CIVIC
- COMMERCIAL
- HIGH RESIDENTIAL
- LOW RESIDENTIAL
- WORKPLACE

MEETING HALL: A building designed for public assembly, containing at least one room with an area equivalent to 10 sq ft per dwelling, or 1300 sq ft, whichever is greater.

NEIGHBORHOOD PROPER: The built-up area of a TND, including blocks, streets, and squares but excluding green edges.

OUTBUILDING: A separate building, additional to a principal building, contiguous with the rear lot line, having at most two stories and a maximum habitable area of 450 sq ft. Outbuildings may be residential retail units. Outbuildings are exempt from building cover restrictions or unit counts.

PARK: A public tract naturalistically landscaped, not more than 10% paved, and surrounded by lots on no more than 50% of its perimeter.

PROHIBITED USES: Uses not permitted in the standard zoning ordinance, as well as automatic food, drink, and newspaper vending machines and any commercial use that encourages patrons to remain in their automobiles while receiving goods or services (except service stations).

SHARED PARKING: A parking place where day/night or weekday/holiday schedules allow the use of parking spaces by more than one user, resulting in a 25% reduction of the required spaces.

SQUARE: A public tract, spatially defined by surrounding buildings, with frontage on streets on at least two sides. Commercial uses shall be permitted on all surrounding lots.

STORY: A habitable level within a building no more than 14 ft in height from floor to ceiling.

STREET LAMPS: A light standard between 10 and 16 ft in height equipped with an incandescent or metal halide light source.

STREET TREE: A deciduous tree that resists root pressure and is of proven viability, in the region with no less than 4-in. caliper and 8-ft clear trunk at the time of planting.

STREET VISTA: The view, framed by buildings, at the termination of the axis of a thoroughfare.

TRACT: A separately platted portion of land held in common, such as a thoroughfare, a square, or a park.

Gary Greenan; Andres Duany, Elizabeth Plater-Zyberk, Kamal Zaharin, Iskandar Shafie; Miami, Florida
The Cintas Foundation

SITE, COMMUNITY, AND URBAN PLANNING

BIBLIOGRAPHY

Saarinen Eliel,
"The City, its growth, its decay, its future", New-York, Reinhold, 1943

Mumford Lewis,
"Technique et civilisation", Paris, Le Seuil, 1950

Mumford Lewis,
"La Cité à travers l'histoire", Paris, Le Seuil, 1964

Choay Françoise,
"L'Urbanisme, utopies et réalités", Paris, Le Seuil, 1965

Gutkind E.A.,
"Le crépuscule des villes" (The twilight of cities, 1962), Paris, Stock, 1966

Mumford Lewis,
"Le Mythe de la machine", Tome 1 et 2, Paris, Fayard, 1967

Girard André,
" Des choses cachées depuis la fondation du Monde ", Grasset, Paris, 1978

Pessin Alain et Torgue Henry-Skoff,
"Villes imaginaires", Paris, Éditions du Champ Urbain, 1980

Chombart de Lauwe Paul-Henry,
"La fin des villes. Mythe ou réalité ?", Paris, Calmann-Lévy, 1982

Savinio Alberto,
" Ville j'écoute ton coeur ", Gallimard, Paris, 1982

Weber Max,
"La Ville", Paris, Aubier, 1982

Schoonbrodt René (sous la direction de),
"Bruxelles vu par ses habitants", Bruxelles, ARAU éditeur, 1984

"Histoire de la France Urbaine. La ville aujourd'hui", (tome V), sous la direction de Georges Duby, Paris, Le Seuil, 1985

Girouard Mark,
"Cities and People", New Haven et Londres, Yale University Press, 1985

Van Effenterre,
"La cité grecque", Paris, Hachette, 1985

Divorne Françoise et alii,
"Ville, forme, symbolique, pouvoir, projets", Paris, IFA / Mardaga, 1986

Culot Maurice (sous la direction de),
"Toulouse les délices de l'imitation", Liège / Paris, Mardaga / IFA, 1986

França José-Augusto,
"Une ville des Lumières. La Lisbonne de Pombal", Paris, Fondation Calouste Gulbenkian, 1988

Corbin Alain,
"Le territoire du vide", Paris, Aubier, 1988

Roullier Jean-Eudes (sous la direction de),
"Villes Nouvelles en France", Paris, Ed Economica, 1989

Dollé Jean-Paul,
" Fureur de Ville ", Grasset, Paris, 1991

Krier Léon,
"Architecture and Urban Design 1967-1992", Londres, Academy Editions, 1992

Cancellieri Anne,
"Habitat du futur", Paris, La Documentation Française, 1992

Papadakis Andreas et Hanson Brian (sous la direction de),
"New Practice in Urban Design", Londres, Academy Group Ltd, 1992

Economakis Richard,
"Buiding Classical. A vision of Europe and America", Londres, Academy Editions, 1993

Lacloche Francis,
"Le temps, le nombre, la ville", Paris, éditions Carré, 1994

Antolini André et Bonello Yves-Henri,
"Les villes du désir", Paris, éditions Galilée, 1994

Schoonbrodt René,
" La participation pour la cité " dans *Espace de Liberté*, Bruxelles, Août-Sept. 1995

Culot Maurice (sous la direction de),
"Trouville, Maisons et Cités-Jardins 1919-1995", Paris, Ed Norma, 1995

Gaiani Marco (sous la direction de),
"La Città senza fine", Florence, Ed Alinea, 1995

Renaud Jean-Claude (sous la direction de),
"Atlas Statistique des Villes Nouvelles d'Île-de-France", Paris, Secrétariat Général des Villes Nouvelles, 1995

Fortier Bruno,
"L'Amour des Villes", Liège / Paris, Mardaga / IFA, 1995

"La ville, peurs et espérances", (collectif), Paris, La Documentation Française, 1995

European Foundation for the Improvement of Living and Working Conditions

Perceive – Conceive – Achieve
The Sustainable City
A European Tetralogy

Part IV – Aesthetics, Functionality and Desirability of the Sustainable City

Luxembourg: Office for Official Publications of the European Communities

1997 – 204 pp. – 21 x 29.7 cm

ISBN 92-827-4923-1 Volume IV Aesthetics, Functionality and Desirability of the Sustainable City
ISBN 92-827-4915-0 Volumes I-IV

Price (excluding VAT) in Luxembourg:
Volume IV: ECU 20; Volumes I-IV: ECU 65